HERITAGE MANAGEMENT AT FORT HOOD, TEXAS
Experiments in historic landscape characterisation

Glynn Barrett, Lucie Dingwall, Vince Gaffney,
Simon Fitch, Cheryl Huckerby and Tony Maguire

Edited by Lucie Dingwall and Vince Gaffney

Archaeopress

Published by

Archaeopress
Gordon House
276 Banbury Road
Oxford OX2 7ED
England
bar@archaeopress.com
www.archaeopress.com

HERITAGE MANAGEMENT AT FORT HOOD, TEXAS
Experiments in historic landscape characterisation

© Institute of Archaeology and Antiquity, University of Birmingham 2007

ISBN 978 1 905739 11 0

All rights reserved. No part of this publication may be reproduced, stored in a retrieval system, or transmitted, in any form or by any means, electronic, mechanical, photocopying or otherwise, without the prior written permission of the copyright owner.

Printed in England by Chalvington Digital

Contents

Contents i
Illustrations iii
Foreword by Lee Foster v
Preface: New Ways in the New World by Graham Fairclough vii

Introduction 1

1. The Origins and Aims of the Fort Hood Historic Landscape Characterisation Project 5
    1.1 Previous archaeological work at Fort hood 6
    1.2 Overview of the data 12
    1.3 Overview of management approaches 12
    1.4 Aims of the Fort Hood historic landscape characterisation project 14

2. Approaches to historic landscape characterisation 15
    2.1 Principles of historic landscape characterisation 15
    2.2 Historic landscape characterisation methodologies 17
    2.3 Developing the Fort Hood methodology 18

3. Fort Hood in Context 23
    3.1 The establishment of Fort Hood as a military installation 23
    3.2 Topography and geology 23
    3.3 Archaeological Review of Fort Hood 23
        3.3.1 Chronology 24
        3.3.2 Processes of continuity and change (Transitions) 29
        3.3.3 Settlement and society 31
        3.3.4 Religion and culture 35
        3.3.5 Transport 37
        3.3.6 Economy and environment 37
        3.3.7 Military 41
        3.3.8 Palaeoenvironment and Geomorphology 42
        3.3.9 Landscape 43
        3.3.10 Oral traditions and documentary accounts 44
        3.3.11 Specific Regional Issues 44
        3.3.12 Methodological and technical development 48
        3.3.13 Managing the resource 48
        3.3.14 Dissemination 49

4. The Fort Hood archaeological database 51
    4.1 Database structures and the Event-Monument-Archive model 51
    4.2 The new Fort Hood database structure 53
    4.3 Implementation of the Fort Hood database 54
        4.3.1 Existing datasets 54
        4.3.2 Standardisation of terminology 55
        4.3.3 Site data 65
        4.3.4 Event data 65
    4.4 Future database developments 68

5. The historic landscape characterisation project 69
    5.1 Creation of the historic landscape polygons 69
        5.1.1 Classification of Landsat data 70
        5.1.2 Classifying aerial photography and merging satellite images 73
        5.1.3 Vectorisation of the classified images 74
        5.1.4 Creation and integration of slope data 74
        5.1.5 Adding attribute data 77
        5.1.6 Creating visibility attributes 82
    5.2 Definition of the historic landscape characterisation types 85
        5.2.1 Experimental raster data analysis 85
        5.2.2 Polygon attribute-based analysis 85
    5.3 Truthing of the historic landscape characterisation data 88
        5.3.1 Desk-based truthing 88
        5.3.2 Ground truthing 91

    5.4 Results and discussion 98
        5.2.1 The HLC data 98
        5.2.2 HLC data and archaeological site distribution 104

6. Conclusions **117**

7. Bibliography **119**

Appendix: The contents and use of the CD **125**

Illustrations

Figures

Figure 1: Fort Hood, location 5
Figure 2: Schematic of evaluation process 8
Figure 3: Fort Hood and recorded archaeological sites 9
Figure 4: Fort Hood, relief and major hydrology features 10
Figure 5: Fort Hood training areas, livefire and impact zones 11
Figure 6: Evaluation plan from Site 41CV988 13
Figure 7: European Pathways to the Cultural Landscape Philosophy for Historic Landscape Characterisation 18
Figure 8: Landscape analysis at Cobham Park, Kent, UK 21
Figure 9: Example of land apportionment map showing early surveys in the Camp Hood area 22
Figure 10: Physiographic regions of central Texas, location and extent of Fort Hood 27
Figure 11: Geological sequence for Texas and local area of Fort Hood 28
Figure 12: Typology of points..29
Figure 13: Data model for the new Fort Hood database 53
Figure 14: Extract from Ordnance Survey 1:25000 mapping 69
Figure 15: Subset of Landsat Scene covering the extent of Fort Hood 71
Figure 16: Initial unsupervised classification of Landsat sub-scene 71
Figure 17: The false colour infra-red aerial photography composite image of Fort Hood 72
Figure 18: Initial polygons derived from classification 72
Figure 19: Location and extent of 5km sample areas 75
Figure 20: Detail of southwestern square sample area 75
Figure 21: 5m contour model and derived TIN (Triangulated Irregular Network) 76
Figure 22: Slope derived from TIN 76
Figure 23: Cumulative viewshed grid 83
Figure 24: Cumulative viewshed reclassified into 5 classes 83
Figure 25: Site polygons superimposed on the terrain model draped with aerial photography 89
Figure 26: Characterisation pilot areas overlaid on the infra-red false colour AP 89
Figure 27: Detail of eastern pilot area (area 2) 90
Figure 28: Eastern pilot area (area 2) HLC sub-type polygons 90
Figure 29: River proximity polygons 93
Figure 30: Flat area polygons and river proximity polygons 93
Figure 31: Potential river terraces 93
Figure 32: Hyperlinking in ArcPad 94
Figure 33: Clear Creek terraces 94
Figure 34: North Nolan terraces 94
Figure 35: House Creek terrace 95
Figure 36: Diversity of the North Nolan Terrace 95
Figure 37: Desk-recorded terraces (brown) shown with field-recorded terraces (green) 95
Figure 38: Example of High Resolution Aerial Photography used in the study 96
Figure 39: Location of Leon River study area 96
Figure 40: Extent of terraces extracted from the HLC data with AP-related field data 96
Figure 41: Detail of AP-related field data 99
Figure 42: River terrace HLC data enhanced by ground-truthing 100
Figure 43: Study area mapped to HLC broad types 101
Figure 44: Study area mapped to HLC sub-types 102
Figure 45: Burned Rock Sites (Mounds, Middens and Scatters) 113
Figure 46: Rock-shelters 113
Figure 47: Sinkholes 114
Figure 48: Open Camps 114
Figure 49: Lithic Scatters 115
Figure 50: LRPAs 115
Figure 51: Historic Military Sites 116
Figure 52: Historic Non-Military Sites 116

Tables

Table 1: Recorded Prehistoric sites at Fort Hood (as of June 2002). 11
Table 2: Recorded Historic sites at Fort Hood (as of June 2002). 14
Table 3: New Fort Hood database - site data structure 54
Table 4: New Fort Hood database - event data structure 54
Table 5: Prehistoric and Historic site types recorded in the Fort Hood Allsites database...........................55
Table 6: Proposed prehistoric site types..56
Table 7: Historic site types recorded in the Fort Hood Allsites database...57
Table 8: Historic site types defined by the Prewitt study 58
Table 9: Variations of historic site type terms used in the Prewitt study's historic site data 58
Table 10: List of historic terms used and preferred terms..59
Table 11: Proposed historic site types..60
Table 12: Proposed historic site/feature types..61
Table 13: New Fort Hood database – example of a site record..66
Table 14: New Fort Hood database – example of a feature record 67
Table 15: New Fort Hood database – example of an object record 67
Table 16: List of fields in the landscape polygon GIS database table..78
Table 17: Broad HLC types 86
Table 18: Attribute groups defined for each broad type 86
Table 19: HLC sub-type definitions..86
Table 20: Count of polygons in pilot areas by HLC broad type 88
Table 21: Sum of area of polygons in pilot areas by HLC broad type 88
Table 22: Count of polygons in pilot areas by HLC sub type 88
Table 23: Sum of area of polygons in pilot areas by HLC sub-type 91
Table 24: Quantification of HLC broad types 98
Table 25: Quantification of HLC sub-types 98
Table 26: Quantification of sites by site type on each HLC broad type...108
Table 27: Count of sites by site type on each HLC sub-type 109

Plates

Plate 1: Military land use at Fort Hood 7
Plates 2 and 3: Aspects of civilian land use at Fort Hood..7
Plate 4: Fort Hood Cantonment..8
Plate 5: Fort Hood South Cantonment with US 190 in the foreground and Killeen in the background 27
Plate 6: Tama Store 31
Plate 7: Antelope Home 1908 35
Plate 8: Karst feature at Fort Hood...39
Plate 9: Flooding at the Old Georgetown crossing of the Cowhouse Creek 39
Plate 10: Historic Black House 40
Plate 11: Training at Fort Hood..40
Plate 12: View from within the live fire zone 45
Plate 13: Cave in the Karst area 45
Plate 14: Smith Mountain...46
Plate 15: A rock shelter at Fort Hood...46
Plate 16: The Leon River Medicine Wheel and the Comanche National Cemetery 50
Plates 17 – 20: Panoramic Photo Mosaics from sample view points 84
Plate 21: Newly-discovered hearth site..99
Plate 22: Military presence in the landscape 105
Plate 23: Cattle grazing at Fort Hood...105
Plate 24: Site of the remains of a historic house at Fort Hood 106
Plate 25: Karst area at Fort Hood 106
Plates 26 and 27: Cowhouse Creek and Table Rock Creek 107
Plate 28: Woodland near Bear Creek 111
Plate 29: Burned rock mound in the Karst landscape..111
Plate 30: Prehistoric camp site by the Cowhouse Creek 112
Plate 31: Prehistoric camp site at Maple Canyon 112

Foreword

For decades, the effective stewardship and management of cultural resources at Fort Hood, Texas, has proven to be a formidable challenge. Balancing this responsibility with the Army mission at Fort Hood, which includes ongoing intensive mechanized training across a 217,000 acre military reservation, has tested the abilities of even the most capable of cultural resource managers. The identification of over 2,000 archaeological sites on the installation, while a great accomplishment, pales in comparison to the demands of determining site significance. Now, with this innovative historic landscape characterization study, the authors have presented us with an extraordinary opportunity to view these resources within the context of a cultural landscape that systematically considers the "multiple roles" of Fort Hood. It is hoped that this will facilitate the move from significance determinations that are site-specific to ones based upon, as the authors state, the "concepts of group value and spatial relationships at a landscape level." Historic landscape characterization, which has begun to gain traction in the United Kingdom, holds great promise for large land managing agencies such as the Army. With appropriate adjustments to enable application in this country, this technique will promote informed cultural resource management that aligns with the agency mission.

Lee Foster, RPA
Deputy Federal Preservation Officer
Office of the Director of Environmental Programs

Preface: New Ways in the New World
by Graham Fairclough, English Heritage

CRM and landscape character

Historic Landscape Characterisation (HLC) evolved, or rather was developed, in the context of at least a century-long British tradition of landscape archaeology and landscape history. This tradition, once, perhaps, best exemplified by the archaeologist O.G.S Crawford and the historian W.G Hoskins, of seeing landscape in terms of ways of understanding the past did not, however, greatly influence heritage management, which remained until well into the 1990s largely and stubbornly site-based. HLC was therefore invented in the early 1990s in order (*inter alia*) to bring a stronger landscape dimension into heritage management and archaeological/cultural resource management as practised by English Heritage and its partners in local government (Herring 1998). It began a process of transferring the focus of archaeologists working in heritage management away from the past and towards the past in the present.

Because HLC began life predominantly as a tool for practical real-world uses, its adaptation to the everyday needs of the US Army's CRM work (Huckerby 2001) is very appropriate. The Ford Hood work is also a valuable step forward in the development of HLC, offering a new stage of experimentation and evolution of the approach in a new rather different landscape and cultural contexts. This is important because whilst HLC as a technique is already about 15 years old, and in some ways well-established, it is still a relative newcomer to archaeological research and cultural resource management and its continued evolution – and extension to new domains - is to be encouraged.

The wider and rather more far-reaching implications of HLC - in effect, the prospect of a new paradigm to lay alongside traditional, site- and monument - based approaches to heritage management - are however only now being fully recognised in policy-making and decision-taking circles. The concept of 'characterisation' in general as used by English Heritage and others (English Heritage 2005) is a way of 'seeing' and understanding that offers an alternative and complementary way of caring for the 'Historic Environment'.

The term 'Historic Environment' is used pragmatically in the UK as a comprehensive and publicly-accessible term that also facilitates integration with other strands of environmental stewardship. It is used in the most general sense of the word, obviously and unarguably including 'pre'-history. It is a term that supports HLC's emphasis not only on the evidential value of heritage for understanding the past but also on the contemporariness of the past as part of the present and as an important part of people's mental and emotional interaction with the world – 'Landscape', in fact (Fairclough 2003, 2006).

This newer way of working brings with it not just a landscape-scale perspective on heritage management and planning, but a readjustment of some of the objectives of CRM (Selman 2006). It encourages land managers to focus not only on site protection in relatively few designated places but to consider to an equal degree how the whole of the historic environment, no matter where separate components may sit on conventional evidential or scientific scales of values, fits into the present and future landscape. This approach is increasingly in Europe being reflected now in official documents such as the European Landscape Convention and others (Council of Europe 2000, Historic Environment Review 2000, Department for Culture, Media and Sport 2001).

Continuing evolution

HLC is methodologically quite young, so experiments such as that of Fort Hood that develop new ways of making an HLC are very welcome. In England, HLC only reached a stable level of methodological development in about 2001, and then only with respect to its particular application at the scale of an English county. English Heritage's first programme, aimed at securing a basic geographical coverage at 'county-level' across all of England (starting in 1994 with Cornwall in the South West), is not yet complete; new techniques and applications continue to be developed, and further stages of work – regional and national overviews - beckon.

Whist young, HLC is nevertheless already established as key component of historic management in Britain and it has been, or is being, adopted, in other countries than England. In near neighbours with similar landscapes, such as Scotland (Macinnes 2004, Dixon *et al.* 1999), and Ireland (in work by the Discovery programme and others), it has been adopted largely unchanged. In other places, as at Fort Hood, landscape differs to such a degree (notably in the partial absence of physical land divisions such as hedges or walls) that different methods must be developed, as in southern Sweden (Nord 2006a, 2006b). Elsewhere, by independent invention during the 1990's, quite different methods have been invented which follow similar broad principles to meet the same objective, as in Denmark and Flanders (DAKD nd, Landscape Atlas of Flanders 2001). In some countries, notably Wales (CAPT nd, Gwyn 2002), distinctive cultural approaches to landscape have resulted in different, very effective techniques.

For all their (healthy) methodological diversity, all these techniques share some basic principles. For example, they all seek (as does the Fort Hood work) to redress the focus that archaeologists' have laid over the past century or so on 'sites'. It is axiomatic that sites do not sit in isolation. They have context and settings and they have relationships between each other; their patterning is as much a part of the archaeological resource, or of the historic environment, as their own individual traits. The very concept of site 'definition' both generic and specific has come under scrutiny, even to the point of recognising that a 'site' is usually just a modern construct drawn from partial (in both senses of that word) data. More to the point, the wider context of a site – commonly referred to as landscape - is in its own right a cultural artefact that calls out to be studied, understood, valued and managed (or protected).

HLC brings at the same time a recognition that the historic landscape's patterns and "sites" (or components) are not just cultural but are also semi-natural and natural. There are semi-natural components such as, for instance, how woodland is distributed and the product of human decisions of action and inaction, how trees are used and exploited can govern their slope, etc, and apparently wholly "natural" aspects such as the use of natural features as sacred sites and landmarks also have cultural significance (the meanings and values, from economic to spiritual, that people place on their environment) and a place in the historic landscape character.

Once all this is recognised, the obsession with antiquity that characterised earlier archaeological practice begins to fade away. It becomes possible to see that the main object of our study and management concerns is the present-day patterns of the environment, with all its historic and prehistoric depths, and most importantly how people relate to these and incorporate them into their perceptions of the world - i.e. into their 'Landscapes' (Brown *et al.* 2005).

Ideas of landscape

Thus we must turn again to this word "landscape", the key concept under-pinning this new heritage paradigm, but a word that means many things to different people. In academic terms, landscape is one of the naturally most multi-disciplinary areas of research, and many disciplines – geography, history, archaeology, architecture, ecology - legitimately lay separate claim to it but often in quite different but mutually helpful ways (Palang and Fry 2003).

Landscape derives, as is well known, from Dutch landscape painting (although there are earlier Italian works). Its meaning was applied initially to the painting itself, the image, but with the passage of time it came to be transferred to the object depicted, to the land itself as viewed by human beings. This meaning brings with it into today's definition part of the sense that landscape is above all else a matter of perception, such as of seeing. There is however a parallel, and much older Nordic or Scandinavian European usage that focuses on territory and community, and in which the geographical, legal and customary aspects – and thus human action, land use and so on - are just as relevant. During the 19th and 20th centuries in North America as well as Europe, further layers of meaning linked to the notion of perception and experiential approaches, and more recently still of cognition. In the later 20th Century natural sciences began to see ecology as a landscape issue and archaeologists began to develop their own, equally diverse landscape theories[1].

In the past few years all of this has been pulled together in the European context into an almost unified construct, best exemplified with the Council of Europe's European Landscape Convention (Council of Europe 2000). This defines landscape as "an area, *as perceived by people*, whose character is the result of the action & interaction of natural and/or human factors"), locates landscape everywhere (e.g. urban and as well as rural, sea as well as land) and, most

---

[1] There is an enormous literature on the meanings of 'landscape' – for example, Schama, S. 1995. *Landscape and Memory*. London: Harper Collins; Cosgrove, D. & S. Daniels (eds), 1988. *The Iconography of Landscape*, Cambridge: Cambridge University Press; Olwig, K.R. 2002. *Landscape, Nature, and the Body Politic: From Britain's Renaissance to America's New World*. Madison: University of Wisconsin Press; Olwig, K.R. 2004. "This is not a landscape": circulating reference and land shaping. In H. Palang, H. Sooväli, M. Antrop & G. Setten (eds), *European Rural Landscapes: Persistence and Change in a Globalising Environment*, 41-65. Dordrecht: Kluwer Academic Publishers; Forman R.T.T. & Godron, M. 1986 Landscape Ecology. John Wiley, New York; Forman, R.T.T. 1995. Land Mosaics: The Ecology of Landscapes and Regions. Cambridge University Press, Cambridge, UK; Ashmore, W. and Knapp, B.A. 1999: *Archaeologies of Landscape*, London, Blackwells; Doukellis, P & L.G. Mendoni (eds), 2004. *Perception and Evaluation of Cultural Landscapes*. Athens: National Hellenic Research Foundation; Hicks, D., McAtackney, L. & Fairclough, G.J. (eds) forthcoming 2007: *Envisioning Landscape Archaeology*; WAC One World Archaeology/ Left Coast Press.

significantly as a departure from traditional selective designation-based approaches, recognises that landscape can have different levels of value and quality (special, outstanding, ordinary, degraded). In this framework, landscape is how people relate to their world, how environment becomes human habitat as well as common heritage, and how people, quite simply, exist in the world.

This particular view of landscape is basically a perceptual one, of landscape as an idea not a thing, and therefore as a present day, contemporary construct. This makes the landscape concept all the more powerful in social and political terms. Past landscapes can perhaps be "excavated" in the sense that we can make reconstructions of past peoples' mentalities from their material culture at landscape scale, but it is only today's landscape that actually exists. The task of heritage managers and archaeologists involved in CRM, as well as protecting the fabric of the past, is also to help people to manage change within the landscape so that our successors "future landscapes" will continue to contain historical depth. They can help people (if they wish to do so) to incorporate the deep past, and sometimes past perceptions, into their present day landscape. This will strengthen the part that cultural heritage plays in present day perception, and also link traditional notions of cultural heritage (sites, monuments, buildings) to the broader and more everyday experience of landscape and lifestyle.

Making an HLC

In this very wide context, the extension of HLC principle and techniques from a European context to an American, New World, one is highly welcome. So too are the significant methodological developments made during the Fort Hood project, specifically the use of remote sensing data and advanced GIS to deal with an area which lacks many of the features or indicators - proxies for landscape characterisation - that facilitated the initial development of HLC in England. Welcome too is the completion of a HLC project which to a larger degree than in Europe has incorporated both the prehistoric 'hidden' layers of landscape and the intangible cultural landscape component of human affiliation and memory. Fort Hood, with its rapid succession of change in only three centuries from hunter-gathering through agriculture to the quintessential 20th century use to support 'industrialised' warfare, also exemplifies very well the important role of change and dynamism in forming landscape character that becomes ever more apparent as landscape's historic dimension is revealed.

Fort Hood's HLC work therefore unlocks several unopened doors on HLC's future evolution. The HLC method evolved in an English landscape whose long story of human activity and change is still visible in the modern palimpsest through field patterns marked by physical boundaries often usually to several centuries' age and through the highly artificial distribution and character of "natural" resources such as woodland, lowland heathland, upland moorland, meadows and so forth. At c.879km^2 in size, Fort Hood is approximately equivalent to the smaller modern English counties, such as West Berkshire (704km^2) or Bedfordshire (1,235km^2 areas) but offers us a landscape that is not characterised by the same range of HLC types or 'indicators', or even the same 'grain' of landscape, and thus it has provided the HLC method with very new challenges in dealing with a different range and indicators and a quite different grain. There are areas of Western Europe (e.g. Portugal, South Sweden) where landscapes characterised by lack of humanly imposed structure might be suitable candidates for using the approach developed for Fort Hood.

The creation of the HLC for Fort Hood has taken important first steps into other methodological areas that HLC has not yet greatly ventured into. One example of this is the more sophisticated use of remote sensing such as *Landsat* data and 'automated' polygonisation; another is how to capture intangible character. On the latter, the Fort Hood work also offers a stepping stone (for instance, combining the HLC maps into Google Earth) towards the even bigger target to finding ways to invite ordinary people – inhabitants, visitors, individuals and communities with a historic link – into the currently essentially expert process of HLC.

The project's re-casting of the Fort Hood archaeological database into an Event/Monument archive as promoted in England by English Heritage is another aspect of a more sophisticated theorisation of knowledge and its meaning. What we commonly called 'sites' (even without complaining that their place in the wider all-encompassing historic landscape is often overlooked) are in fact simply the site of records made or of artefact survival. The primary and most important fact about them therefore is the circumstances by which they were found, noticed and recorded – the 'event'. All flows from this first piece of information – the character of data, and its detail, reliability, completeness, more importantly, its limits, why the area next to the site is "empty" in our distribution maps, even sometimes, given that archaeological interpretations vary through time, to what category the site is attached. 'Monuments' in this scheme are explicitly recognised as being intellectually constructed, not 'real' predetermined things. Recasting the database is a corollary of HLC, in other words.

Uses of HLC

The Fort Hood 'experiment' (if that is an appropriate label for so successful an outcome) therefore not only migrates a European philosophy and its techniques into the New World, but expands and refines the method in a variety of useful ways. Most useful of all, it does this in the context of hard, practical applications founded firmly on real-world land use conflicts and managements.

Whilst primarily in origin an applied practical tool (Clark *et al.* 2004, Bloemers 2002), HLC also has research and understanding benefits, for the general public as well as for specialists (Turner 2006, Williamson 2006). These are only beginning to be realised in England and another welcome step forward in the Fort Hood work is therefore its experimentations in this field, preliminary correlations between HLC and site distribution, for example. This is also a practical application, of course, which allows HLC to become a means of defining the limits of our knowledge, contextualising what we think we know and pointing out some directions for future research.

HLC and the event-based database are both first and foremost management tools. Site data in the context of HLC provides the evidence base for decision-making, from the most basic uses (e.g., do we know of any archaeological remains that development changes, activity or land use might destroy or damage?) to the more sophisticated (e.g. major infrastructure planning – where best a new Highway might fit in the landscape (Highways Agency Guidance 2007). In England, most of these decisions take place with local government's "Historic Environment" services. The larger landowning estates maintain similar systems and procedures, however, particularly in the public sphere such as the National Trust, the Forestry Agency and the Ministry of Defence which, as in the USA, manages large areas of prehistoric and historic landscape of which the Salisbury Plain training area around Stonehenge is only the largest (yet at 380 km^2 is much less than half the size of Fort Hood) and most famous example.

The practical, curatorial, uses for HLC form part of a larger new paradigm, known under the shorthand of 'characterisation'. Characterisation, in its essentials, adopts area-based and landscape (in perceptual as well as spatial senses) approaches to cultural heritage management. It seeks a generalised overview of the whole historic environment that is designed to be used strategically in spatial planning, land management and other form of land use decision-making. Traditional approaches based on detailed site-based understanding remain necessary of course. Even when taken together, however, they rarely cover all the needs of cultural heritage management, and when, as often, the site-based approach is implemented by way of selection based on national register or list criteria, its applicability to spatial planning and land management become even more partial.

In contrast, HLC, and characterisation approaches in general (English Heritage 2007), offer the chance to break out from this mould and to allow the wider historic environment to be taken into account, albeit at a higher level of generalisation. In England, this is already paying dividends in relation to integration with mainstream land use policies (rather than just sectoral protectionist laws) and to inter- and trans-disciplinary collaboration both across the natural-cultural spectrum and between all landscape disciplines. The Fort Hood HLC and database will surely prove to be just as useful to the US Army in its land management and cultural resource programme.

Introduction

The landscape of Fort Hood, in central Texas, presents archaeologists and cultural resource managers with some of their most exacting but absorbing challenges. That much is clear from the activities of the many archaeologists and heritage managers who have sought to use the extensive cultural database and unique landscape of the base as a test bed for research and management methodologies. It is, for instance, no coincidence that some of the earliest, and most influential, papers on the use of geographical information systems in archaeology were built upon research carried out at Fort Hood (Williams *et al.* 1990a; 1990b). The Fort Hood Historic Landscape Characterisation Project has, therefore, a larger historic and research context that stretches beyond the perimeter of the camp itself or, indeed, the regional archaeology of Texas. It, perhaps, finds a place in the tradition at Fort Hood for the development of methodologies for archaeological research and the application of novel technological solutions for cultural resource management at a general and more substantive level.

This project, carried out as an international collaboration between the Fort Hood Cultural Resource Management Team and the Institute of Archaeology and Antiquity (University of Birmingham, UK), sought to provide a novel application of historic landscape characterisation methodologies at the base. As is becoming clear, historic landscape characterisation offers a novel and reflexive solution to the management of large cultural landscapes. In classical applications, characterisation provides a useful tool to manage the cultural landscape as a whole, providing broad classifications of the landscape on the basis of current land use and with reference to the physical remains of past cultural practice that survive as part of the contemporary landscape. In attempting this there is, within historic landscape characterisation, the potential to resolve a primary resource management paradox. That in which we attempt to reconcile our desire to understand the past in its entirety whilst basing our resource management procedures on strategies which artificially isolate small areas for protection without any consideration of the wider landscape in which they previously existed, or the modern landscapes within which they achieve a contemporary, cultural value.

It must be acknowledged that historic landscape characterisation is frequently associated with European landscapes and most strongly with Britain. This, ultimately, is where the methodology was first conceived and developed (Fairclough *et al.* 1999). There is, however, no reason to believe that landscapes outside Europe would not benefit from promoting similar programmes. Human behaviour, whilst infinitely variable in detail, also possesses some fundamental commonalities and the broad principles and generalising methods applied through landscape characterisation can provide useful information and still avoid judgementalism. Each historic landscape characterisation project should be the outcome of a specific historical trajectory and, to date, completed projects support such principles in terms of the value of the output. However, it is equally true that the landscapes of central Texas, and Fort Hood specifically, differ significantly from those of Europe, and this is despite the intriguing fact that the area of the fort was chosen because the "the rolling hills in the western part of Fort Hood are similar to central Europe" (General Shoemaker 1989). These differences are not solely to be seen in environmental terms, there are also distinctions in colonial landscapes which possess associations with historic, indigenous populations, the substance of which frequently remains elusive within the published literature or even the archaeological record itself. In these circumstances the concept of value or significance can become contentious and an appeal to external process, including land characterisation, make considerable sense. There is also a major contrast in the issue of the administrative organisation and function of Fort Hood itself and the continuing association of the military with an area of no less than 88,221 hectares (218,000 acres). Fort Hood is currently one of the largest military bases in the world and certainly the largest federal landholding within Texas itself. Hundreds of farmsteads and more than fifty communities were established as historic objects following the enforced movement of population associated with the establishment and expansion of the base. This is not an abstract issue and it is clear that these are emotive subjects with respect of the wider communities of Bell and Coryell Counties, many of whom retain links with these historic settlements and their archaeological remains. The base, of course, takes the stewardship of this landscape seriously and the Fort Hood Cultural Resource Management Team supports the recording and conservation of more than 2,000 archaeological sites, the curation of a significant text and material archive and implementation of an active outreach programme. Despite this, it is critical that resource management at Fort Hood involves a *modus vivendi* that incorporates the requirement for military training, the maintenance of public access to areas of the base for leisure pursuits, respect of indigenous rights and the protection of the cultural heritage with regard to the sensitivities of the general public and for broader ethical reasons.

Historic landscape characterisation offers the opportunity to consider the base and its multiple roles overall and the prospect to step beyond the repetitious, if necessary, testing of sites for eligibility within the National Register. Instead the process encourages a more reflective position on the overall cultural landscape and the wider significance and group value of cultural monuments within such a landscape.

To do this much should be little more than the aspiration of any historic landscape characterisation project set within the legislative context of the United States. However, in the case of the Fort Hood project there has also been the requirement to step beyond the standard historic landscape characterisation process in the initial construction of the project archaeology database, which was derived from disparate sources of varying quality. This has been an opportunity, as well as a task. The proposed, and partly implemented, restructuring of the database provides real opportunities for regional archaeologists to engage more substantively with the data at Fort Hood and more widely across central Texas, to ask different questions of the data and to present the resource more effectively to a wider public.

More significantly, the environmental and map data required to implement the characterisation programme proved particularly challenging. In this instance, at least, Fort Hood is not the average English county! Primary data sources for mapping were largely digital (satellite and aerial photographic imagery). This, along with the absence of detailed cultural mapping for some recent periods and the monolithic nature of military land use since 1942, encouraged the team to regard the process in a manner comparable to multispectral imaging, and the final methodology became a highly automated process. In this the Fort Hood project is currently unique amongst published HLC programmes. The utility of the process seems to be indicated by successful ground-truthing of results by UK student Simon Fitch undertaken as part of his MA placement at Fort Hood. Consequently, the results published here should be a strong endorsement not just of the essential principles of historic landscape characterisation, but also that the process has a wider applicability to regions with radically different histories and areas where available supporting data is of variable quality. The importance of appropriate technical and resource management expertise within management terms should be equally clear from this work.

All the authors felt that the experience of working in such a wonderfully diverse landscape was profound, whilst the support offered by the Fort Hood authorities was consistent and of immense value. Above all, however, was the sense that the project fitted into a wider tradition of innovative academic development and cooperation characterised, and fashioned, by the immense amount of work already carried out at the base. These activities have contributed to Fort Hood's pre-eminent position in the academic consciousness and ensure that this area of central Texas remains a landscape of international significance. As a group we would hope that future research, carried out in a similar spirit, will guarantee that this position is maintained.

Vince Gaffney and Cheryl Huckerby
Birmingham   Washington
October 2006

ACKNOWLEDGEMENTS

Thanks are due to all the CRM staff at Fort Hood, especially Karl Kleinbach and Kristen Wenzel, for giving their time, knowledge and hospitality so freely along with Sunny Wood and Gil Eckrich for help with the photos. Thanks are also due to all the archaeologists in Texas who took time out of their busy schedules to attend the seminar at the University of Texas in Austin, and in particular to Doug Boyd for the additional information he provided. In the United Kingdom we would like to thank Dr Chris Gaffney for assisting with geophysics training at the Fort Hood Field School. Exegesis encouraged and facilitated Lucie Dingwall's participation in the later stages of the project; Harry Buglass prepared the superb cover illustration. Within Birmingham, Dr Mark Bunch assisted in the creation of the Google Earth data, Helen Gaffney helped format the text, multiply, whilst Helen Goodchild cast her expert eye over the final draft. Caroline Raynor managed the finances of the project with her usual efficiency and good humour and Professor John Hunter supported and encouraged the team throughout the time of the project.

This report is dedicated to the memory of Tony Maguire.

Glynn Barratt, Lucie Dingwall, Vince Gaffney, Simon Fitch and Cheryl Huckerby

1. The origins and aims of the Fort Hood historic landscape characterisation project

The Fort Hood Historic Historic Landscape Characterisation (HLC) project was a collabration forged by the head of the cultural resource management program at Fort Hood, Dr Cheryl Huckerby with the Institute of Archaeology and Antiquity at the University of Birmingham (UK). The goal of this partnership was to explore new methodologies for the purposes of heritage management at Fort Hood in Texas. This vision led to an exciting collaboration between archaeologists from the United States of America and Europe and drew on a two-way exchange of knowledge and ideas, enabling the development of a pioneering landscape characterisation project. The programme was designed to satify the exacting land management requirements of the base, support decision-making related to the conservation of the natural and cultural heritage of the area but also to facilitate the complex interaction of a range of military and civilian uses of the landscape.

Although a more detailed background to Fort Hood is provided in Chapter 3 some consideration of the base and the activities associated with its landscape must be provided at the onset in order to understand the origins and aims of the project. Fort Hood is the largest active armoured post in the USA covering an area of approximately 218,000 acres (88,221 hectares). Located on the Edwards Plateau in Central Texas, and straddling Bell and Coryell counties, the base is adjacent to the small town of Killeen, approximately 60 miles north of Austin and 50 miles south of Waco. It lies immediately west of the Belton reservoir. Fort Hood was originally established as a military training camp in 1942 as a result of American involvement in World War II, and had become a permanent military installation by 1951.

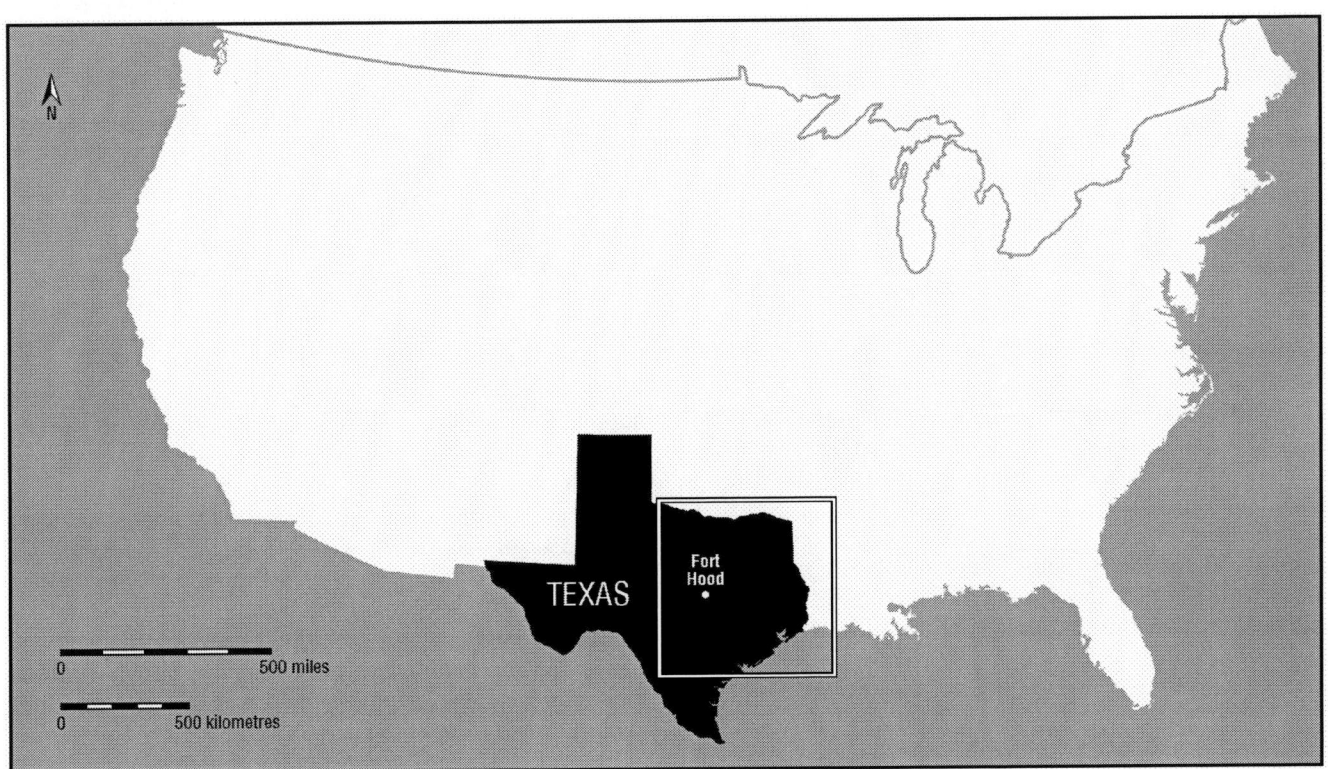

Figure 1: Fort Hood, location

The cultural resource management programme at Fort Hood encompasses multiple roles, which, as in comparable landscapes throughout the world, have the potential to conflict with each other. However, Fort Hood is a unique place in cultural resource management terms and represents unique challenges. It combines the role of being an archaeological landscape of international significance with that of being one of the largest military bases in the world, and the project was undertaken during a period when awareness of military training needs was exceptionally heightened, immediately following the terrorist attacks on the USA in September 2001.

There are also significant civilian demands on the land which have to be considered by the cultural resource management programme, for example the base is used extensively for hunting, and there is still a limited amount of cattle grazing in certain areas (plates 2 and 3). In addition, and of great significance to the considerations of the cultural resource management programme, there are strong local cultural ties to the land at Fort Hood, both in regard to the historic communities from which the population was abruptly removed when the base was established, and, amongst indigenous commmunities, to the Native American sacred sites asscoiated with the area (the Comanche National Cemetery and the Leon River Medicine Wheel, Quigg et al. 1996). The challenge faced by the project team was to use innovative techniques to inform balanced and integrated management approaches that would be appropriate for such a significant resource with such huge potential.

1.1 Previous archaeological work at Fort Hood

The primary legislation under which the cultural resource management program at Fort Hood operates is the National Historical Preservation Act of 1966, the Archaeological Resources Preservation Act of 1979 and the Native American Graves Protection and Repatriation Act of 1990. In 1990, Fort Hood entered into a programmatic agreement with the United States Army, the Texas State Historic Preservation Officer (SHPO) and the Advisory Council for Historic Preservation. In accordance with this agreement, a Historic Preservation Plan was developed. This was renewed in 1994 as a cultural resource management plan (Jackson 1994), which established long-term goals for managing Fort Hood's cultural resources.

The facility has been subject to intensive archaeological investigations since the late 1970s, and by the time that this project began in 2001, 98.6% of the Training and Cantonment Areas, and 71.1% of the Livefire and Impact Area had been surveyed (Huckerby 2000). These surveys have been conducted in order to comply with federal legislation that requires federal agencies to inventory and evaluate their cultural resources, to nominate those potentially eligible for inclusion on the National Register of Historic Places (NRHP), and to ensure proper management of these significant resources, either through preservation or data recovery. Overall policy at Fort Hood has been to focus on the protection of all NRHP eligible and potentially eligible cultural resources (Huckerby 2000), whilst minimising restrictions on the military mission. So far the cultural resource management programme has been primarily directed towards the assessment of sites for NRHP eligibility (figure 2). This has been approached differently for the prehistoric and historic resources. There has been an emphasis on historic document review for the historic resource, whilst the approach for the prehistoric resource has consisted of shovel testing proceeding to National Register testing, prioritised on the basis of mission needs.

The original surface inventory of prehistoric sites did not involve consideration of the geomorphological context of sites nor did this include sub-surface shovel testing. However, since 1992, known sites have been re-visited, assessed for their geomorphology, and those assessed as having a potential for intact deposits have been systematically evaluated by shovel testing. Some new sites were also discovered and evaluated. Since 1993, test excavations consisting of formal testing of sites with uncertain research potential have been carried out, with some proceeding on to data recovery excavations for sites which could not be preserved and protected (Ellis et al. 1994). A basic geomorphological history was established for the deposition of alluvial sediments in the major drainages (Nordt 1992).

With regard to the Historic period, the Historic Document Review that was underway at the initiation of the project resulted in chain of title information for all properties associated with historic archaeological resources, an archaeological integrity assessment of all historical archaeological sites, an historic context for the 1942-3 land acquisition properties and a popular history of European life on the pre-Fort Hood landscape. This provides information required to support site assessments for National Register eligibility (Blake 2001, Dase et al. 2003, Freeman et al. 2001, Pugsley 2001, Sitton 2003, Stabler 1999, Ward et al. 2000).

In addition to these intensive National Register testing surveys, a number of research projects have also been undertaken at Fort Hood. In many cases, these studies utilised the unique combination of resources provided by Fort Hood to develop innovative strategies for research and management. One of the most significant of these studies was the attempt at classification of prehistoric and historic sites at Fort Hood using exploratory data analysis to define groups of related sites. The study was carried out by Williams, Briuer and Limp in the 1980s, and, as one of the first uses of GIS in archaeology, it is illustrative of the seminal research that has been made possible because of the archaeological resource at Fort Hood (Williams et al. 1990a and 1990b). Predictive models for Fort Hood were developed in the 1980s and subsequently revised for prehistoric and historic site locations at Fort Hood (Carlson et al. 1994). On the basis of this, a model for prehistoric land use was developed that identified general trends and focused on the increasing use through time of food sources with comparatively lower cost benefit ratios (Thoms 1993, 61). In the early 1990s, a study was carried out which was aimed at developing a prehistoric research design for Fort Hood (Ellis et al. 1994). The study determined that the simplistic cultural-historical perspective that had prevailed throughout the history of archaeological research in Central Texas was not providing satisfactory results. The resulting document defined the ultimate goals of prehistoric archaeological research at Fort Hood and established a set of significance standards, under NRHP inclusion criteria, for judging the research potential of individual prehistoric sites. More detail about previous work at the base is provided in the Archaeological review of Fort Hood in Chapter 3.

Plate 1: Military land use at Fort Hood – photo by Gil Eckrich

Plates 2 and 3: Aspects of civilian land use at Fort Hood – photos by Gil Eckrich

Plate 4: Fort Hood Cantonment – photo by Gil Eckrich

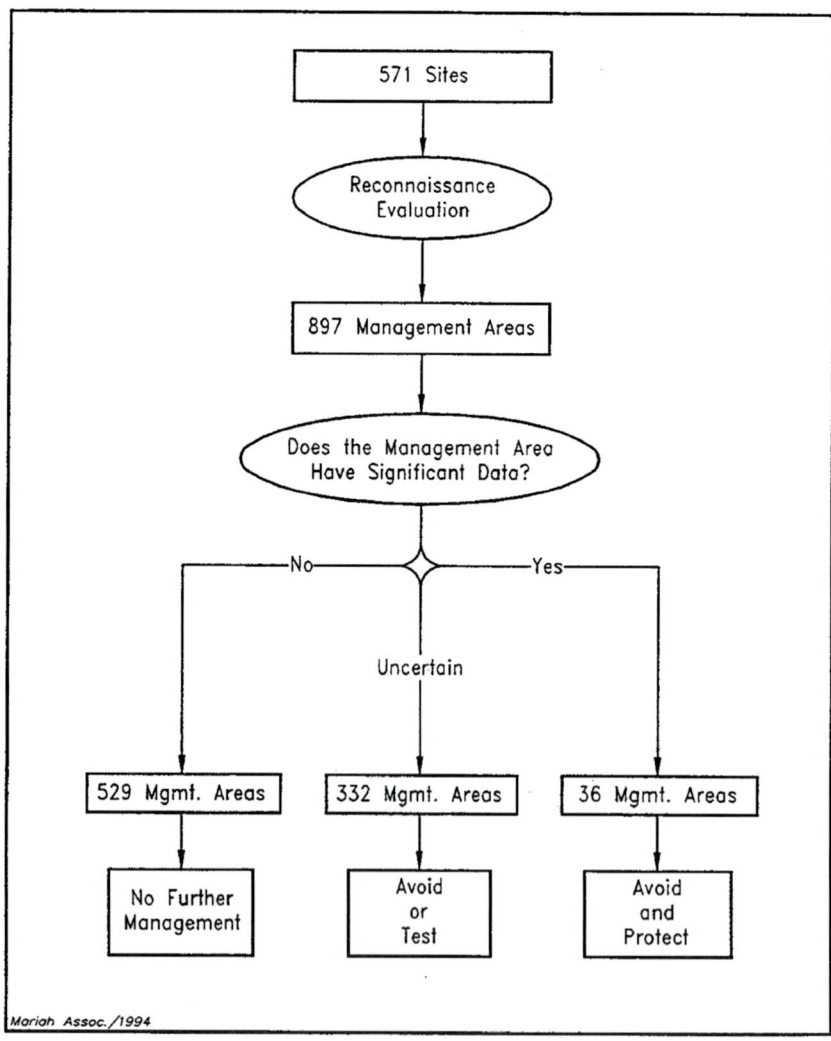

Figure 2: Schematic of evaluation process (Trierweiler 1996a, figure 2)

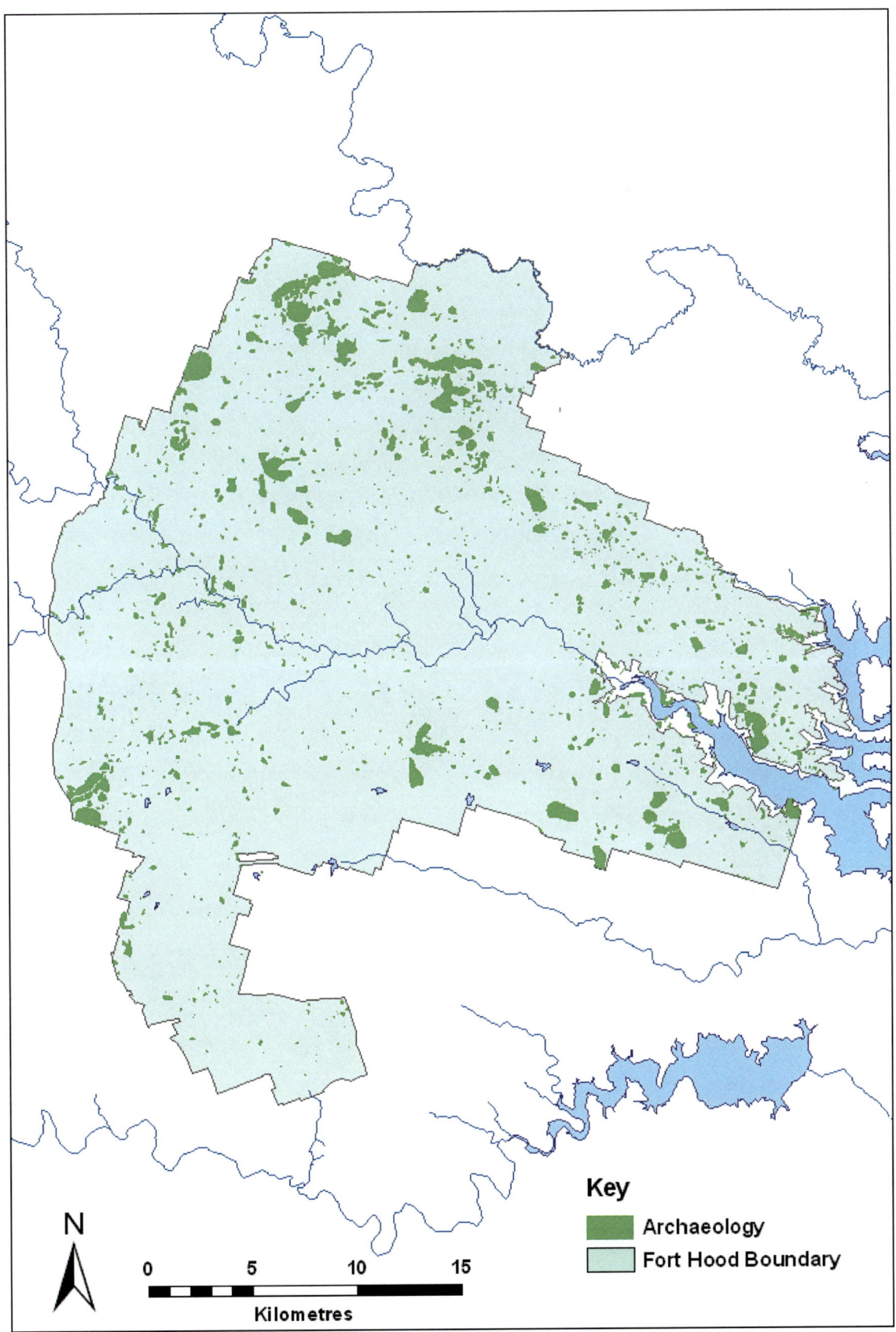

Figure 3: Fort Hood and recorded archaeological sites

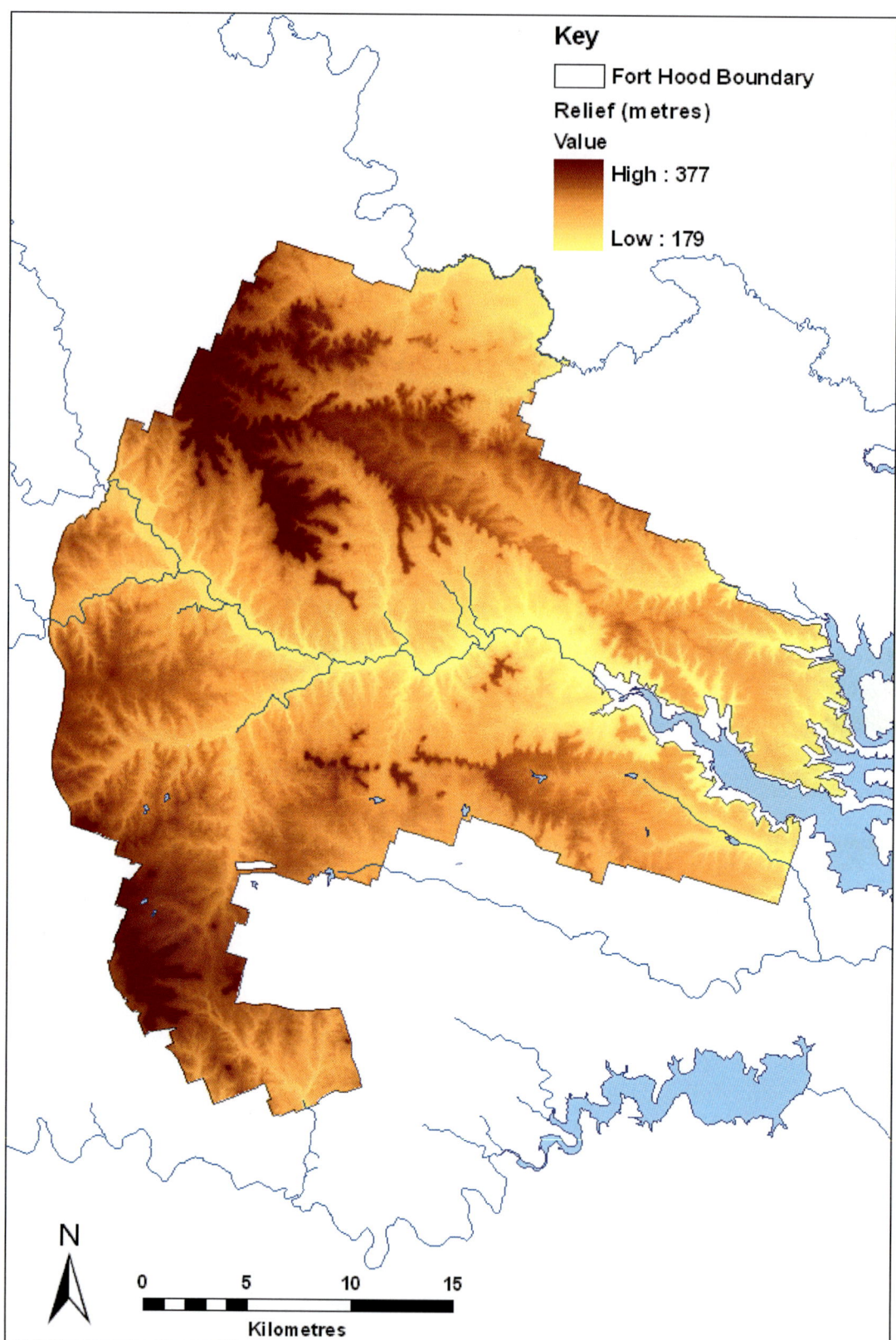

Figure 4: Fort Hood, relief and major hydrology features

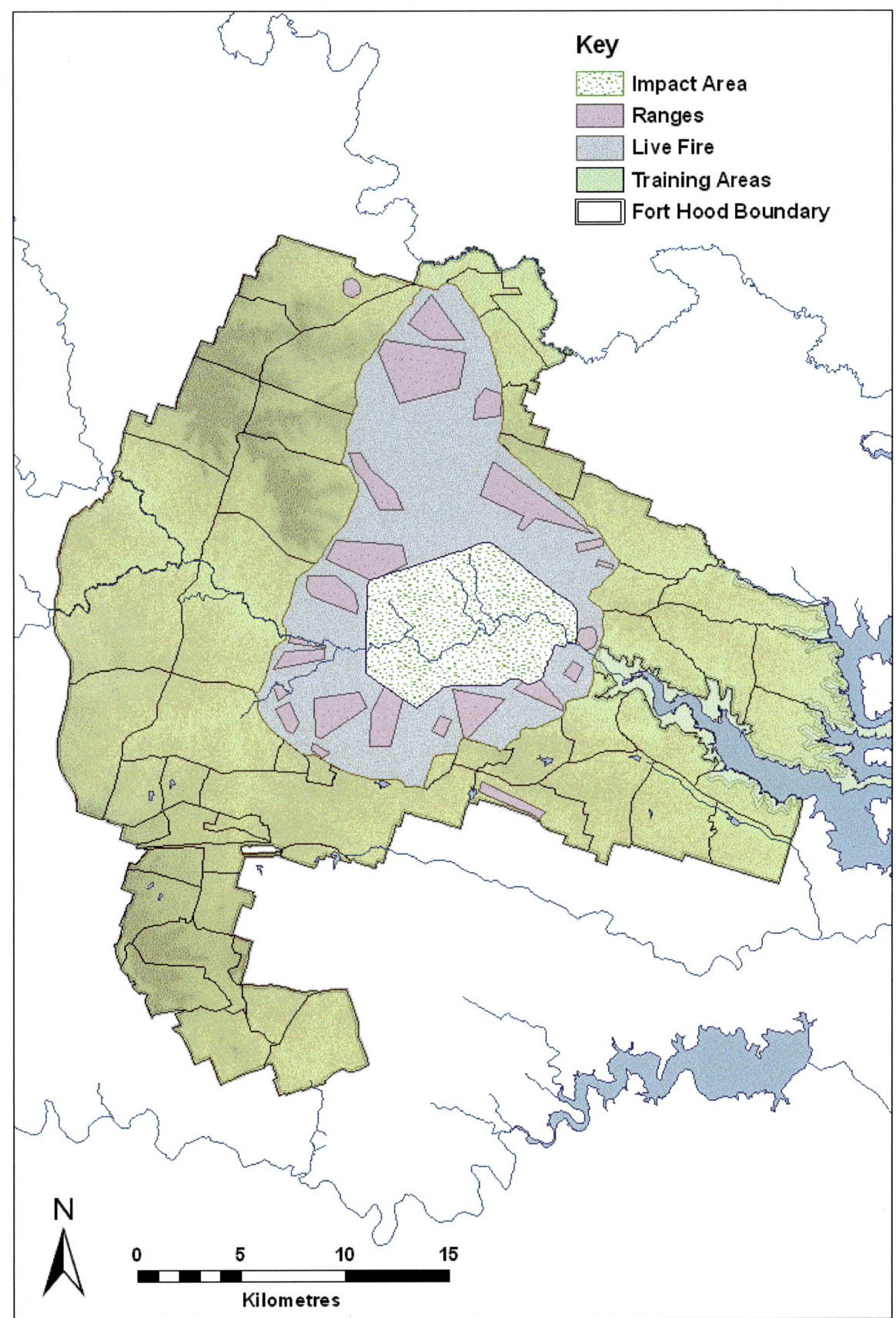

Figure 5: Fort Hood training areas, livefire and impact zones

1.2 Overview of the data

The intensity of survey on the base and the relative comprehensiveness of the inventory of cultural resources for large areas of Fort Hood make its potential as a research tool very high. Information on prehistoric and historic archaeological sites is held digitally in Esri's ArcView GIS as polygons, together with some attribute data. The quantity and range of natural environmental data for the whole of Fort Hood, also held in ArcView, is an extremely valuable resource, and the potential for integrated analysis with archaeological data via the use of GIS technology is enormous. As well as a wealth of data relating to present-day human activity, including urban areas, buildings, infrastructure, political and administrative boundaries, the data includes contour information, a 30m resolution Digital Elevation Model and derived products (slope, aspect, hillshade), detailed information on hydrology, land-use and vegetation cover, geology, soils, major geomorphological formations, and also an analytical layer relating to ease of movement across the terrain.

A consequence of previous assessments of the prehistoric archaeological resource at Fort Hood is that our knowledge of these periods is restricted largely to the locations of individual sites and the identification of eligible and potentially eligible NHRP features. The testing program has also been targeted at sites in areas most at risk, so there is less data available for sites in lower-risk areas, such as environmental set-aside areas.

A major gap in the data is the establishment of a detailed geomorphological/ palaeoenvironmental context. Nordt's geomorphic history covered the major drainages, but the study did not extend into smaller drainages and did not deal with colluvial processes or landforms. A more detailed study building on the earlier baseline information would contribute towards the understanding of critical research issues such as past climate change. Detailed mapping of archaeological and palaeohydrological features from remotely sensed data (aerial photographs and satellite imagery) is also lacking. Aerial photographs are held digitally at the base but require rectification and interpretation as part of a larger mapping programme.

While the level of archaeological and environmental data available is comparatively high, and there is detailed data available for individual sites, the data has mainly been collected for very specific purposes and it exists very much as raw data, with little integrated analysis and interpretation. This is particularly apparent in relation to the group value of sites, which are usually considered in isolation, and the relationship to sites or groups of sites to the wider landscape. The situation for the prehistoric period is summed up very succinctly by Ellis's statement that "we have accumulated a wealth of data but we have very little information" (Ellis 1994, 25).

Knowledge and analysis of the historic archaeological resource is more developed. However, a significant gap in the data for the historic period is comprehensive digital historic mapping. GIS layers containing the original land grant maps for the relevant sections of Bell and Coryell counties, and the boundaries of pre-acquisition land tracts and associated ownership histories would be valuable. The historic sites at Fort Hood represent an almost unique resource for the study of community development, due to the abrupt cut-off of entire communities with the establishment of Camp Hood in 1942 (Williams *et al.* 1990), and the potential for high-level spatial analysis of these communities is very high. Moreover, many of the present-day communities surrounding Fort Hood still retain links with these historic communities. This peculiar context considerably enhances the research potential of the base, the significance of the known sites in landscape terms and, not least, the perceived value of historic sites to the contemporary population.

1.3 Overview of management approaches

There are a number of inter-related issues arising from past approaches to cultural resource management at Fort Hood that require some comment, particularly in relation to the prehistoric period. The quantity of data gathered together at Fort Hood provides a major opportunity for synthesis and analysis (tables 1 and 2 below show the number of recorded Prehistoric and Historic sites at Fort Hood, broken down by site type). This is a fundamental point as in order to protect cultural resources effectively, it is necessary to know not just where they are, but what their significance is (in terms of either contemporary or past populations). Knowing the significance of a site in academic/research terms will also establish its significance in management terms, leading to the correct and most efficient management of cultural resources. Although the site inventory is comprehensive for large areas, it remains, essentially, a record of individual components with few means of demonstrating context and continuity. The research potential of the inventory as a whole is far greater than the sum of sites considered individually. There has been little consideration of group value or landscape context in the testing and data recovery programmes in relation to the cultural landscape of Fort Hood. Consequently, the significance of sites has therefore been evaluated purely from the perspective of the physical remains associated with the site under investigation and presented devoid of any larger context.

Group value is now recognised as crucial when considering significance, as the value of a particular site may be enhanced either by its association with other sites of different types and periods, or by clustering with other sites of the same type (Startin 1994). Whilst it is true that there is some provision for assessment of group value of historic sites within the Fort Hood Standards of Significance for Archaeological Sites, under the banner of 'Community Districts', there has been no substantial effort to extend the concept of group value to prehistoric sites on the base (Ellis *et al.* 1994, Jackson 1994).

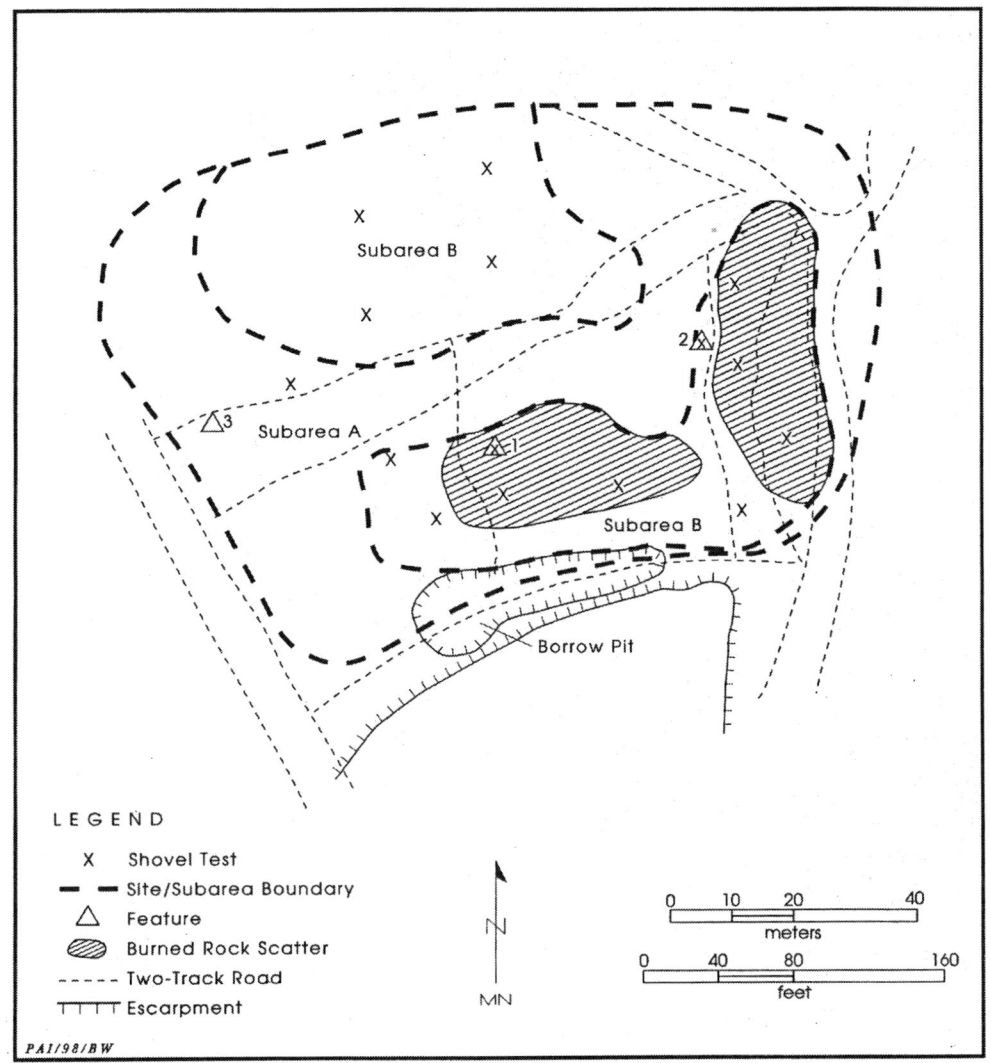

Figure 6: Evaluation plan from Site 41CV988 (Kleinbach 1999, figure 19)

However, implementation of such models is increasingly present within the wider domain of heritage management (Clark *et al.* 2004). New theoretical and management procedures are now being applied, that steer away from solely using individual sites as the basis for understanding, and move towards more broadly-based methods which can relate to extensive areas and to inter-relationships and interactions.

In some cases sites which may, apparently, have a lesser archaeological value in respect of their physical remains may achieve significance through their relationship to other sites or even the surrounding landscape (in respect of military history the significance of context may be illustrated by reference to the Defence of Britain project at http://www.helm.org.uk/server/show/category.7766 and English Heritage 2003).

Site Type	Number
Artifact scatter	5
Burned rock midden	61
Burned rock mound	54
Burned rock scatter	220
Find spot	1
Hearth	1
Lithic scatter	358
Lithic resource procurement area (LRPA)	78
Medicine Wheel	1
Open camp	196
Other scatter	1
Rockshelter	150
Sinkhole	4
TOTAL	1130

Table 1: Recorded Prehistoric sites at Fort Hood (as of June 2002)

Site Type	Number
Animal dip tank	6
Artifact scatter	323
Bridge	13
Building	3
Cattle dip tank	3
Cattle trough	1
Cemetery	13
Church	1
Cistern	16
Corral	11
Culvert	1
Dump	40
Farm/ranch	549
Farmstead	1
Fence	1
Firing range	1
Foundation	2
Hearth	1
Historic graffiti	1
Military site	7
Military training site	1
Mound	1
Quarry	1
Railroad	1
Rockshelter	2
Rock wall	1
Root cellar	3
Rubble	1
School	8
Settlement	2
Sheep dip tank	1
Site	21
Spring house	1
Stock pen	3
Stock tank	2
Structure	1
Trough	2
Water pipe	1
Water storage site	19
Water supply site	23
Water tank	7
Water trough	4
Well	14
Well head	2
Windmill base	2
TOTAL	**1118**

Table 2: Recorded Historic sites at Fort Hood (as of June 2002)

In the past, the entire focus of the cultural resource management programme at Fort Hood has been on National Register eligibility testing, with data recovery viewed both as a final compliance step and as the only mitigation option (Huckerby 2000). This has been partly a result of, and partly a cause of, the issues raised above. With this type of approach, the elements so protected are often no more than a small and often unrepresentative fragment of the complex whole (Herring 1998). Where groups of people lived, why they chose to live there, and what their relationship was with the surrounding area, and with other groups of people, are questions that most geographers, ethnologists, anthropologists and archaeologists routinely ask (Stančič et al. 1996). So far, approaches to the evidence have not enabled these questions to be answered.

The fundamental managment problems associated with such an attitude are raised in the 1994 document concerned with developing significance standards for Fort Hood. It states that "non-sites (by definition) have no data content bearing on the research issues and are determined non-significant.....Sites with contextual fatal flaws (again, by definition) have no significance regardless of the amount of data actually present." (Ellis et al. 1994, 181). Such a position was always contentious given the early recognition of the value of 'non-site' archaeology within the United states (Gaffney and Tingle 1984) but, in recent years, there has also been an increasing appreciation within cultural resource management of the importance of landscape in understanding the past, and of the concept that spaces between individual sites can be as important and tell us as much about the past as the sites themselves. As a result, there has been an attempt to move beyond site-focused designations of archaeological importance, with the aim of analysing landscapes as a whole. This approach does not leave 'white areas' that appear to be judged as having no value whatsoever in cultural terms. This does not imply that all areas are nationally important, but allows sensible decisions to be made based on a more complete understanding of past land-use (Fairclough et al. 1999; Clark et al. 2004).

As a consequence of previous practise there is therefore a real imperative to find an alternative approach which will lead not only to a greater understanding of the cultural resources at Fort Hood, but will enable a range of different management approaches to be carried out, thus providing the basis for attempting flexible, integrated and positive management for the whole landscape, not just the "rigid protection of some of its parts" (Fairclough et al. 1999). A succesful approach would also be concerned with the relationship between human activity and the natural environment as this may help to answer some of the questions that are central to current research, such as understanding the relationship between burned rock sites, climatic changes and cultural adaptations in subsistence strategies (Ellis et al. 1994). The Fort Hood Historic Landscape Characterisation project was born out of this need for informed, relexive management strategies.

1.4 Aims of the Fort Hood historic landscape characterisation project

The Fort Hood historic landscape characterisation project sought to provide a management framework that would support the co-existence of a modern, sophisticated cultural resource management programme, in a unique and complex historic landscape, with the requirements of an active military training program and with current civilian land-use.

The broad objectives of the project were:
- To apply novel management practises to the cultural data at Fort Hood and thereby assist heritage managers at the base in their desire to support key research programmes
- To develop new approaches to assessment that moved beyond site-focused designations of significance, considering landscape perspectives such as the group value of sites, the 'blank' areas between sites, local distinctiveness and significant natural places in the landscape
- To provide a framework that would allow a range of different management approaches for the whole landscape, so that all of the landscape could be effectively and sustainably managed, thus avoiding the situation where individual parts are artifically preserved within a setting whose archaeological and historical value is otherwise completely ignored
- To provide a broad-brush landscape study that would form a baseline from which future, more detailed research and assessment could follow
- To support the Fort Hood Cultural Resource Management Programme's core functions, and facilitate the integration of the cultural resource management program with other environmental and conservation programs at Fort Hood
- To continue the tradition of innovative archaeological work at Fort Hood by exploring the use of landscape characterisation techniques that were developed for a very different, European archaeological landscape, and adapting them in novel ways for this unique and exciting landscape.

2. Approaches to historic landscape characterisation

2.1 Principles of historic landscape characterisation

Before considering issues related to the implementation of historic landscape characterisation, it is important initially to consider the terms that are being used, and to understand what is actually meant by 'historic landscape'. The term 'historic' as used in this context encompasses all previous human activity from the earliest humans up to the present day, and does not refer solely to that commonly known as the 'Historic' period in Central Texas. The term 'landscape' is an entirely human concept of an area of land, and it is the human perception that makes an area into a 'landscape'.

The *historic landscape* can be defined as a spatial and temporal entity, which is dynamic and ever-changing, and reflects a number of different factors. These include the physical evidence of human interaction with nature, the role of prehistoric and historic processes in shaping the present landscape, the inter-relationship and distribution of features within the landscape (Fairclough *et al.* 1999, Clark *et al.* 2004), and also the way in which humans perceive and observe the present-day landscape. The historic landscape can encompass topography, habitats, semi-natural features and palaeoenvironmental deposits as well as archaeological sites, sacred sites, historic buildings, and the modern built environment (Department of the Army 2000). It can also encompass wholly natural features, and intangible and non-visual elements such as cultural and psychological perceptions, and historical associations (Fairclough 2001).

The dominant landscape character exhibited today is dictated by recent land use, but even this has also been shaped by more subtle histories of human activity that may extend back into prehistory. Historic landscape characterisation (hereafter referred to as HLC) is primarily concerned with mapping the historic dimension of the present-day landscape, and the key principle is that it is a non-selective, interpretative approach to managing change in the landscape. It is designed to produce a generalised understanding of the historic and archaeological dimension of the present-day landscape, and is based on the appreciation that every aspect of the landscape has been influenced by, and in many respects physically shaped by, human activities. The end result is a tool for understanding the processes of change in the historic environment as a whole, for identifying what is vulnerable, and for maintaining diversity and distinctiveness in the local scene.

HLC has been applied extensively in the United Kingdom and elsewhere in Europe, although its origins lie in England in the early 1990s. In September 1991, the Government White Paper "This Common Inheritance" invited English Heritage to prepare a list of landscapes of historic importance (English Heritage 1991), similar to its Register of Parks and Gardens of Special Historic Interest. The intended purpose of this work was to define areas of landscape deemed to be more 'historic' and, therefore, more worthy of preservation than the surrounding areas. Subsequently, English Heritage instigated a number of pilot projects to assess appropriate methodologies for identifying 'historic landscapes' (summarised in Fairclough *et al.* 1999). The results led to the view that a more holistic approach to historic landscape assessment than that originally envisaged was appropriate and a fuller understanding that the "requirements for historic landscape conservation would not be met by a selective register" (Fairclough 1994, 35).

A more holistic approach was anticipated to characterise all areas within the landscape with reference to agreed criteria, and not concentrate on the identification of key 'historic landscapes'. Such an approach, in which the whole of an area of landscape is assessed and characterised, is in line with methodologies of landscape assessment frequently undertaken for non-historical reasons and often presented as development or spatial plans. The general purpose of these has been defined by the Countryside Agency (Countryside Commission 1993, 1998; Countryside Agency 1999) as assisting local authorities, land use and conservation agencies and the private sector to:

Understand how and why landscapes are important.
- Promote the appreciation of landscape issues.
- Successfully accommodate new development within the landscape.
- Guide and direct landscape change.

HLC is concerned with recognising the ways in which the present landscape reflects how people have exploited, changed and adapted to their physical environment through time, with respect to different social, economic, technological and cultural aspects of life. The resultant pattern of physical features varies consistently from one place to another because of these consistent underlying constraints and influences of geography, history and tradition. Fairclough has defined historic landscape character assessment as "...the ways in which, in the present landscape, we can see and interpret physical remains as indicators of how the landscape's character has been created over thousands of years by the interaction of people and their environment." (Fairclough *et al.* 1999, 3).

HLC allows the landscape to be seen as a palimpsest within which preceding land use informs succeeding settlement. It provides a broad analysis of the physical remains of past social practices as they survive within today's landscape, and aims to trace the changing ways in which the different parts of the landscape have been inhabited over time, on the basis of the *visible* evidence within the modern landscape. Consequently, it provides a broad impression of how historical forces have contributed toward landscape change. It is important to recognise that HLC data should not be regarded as a stand-alone tool, nor as a replacement for other datasets such as Sites and Monuments Records. Rather, it is intended as a complementary dataset that can be used in conjunction with other information to aid integrated management (Clark *et al.* 2004).

The broad principles outlined above have more recently been simplified and codified for use in a wider European context as part of the Culture 2000 *European Pathways to the Cultural Landscape* programme (www.pcl-eu.de/project/agenda/philo.php, Fairclough and Rippon 2002 and Clark *et al.* 2004). These principles are produced complete in the box below as useful shorthand to the philosophical framework for the process of Landscape Characterisation.

Philosophy for Historic Landscape Characterisation
Adapted by the EU Culture 2000 network
'European Pathways to the Cultural Landscape'

Within the general definition of landscape established by the European Landscape convention:- *"an area, as perceived by people whose character is the result of the action and interaction of natural and/or human factors"*

The EPCL (along with other types of archaeologically based landscape work) adapted the following principles:

- **Present not past; landscape as material culture:** it is the present-day landscape that is the main object of study and protection
- **Landscape as history not geography:** the most important characteristic of landscape is its time-depth; change and earlier landscapes exists in the present landscape
- HLC-based research and understanding is concerned with **area not point** data - landscape not sites
- All aspects of the landscape, no matter how modern, are treated as part of landscape character; **not just 'special' areas**
- Semi-natural and living features (woodland, land cover, hedges etc.) are as much a part of landscape character as archaeological features; **human landscape – bio-diversity is a cultural phenomenon**
- A characterisation of landscape is a matter of **interpretation not record, perception not facts**; "landscape" is an idea not a thing, although constructed by minds and emotions from the combination of physical objects; **landscape not environment**
- **Peoples' views:** an important aspect of landscape character in EPCL will be the collective and public perceptions to lay alongside more expert views.

Figure 7: 'European Pathways to the Cultural Landscape' Philosophy for Historic Landscape Characterisation reproduced from Aldred and Fairclough 2003, 21.

2.2 Historic landscape characterisation methodologies

Although HLC methodology has developed and evolved through time, the fundamental principles have remained (Aldred and Fairclough 2003). The first stage of any HLC project consists of assessing every distinguishable land parcel of the study area and assigning it to the type which best represents its predominant historic landscape character, as far as this is determinable (Herring 1998). Once detailed HLC types have been defined, simplified and interpreted cultural landscape zones can be derived. The significance of these zones can then be evaluated using systematic assessment criteria, and appropriate management strategies implemented, and if required, integrated with existing natural resource assessments and management strategies. Sources used to determine HLC types should be systematic and consistent across the whole of the study area. The procedure is recursive, with the data collection stages and data analysis stages having the potential to inform each other. This approach enables general patterns of the cultural landscape to be discerned, while providing a basis for more detailed, localised work if necessary. The aim is to transform the presence and distribution of archaeological sites into qualities of the landscape, visible in the displays and maps created by the characterisation. One of the perceived strengths of this approach is that it addresses the cultural resource in its entirety.

Such a broad-brush approach emphasises analysis and understanding and as such enables research to move from the general to the particular, from a position of understanding (English Heritage 1994). It provides a conceptual framework within which all future archaeological and historical work can potentially be fitted so that there is a reflexive relationship between the characterisation and any archaeological recording, analysis and interpretation, and historical research (Herring 1998). It can also form the basis for new ways of telling the story of what is contained within the historic landscape to the communities who are associated with it today.

The Fort Hood HLC project design sought an approach based upon a broad survey of examples of similar work carried out in England. It is therefore appropriate to examine here the evolution of HLC in England and to assess the value and impact of the procedures to heritage managers in England. The first stage of English characterisation has been carried out on a county basis and has evolved within this county framework. Consequently, whilst following the same guiding principles no two applied methodologies are exactly the same. Elements of several such projects have proved influential in the design of the Fort Hood HLC methodology, ranging from the pilot HLC project undertaken in Cornwall in the early 1990s (Herring 1998) to the more recent Shropshire and Lancashire models (Wigley 2001). More recently, analysis of HLC methodologies by Aldred and Fairclough (2002, chapter 2) has suggested that such schemes tend to break down into four broad types of project: which, to some extent, represent a chronological development;

- Classification-led - early HLC projects which used prescriptive, pre-defined and implicit classifications, using map-based field morphologies to build HLC data models
- Document-led - prescriptive, pre-defined and implicit classifications which are primarily associated with the use of historic mapping to provide a historic rationale to classification-led schemes
- Attribute-led - classifications derived from, usually, computer-based modelling of a range of attribute data associated with field morphologies generating models with explicit data structures
- Multi-mode - more recent projects using a blend of prescriptive and descriptive attributes associated with morphological criteria, and within computer-based analysis, and aimed at creating models of landscape character

The categorisation of HLC schemes provided by Aldred and Fairclough indicates that, following the inception of HLC, probably the most significant aspect of the evolution of basic methodology has been the migration of characterisation mapping from conventional paper-based cartography to Geographical Information System technology. It is worth noting that this period of evolution of characterisation has closely matched the adoption and assimilation of GIS within the English Heritage Management community as a whole. The effect that the use of GIS has had on HLC has not been restricted merely to the way in which data is held and displayed. GIS has substantially changed the way in which data is collected, analysed and used in two very significant ways.

The first is that GIS allows much greater flexibility than static mapping in manipulating and analysing the data to create a range of classifications, interpretations and management implementations. In the earliest paper-based projects, after the initial HLC land types had been created, decisions had to be made regarding classifying HLC polygons into larger zones for management and interpretation purposes. Once such decisions had been made and maps created, it could then involve a great deal of work to change the level of classification and interpretation. GIS, however, makes it relatively easy to create a range of classifications and interpretations in order to address differing requirements. Secondly, GIS databases enable the decisions and interpretations that have led to the attribution of an area of landscape to a particular HLC type to be recorded and made transparent, thus allowing future users to assess the subjectivity of the characterisation and, if necessary, defend any planning decisions made on the basis of an HLC characterisation programme (Fairclough 2001).

With the gradual adoption of GIS, HLC projects in England have refined the methodology that was developed for the earlier projects, and have tended to move from a classification-led method to an attribute-based system. In classification-led or 'prescriptive' approaches, the level of interpretation is decided and HLC types are defined, at the start of the project, and areas of land are then allocated to types on the basis of interpretations and observations. This method was followed by earlier projects including the Cornwall HLC (Herring 1998). Attribute-based or 'descriptive' approaches first assign a range of attributes to each polygon and then implement a GIS analysis to determine the HLC types to which each polygon should be allocated. The HLC types are defined through analysis of the combinations in which certain attributes occur. For example, in a UK example, areas of predominantly small fields (Attribute 1), that have predominantly sinuous boundaries (Attribute 2), some or all of which have 's-curve' morphology (Attribute 3), can be defined as 'piecemeal enclosure' character type. The HLC types are therefore generic in nature and may occur in different parts of the landscape, but in each case they are defined by the same combinations of attributes (Wigley 2002). This method attempts to maintain the characterisation processes itself as 'value free' as possible, making the resulting HLC types defensible as being based on a consistent set of criteria. This method also allows the generation of many different classifications and interpretations. This type of methodology has been followed by the more recent characterisation exercises undertaken in the counties of Herefordshire, Shropshire and Lancashire (White and Ray 2000). As indicated by Aldred and Fairclough (2002) it has, in practice, been possible to utilise elements of each approach, for example to define a simple framework of broad HLC types into which to fit more detailed HLC types derived on the basis of GIS analysis of polygon attributes. Not surprisingly, perhaps, multi-mode approaches with increasing sophistication, including an enhanced use of time-depth as a variable within classification, are emerging as the dominant mode of analysis and are perceived as the most profitable route for further development (Aldred and Fairclough 2002, 20).

Elsewhere in the UK, Wales and Scotland have followed slightly different approaches to the historic landscape, although the difference lies in methodology rather than aims and principles. In Wales, the '*LANDMAP*' national land information system separates the landscape into five Aspects for evaluation: *Geological Landscape, Landscape Habitats, Visual and Sensory, Historic Landscape* and *Cultural Landscape* (Countryside Commission for Wales 2004). In Scotland, '*Historic Land-use Assessment*' is the methodology used for analysing past and present land-use. Each area with similar origins is given one of 55 '*Historic Land-use Types*', and is also allocated a '*Category Group*', or a '*Period of Origin*'. Wherever past land-use has been detected, an area is also allocated '*Relict Category*', '*Relict Period*' and '*Relict Type*' (RCAHMS 2006).

However, although the principles underpinning approaches to historic landscape in the UK and Europe are still relevant and adaptable to other areas of the world, devising the methodology for the Fort Hood HLC project raised a number of new questions and challenges. It was these challenges that fuelled the experimentation and novel application of HLC techniques and principles that exemplify the Fort Hood HLC project.

2.3 Developing the Fort Hood methodology

As outlined above, one of the fundamental principles of HLC is the use of consistent and comprehensive source material. The primary inputs within an HLC analysis were characterised by Aldred and Fairclough (2002, 22) as;

- morphological analysis (mainly of field patterns);
- recording of historic maps;
- use of documentary evidence;
- recording present-day land-use;
- archaeological interpretation;
- air photo evidence;
- assessing past land-use;
- other research.

However, it was apparent from the project-planning stage that different types of primary data sources would have to be used for the Fort Hood characterisation than those that have been used in the UK. HLC in Britain and Europe has been developed to characterise a landscape which is clearly a *palimpsest*, where the remains of numerous episodes of human presence are retained in the present day landscape. In such countries the formalised field patterns which have become established, often over several thousand years, have provided a good starting point for characterisation. Often old maps, perhaps going back from the present day as far as the 16th century are available, and these may be used to identify and date the changing phases of enclosure and the age and duration of boundaries. An example of such longevity in terms of cartography can be seen in the two map extracts below of a recent landscape analysis carried out at Cobham Park in Kent, England. As part of an evaluation of the archaeological content of the Cobham Park Estate an initial historic landscape characterisation was carried out using available mapping and aerial photography. In the example below, field boundaries which were extant at the time of the earliest available map, the Thomas Norton Map of 1641, can be seen persisting in the modern day landscape, clearly visible in current aerial photography (Barratt and Litherland 2003).

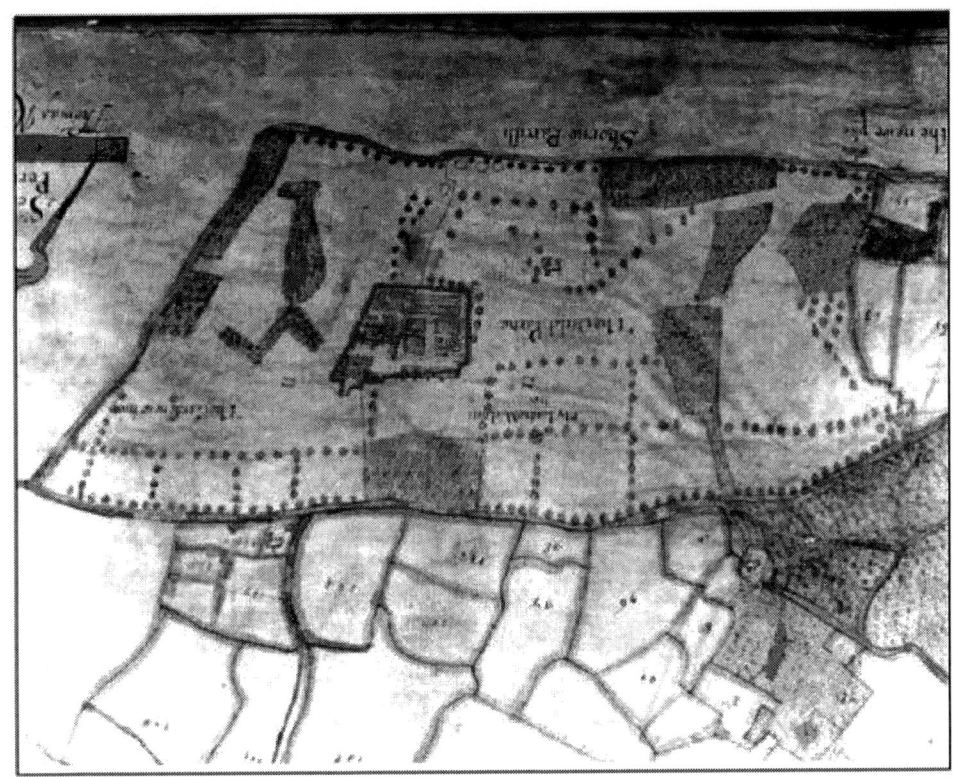

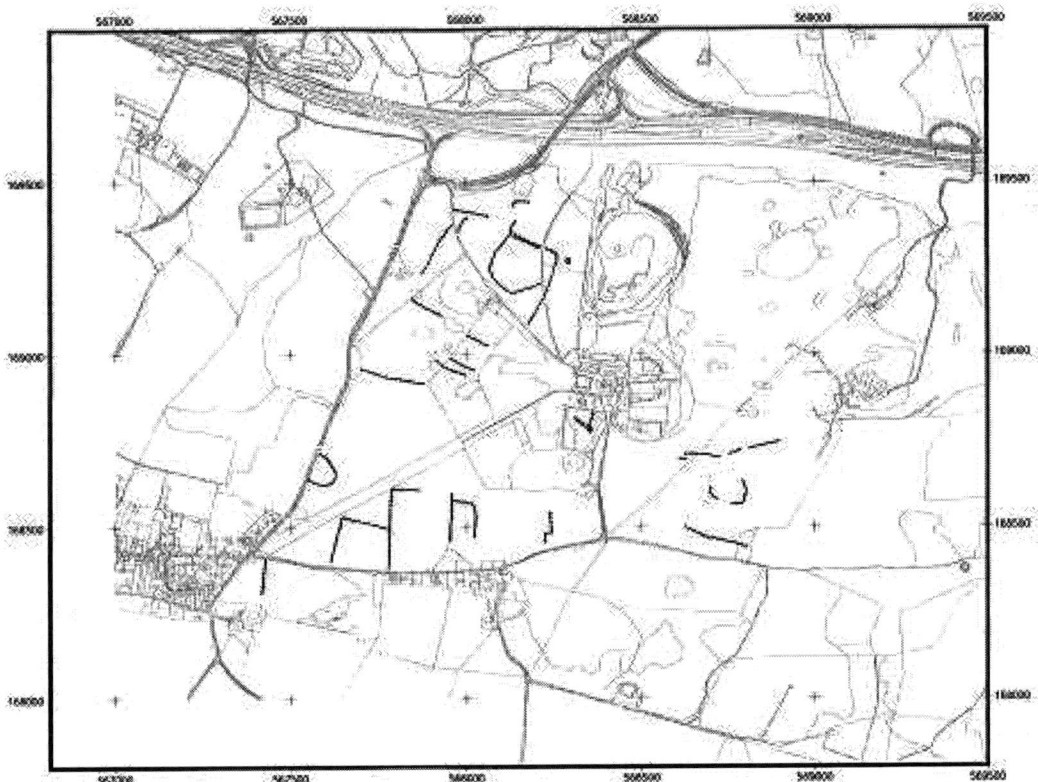

Figure 8: Landscape analysis at Cobham Park, Kent, UK. The Map on the top, from 1640, shows rectangular fields at the centre. These persist in the present landscape as evidenced by the aerial photographic transcription to the bottom. © Crown Copyright/database right 2007. An Ordnance Survey/EDINA supplied service.

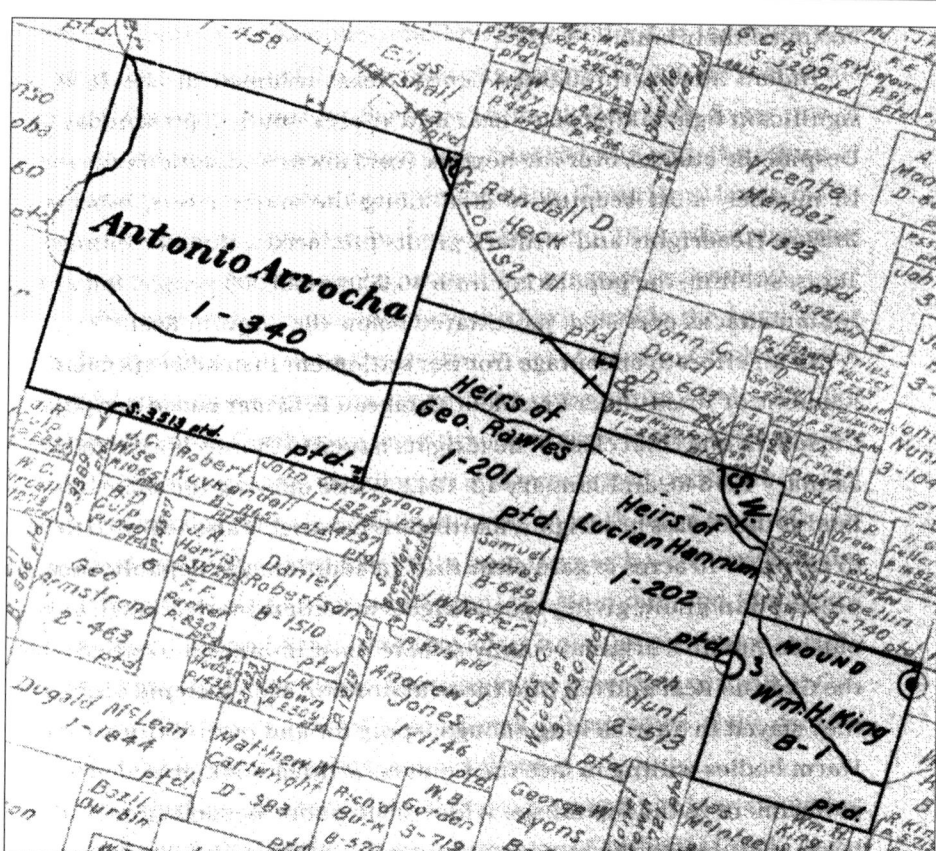

Figure 9: Example of land apportionment map showing early surveys in the Camp Hood area, from the General Land Office, and reproduced here from Pugsley W.S. 2001

Such survival is not unusual in examples of landscape from the UK, making it possible to assemble landscape units and basic categories for characterisation from an examination of the field boundary morphology. Indeed, most of the English characterisation projects are in large part an analysis of boundaries. Boundaries feature less prominently in areas of Scotland and Wales where there is more unenclosed upland, and for the most part, as in England, these areas tend to have been classified relatively homogenously. However, in countries where agricultural settlement has been more recent, such as North America, there is no comprehensive, detailed, cultural and historic mapping available. Furthermore, the radical differences in landscape, both environmental and cultural, mean that the field pattern is likely to be less useful, being relatively recent in origin and reflecting a combination of soil types and the land apportionment survey grid (figure 9).

Another major issue with the Fort Hood HLC project is the series of abrupt and wholesale changes that have occurred over the landscape within a relatively short space of time. The removal of the indigenous Native American population, who employed a hunter-gatherer way of life with minimal use of agriculture, was followed, after a hiatus, by the settlement of European farmers in the 19th century. Colonial advance was associated with a radically different use of the land for permanent settlement, farming and ranching. The European farmers were, in turn, very suddenly supplanted and their farming lifestyle replaced by monolithic military use of the land. There is nowhere in Europe where large-scale land-use has changed from hunter-gathering to developed farming to industrial-scale military use all within the space of 300 years. The nature of indigenous land-use at Fort Hood, including the significance of perception of landscape (Ingold 1986; 1992; 1993), and how to reflect this adequately using HLC techniques, was one of the key challenges of the project. It is notable, however, that some of these issues had already begun to be addressed in European methodologies. As Fairclough states, "A greater challenge is to expand HLC to embrace the intangibles of landscape, such as cultural and psychological perceptions and historical associations: the ways in which 'landscape' embraces all the senses of belonging or alienation, familiarity or strangeness. HLC needs to incorporate how people react to landscape, often not through the accepted rules of aesthetics." (Fairclough 2001, 26). In fact, HLC techniques lend themselves very well to the study of such landscapes due to the emphasis on viewing the landscape as a whole. Approaches to aboriginal cultural landscapes in Canada by the National Park Service have highlighted issues that are directly relevant to Fort Hood. Their guidelines for the identification of aboriginal cultural landscapes refer to landscapes in Australia where "many Aboriginal sites are discrete areas separated by long distances but interconnected by trading routes or the paths of ancestral beings. They are most clearly understood when they are recognized as parts of a network rather than individual components. (Bridgewater and Hooy, 1995: 168)" (Parks Canada 2004).

In examining how to reflect and value intangible aspects of the landscape, it is necessary to return to the definition of landscape as 'an area as perceived by people' and acknowledge that different peoples and cultures perceive the landscape in different ways which must be accorded due consideration and validity. As has already been mentioned in the introduction, in a landscape such as Fort Hood, the concept of value or significance can become contentious. Indeed this has already proved to be so in the case of the Leon River Medicine Wheel at Fort Hood, where western archaeological values and ways of thinking about the past appeared to conflict with Native American perceptions of the site as sacred (Quigg *et al.* 1996). One of the aims of the Fort Hood HLC methodology was to provide a framework for beginning to address issues like this. Again, HLC is a logical approach for achieving this because at the core of HLC is the acknowledgement that every part of the landscape has significance, and that local perception and distinctiveness can influence the significance of an area of landscape as much as national designations of importance.

Another consideration when developing the Fort Hood HLC methodology was the often erroneous assumption that European settlers in North America moved into an empty landscape of pristine wilderness. However, it is now recognised that aboriginal populations were, and are, capable of widespread modification of their environment, transforming it into humanised landscapes. It was therefore necessary to ensure that the project methodology adequately embraced the integrated nature of HLC, and the emphasis on the way in which the physical remains of all past human activities underpin the distinctiveness and diversity of present-day landscapes. Indeed, there are very few landscapes within which human settlement is undertaken without reference to the land itself, past land-use or settlement. The landscape characterisation model for Fort Hood sought to establish the wider context of both the prehistoric and the historic periods, appreciating the roles of indigenous groups, European settler groups, and the natural environment in creating the present visible landscape.

The overall structure of the Fort Hood HLC project took the following form:
- Re-assessment of the nature and extent of available data
- Re-design of the Fort Hood database
- Definition of base landscape polygons
- Polygon attribute-based classification
- Desk-based and ground-based truthing of sample areas

The actual characterisation process in the Fort Hood HLC project, as with English HLC projects, was limited to a relatively short period, in this case of 18 months duration, and the methodology adopted therefore had to be fairly simple in design and rapid in implementation. The method eventually chosen for implementation is fundamentally an attribute-led approach, and for reasons already described above, the characterisation methodology employed at Fort Hood could not be based on the use of detailed mapping and the division of the landscape into units based on field boundaries. Aldred and Fairclough make the point that "the range and use of source material is the one of the principal determining factors in HLC methodology, but closely linked to questions of data structure. What is used and how it is used ultimately influence the decisions made in defining HL character." (Aldred and Fairclough 2003, 41). It was critical, therefore, whilst formulating the project methodology, to establish the core data sources and methods for dividing the landscape into sensible units for analysis. It was decided to use Landsat satellite data, supported by aerial photography, as the base data and starting point for classifying the landscape into homogeneous but distinct types. These basic classifications could then be built on and supplemented by gathering data on a range of natural environmental and cultural attributes, both prehistoric and historic, which could be collated and analysed within a GIS to create the characterisation types. A detailed description of the project methodology is provided in Chapter 5, but it should be noted here that the Fort Hood HLC project is indebted to all who have gone before and helped to map out the way.

3. Fort Hood in context

3.1 The establishment of Fort Hood as a military installation

By 1941 the involvement of America in World War II had created an urgent need for an expansion in military training facilities, particularly for training in tank warfare. This need led to the initiation of a selection process for a substantial tank training base to be located in Central Texas. Initially the preferred site was centred in the flat Valley Mills area some twenty miles west of Waco. However the area between Killeen and Gatesville was also considered as a possible alternative site. The subsequent investigation into the suitability of the sites resulted in the selection of Killeen, sanctioning the location of the base at Killeen on January 15th 1942. This selection followed the successful driving of a borehole into a substantial aquifer on January 10th 1942. The location of this substantial water source, and some determined lobbying by influential members of the Killeen community, finally convinced the military that Killeen was the best site. The new base was named Camp Hood after the Confederate General, J.B Hood (McMurry 1992) and the site was expanded by land acquisitions in 1943.

Following the ending of the war, all of the training bases established during the conflict were reviewed, to see which should be closed and which made into more permanent facilities. It is at this time that the distinctive nature of the topography at Camp Hood became recognised as being of strategic military importance. These distinguishing features were later summarised in 1989 by General R. M. Shoemaker, who noted that "the rolling hills in the west are similar to central Europe", the steeper hills of the central area of the camp are "much like mountains" while in the east, the dense woodland is "ideal for training for war in jungles" and "the dusty grey soil along the slope bottoms approximates desert sands" Fort Hood therefore offered as a military training facility a microcosm of the future perceived theatres of conflict. These strategic considerations ensured that by 1951 the installation, which was by then called Fort Hood, had become permanent. Further acquisitions of land followed in 1953 and 1955, increasing the size of the military reservation to become today the largest active armoured post in the U.S.

3.2 Topography and geology

The geology and landscape evolution of the landscape forms noted by Shoemaker is no less significant in understanding the past cultural use of the landscape. The placement of tracks and roads, establishment of communities, ancient and less ancient, are all influenced, at least in part, by the topography and the geological forces that shaped the broad characteristics of the *Edwards Plateau, Balcones Escarpment* and the *Lampasas Cut Plain*, the fundamental major landforms of the area.

The Edwards Plateau is a series of undulating, scrub oak-clad hills that form the backbone of the Texas Hill Country. The Balcones Escarpment forms the outer edge of the escarpment, falling steeply to prairie lands along its southern and eastern edges with the Lampasas Cut Plain, an area of prominent, flat-topped ridges bounded by broad, low-lying eroded stream valleys to the north and west of the escarpment. The counties of Coryell and Bell, straddled by Fort Hood, lie largely within this plain on the dissected eastern margin of the Edwards Plateau.

The geology of the Fort Hood area can most easily be understood as a layer-cake stratigraphy. The geology is comprised of a relatively simple bed, which has a shallow dip. All of the hard rock geology of the study area is of Cretaceous age (136 to 64 Ma [approx.]). These carbonate rocks have been formed as a result of marine flooding of a shallow basin. Barnes (1979) provides a useful division of these rocks. The soft rock geology is largely based on Quaternary to recent (64Ma to present) alluvial deposits situated close to the present day river courses. These deposits are largely composed of the erosional products of the surrounding Cretaceous rocks.

3.3 Archaeological review of Fort Hood

The purpose of this section is to provide a thematic outline of the evidence for prehistoric and historic archaeology at Fort Hood; to place this within a regional context, define current gaps in knowledge, and to explore the potential of the resource to answer specific research questions through specified actions.

Regional research on prehistoric archaeology in Central Texas, and research designs produced for Fort Hood, have been underpinned by hunter-gatherer theory and Middle Range research (Binford 1980), and have focused on the site as the primary subject for analysis and excavation as the primary means of obtaining archaeological evidence (Binford 1972, 150-161). Overviews are provided by Black (1989, 25-32) and Collins (1995). A prehistoric cultural-historical framework has been defined by Prewitt (1981, 1985), and revised cultural chronologies of the region have been provided by Johnson and Goode (1994) and Collins (1995). Background on the broader history of archaeological method and theory, and the formulation of a prehistoric research design for Fort Hood has been provided by Ellis *et al.* (1994), and a planning document for the treatment of prehistoric archaeology has been produced more recently (Boyd *et al.* 2000). Research on the Historic Period has focused on histories of land tracts and developing the historic context (Stabler 1999; Ward *et al.* 2000; Freeman *et al.* 2001), and a popular history of Fort Hood has also been published (Pugsley 2001). We do not need to duplicate or emulate these studies here, as these were carried out with very different aims and priorities. Neither do we seek to provide a comprehensive account of all that is known about Fort Hood within this publication. Instead, this section aims to address cultural processes and management issues through a series of broad study themes, and to suggest different ways of approaching the evidence, emphasising the need to move away from site-based approaches and instead to study the landscape as a whole. Many chronological issues are encompassed within the thematic section, but a separate section on chronology has been included in order to provide some basic background information for those not familiar with the archaeology of Central Texas, and to highlight some key chronological themes. This review provided a baseline for the historic landscape characterisation project, and was based on the state of knowledge of the archaeological and historical resource at the start of the project in 2001.

3.3.1 Chronology

It has been noted by several archaeologists (Collins 1995; Trierweiler 1996b) that in the past, prehistoric archaeological study around the Fort Hood area, and Central Texas in general, has concentrated heavily on establishing elaborate chronologies, typological sequences of artefacts and cultural-area affiliations. It has been suggested by Collins (1995, 362) that this may have been at the expense of understanding the nature of the archaeological record, although it could be argued that this emphasis was consistent with contemporary issues (Trierweiler 1996b, 35).

Various cultural chronologies have been developed for the region, namely by Prewitt (1981, 1985), Johnson and Goode (1994) and Collins (1995). The general framework established by Prewitt appears to be valid and has been widely used, although in the light of continuing investigation, deficiencies have been recognised (Ellis *et al.* 1994; Collins 1995, 371). More recently, chronologies have moved away from using the term 'phase' to describe cultural-historic units, and towards using 'interval' or 'pattern' within broader periods (Mehalchick *et al.* 2000), and Collins' more recent chronology is based on a relatively precise radiocarbon-dated projectile point sequence (Collins 1995; Mehalchick *et al.* 2000, 9). There are, however, still some reservations about chronology. Black asserts that a single regional chronology is not yet viable, and Hester (1986) emphasises the significant localised differences in the Central Texas archaeological area (Trierweiler 1996b, 36).

Pre-Clovis
The potential of Pre-Clovis occupation of the Americas is an increasingly significant research theme in American archaeology (Collins 2000). At present, there is no firm evidence for Pre-Clovis material in Central Texas, and identifying such evidence is likely to be problematic, as valleys were scoured out immediately before the Clovis period, rockshelters of this date may be highly degraded and upland landforms do not usually produce good stratigraphic contexts (Collins 1995, 381). However, important new sites producing material of Clovis date, such as the Gault site, may well provide some clues to the origins of Clovis culture (Collins and Hester 2001). It is also possible that Pre-Clovis evidence will survive in secondary deposits including natural sediment traps, or be detected through proxy indicants including palaeoenvironmental data.

Palaeoindian (11599-8800BP)
Few intact Palaeoindian components have been intensively investigated in Central Texas and, other than isolated artefacts, remains of this period are poorly represented at Fort Hood (Trierweiler 1996b, 37). Much of our knowledge and understanding of this period in Central Texas has been extrapolated from other areas (Trierweiler 1996b, 31). Collins divided the period into two sub-periods, the early sub-period consisting of two style intervals: Clovis and Folsom. Interpretation of human lifestyles in the Clovis interval has undergone considerable change in recent years, moving from the fundamental defining criteria of Clovis communities as big-game hunters towards the view that Clovis artefacts indicate a more generalised hunter-gatherer lifestyle, making use of a wider array of subsistence resources, including plants and smaller animals. Recent investigations at sites such as the Wilson-Leonard site (Collins and Weir 2001) and the Gault site (Collins and Hester 2001) support this view of a less mobile society and a more diverse resource-base than previously thought. Folsom artefacts are considered to be more representative of specialised hunting, especially of bison (Mehalchick *et al.* 2000, 11). Collins divided the Late Palaeoindian sub-period into a number of style intervals which display traits more usually thought of as Archaic, indicating that this may be a transitional period from the Early Palaeoindian to the Archaic.

A clearer definition of the chronological and cultural significance of the style intervals in this late sub-period is required. Collins has also identified the need to draw on data from outside Central Texas which may have implications for a better understanding of local evidence (Collins 1995, 381). Furthermore, although information from the Gault and Wilson-Leonard sites will provide new insights, data from a broad spectrum of sites is still needed in order to identify meaningful patterns (Hester 1986)

Archaic 8800-1300BP
The Archaic period represents a large proportion of the prehistory of Central Texas, in which the development of patterns distinctive to Central Texas developed, such as extensive use of burned rock. Distinctive changes within the archaeological record associated with this period are generally understood as a shift towards a long-term, successful adaptive strategy based on hunting and gathering of a wider array of resources and a decrease in group mobility (Mehalchick *et al.* 2000, 12).

Plate 5: Fort Hood South Cantonment with US 190 in the foreground and Killeen in the background – photo by Gil Eckrich

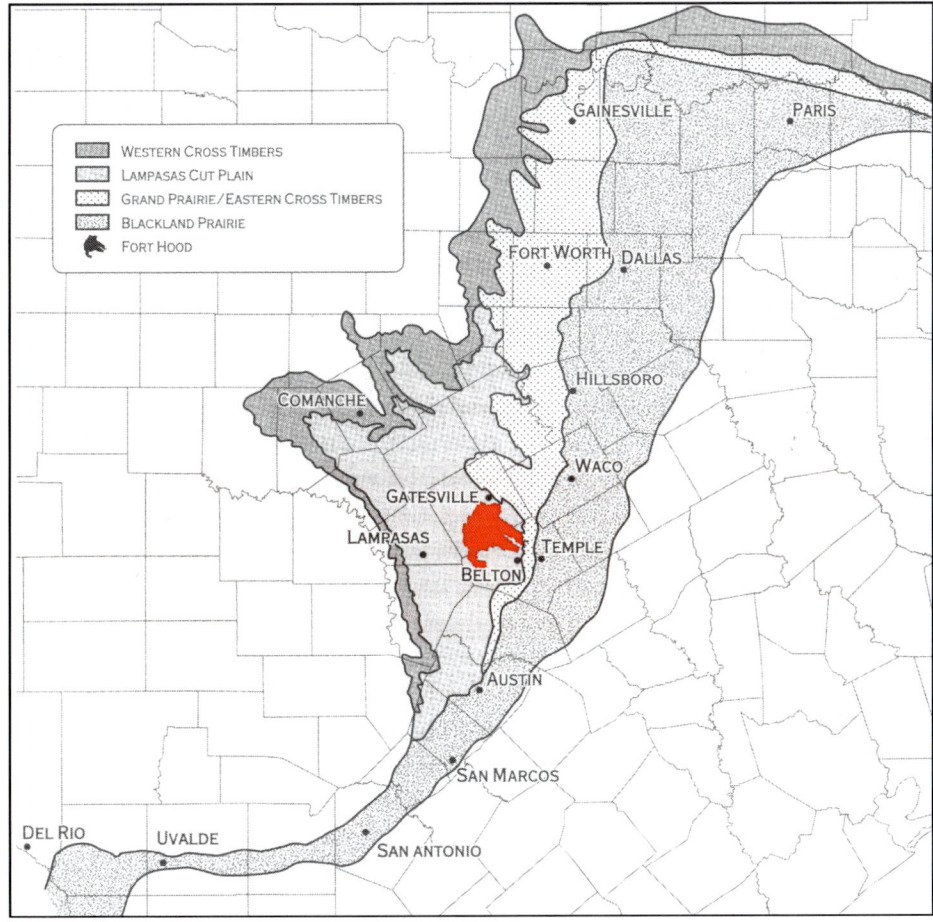

Figure 10: Physiographic regions of central Texas, location and extent of Fort Hood (Adapted from Hill 1901)

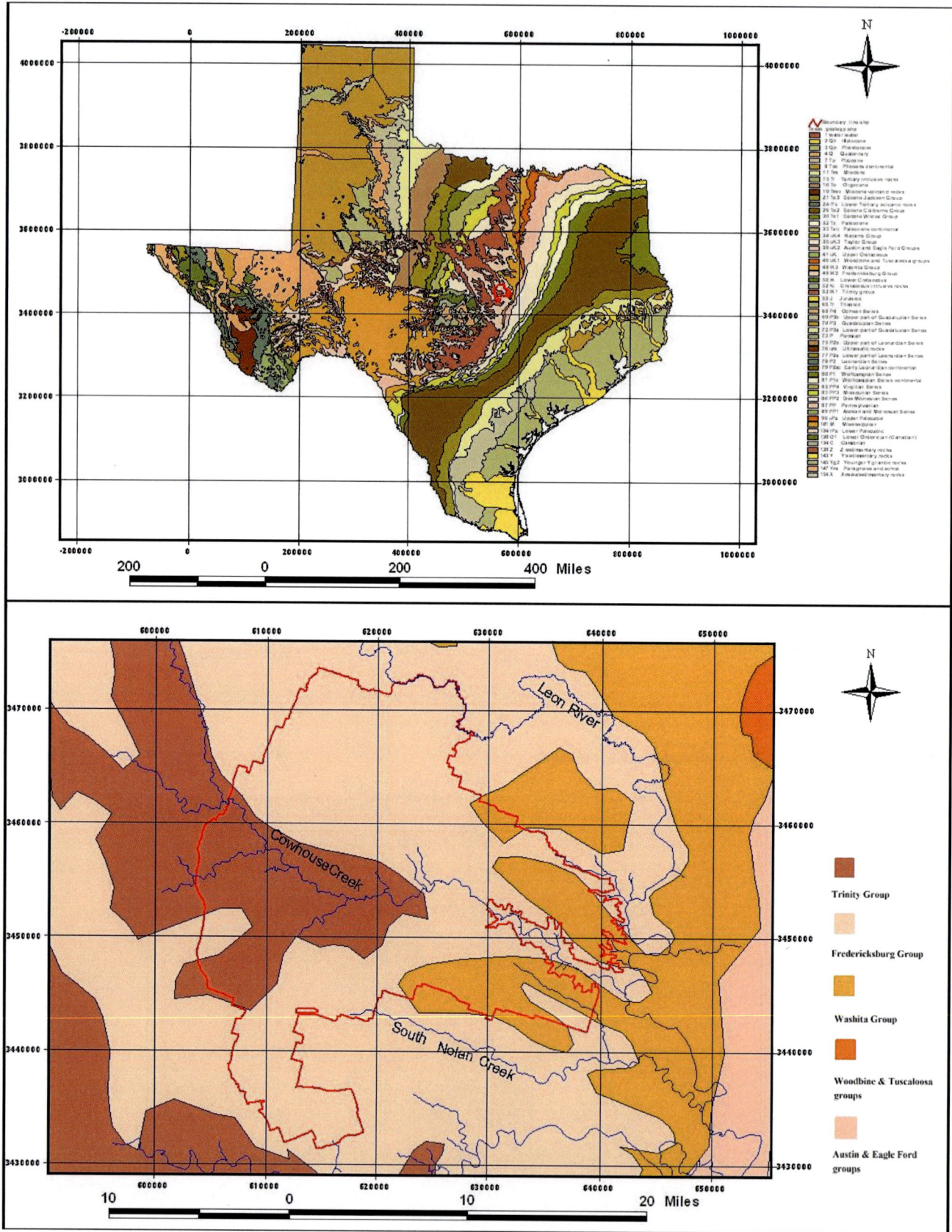

Figure 11: Geological sequence for Texas and local area of Fort Hood

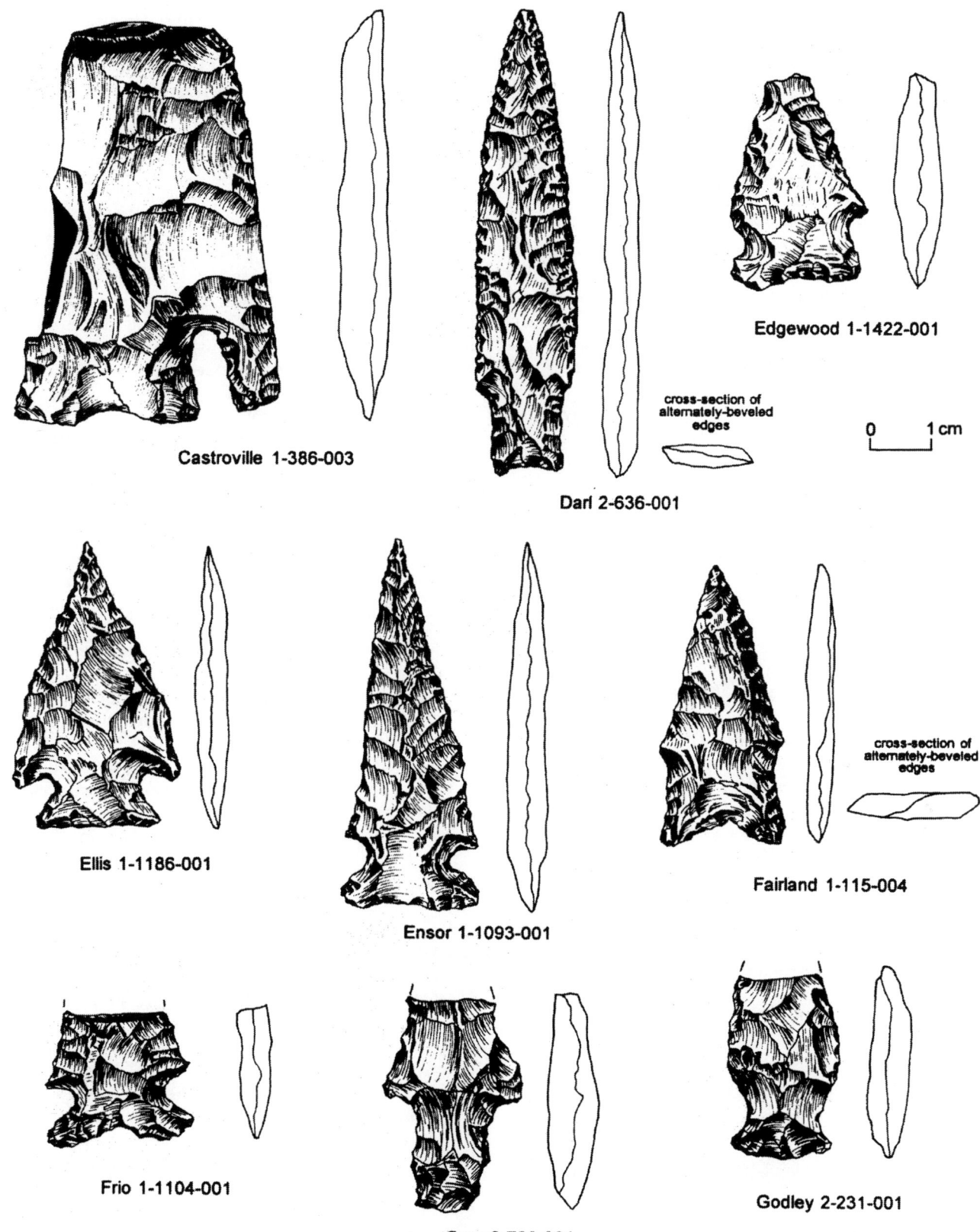

Figure 12: Typology of points (Trierweiler 1996a, Appendix D D3 Projectile Point Typology)

Early Archaic 8800-6000BP

Early Archaic sites appear to be concentrated on the eastern and southern margins of the Edwards Plateau, where there were reliable water sources and a diverse array of subsistence resources (Mehalchick *et al.* 2000, 12). This apparent concentration has been associated with evidence for increasing aridity (McKinney 1981). Prewitt has suggested that population density was relatively low and groups were highly mobile (Prewitt 1985, 217). Three style intervals have been assigned to this period, and sites including the Sleeper site show evidence of intensive plant processing. Burned rock features including hearths and ovens occur. Evidence from Fort Hood indicates that use of larger burned rock middens began in this period (Trierweiler 1996b, 38). At Fort Hood, the Early Archaic period is not much better represented by intact components than for the Palaeoindian period, although some occupation sites which lack charcoal and diagnostic points may in fact date to the Early Archaic. Many sites containing artefacts projected for this age are also palimpsest accumulations. The small sample size of excavated sites makes it difficult to answer specific research questions associated with this period (Trierweiler 1996b, 38).

Middle Archaic 6000-4000BP

This period is far better known than the preceding period in Central Texas. Information is largely based on numerous excavations of burned rock middens and rockshelters. Until recently, it was thought that burned rock middens first emerged in this period, but evidence from Fort Hood has shown that these sites were already in use by the Early Archaic period (Trierweiler 1996b, 38). Three style intervals span this period, and the tool types indicate that hunting remained an important pursuit, despite a possible shift in emphasis of the subsistence base represented by the extensive use of burned rock middens. It has been postulated that this change may have been a response to drier climatic conditions associated with the need to exploit more diverse resources and requiring a different technology (Johnson and Goode 1994, 26). The number and size of sites may suggest an increase in population during this period (Prewitt 1981, 73).

Late Archaic (4000-1300BP)

This period is represented by a number of investigated sites, many with stratified components, but there are also significant gaps in our knowledge or understanding of the archaeology of this period (Collins 1995, 384). Collins recognises six style intervals during this period, and Johnson and Goode (1994, 37) divide the period into Late Archaic I and Late Archaic II based on increased population densities and evidence of spreading eastern religious influences. However, Collins (1995, 385) argues that these interpretations will require substantiation through archaeological investigation. There is a greater diversity of site types in Central Texas in this period, including large cemeteries, and much knowledge comes from investigation of palimpsest middens. Evidence now suggests an increased use of burned rock middens in this period (Trierweiler 1996b, 39), and this high level of usage continues into the Late Prehistoric period (Mehalchick *et al.* 2000, 13). The extensive use of burned rock middens and the low ratios of projectile points to other tools in site assemblages may indicate a decrease in the importance of hunting (Prewitt 1981, 74, Mehalchick *et al.* 2000, 13).

Late Prehistoric (1300-300BP)

The period is divided into two sub periods, variously called the Early Late Prehistoric, Late Prehistoric I or Austin, characterised by Scallorn-Edwards points, and the Late Prehistoric, Late Prehistoric II or Toyah sub period, characterised by Perdiz points. The three defining traits of the Late Prehistoric period in Central Texas are the introduction of the bow and arrow, the use of ceramics and evidence of agriculture, although from where and how these traits were introduced is as yet unclear, whilst agriculture appears to have played a relatively minor role in Central Texas. It is clear from recent investigations (Mehalchick *et al.* 2001, 13) that the use of burned rock middens continued throughout the period, and that basic methods of hunter-gatherer subsistence practiced in the Archaic period continued to be important. It has been suggested that the break between the Archaic and the Late Prehistoric periods could just as easily be placed in between the Late Prehistoric I and II sub-periods (Collins 1995, 385) This is supported by the evidence from Fort Hood, where there is very little change in the tool assemblage, raw material use pattern or subsistence resources in the Late Prehistoric I sub-period (Trierweiler 1996b, 681). It has been suggested that the population declines from the Late Archaic period (Prewitt 1985), although the evidence for this is not actually conclusive, and there appears to be a relatively intense use of rockshelters. It has been suggested that shelter use may be linked to protection from other groups in the area (Trierweiler 1996b, 682), perhaps linked to evidence of conflict from excavated burials of the Late Prehistoric I period which contain arrowheads that may actually be the cause of death rather than appearing as grave goods (Prewitt 1981, 83).

The Late Prehistoric II or Toyah sub-period is one of the better-documented and dated phases, and is supported by data from recent, large-scale excavations in West Central Texas, including those at the O.H. Ivie Reservoir (Trierweiler 1996b, 41). It is also the best represented period in terms of stratigraphically discrete occupation units (Collins 1995, 385). There appears to be a major shift in subsistence from the Austin to the Toyah as groups became more mobile and bison became increasingly important, as testified by tools related to bison processing. However, the introduction of ceramics clearly did not stop the use of burned rock middens. Likewise it does not seem to have altered the stone tool assemblage, either indicating that ceramic technology was probably not fully integrated (Trierweiler 1996b, 687), or that we do not understand what burned rock and stone tools were used for, and ceramics were not relevant to the function.

Historic 300BP

The early part of the historic period is not well-documented, as Spanish missions and immigrant groups skirted around the area. There are sparse contemporary accounts of native groups living in the area, and equally scant archaeological evidence. None of the indigenous groups living in the area in historically documented times are considered to be directly related to the prehistoric groups that inhabited the area. The Tonkawa were once thought to have had their long-ancestral homeland in Central Texas, but this has proved not to be the case. The Native groups encountered apparently consisted of displaced groups escaping Spanish oppression and the newly arrived, mounted Apache. It was not until the 18th century that the first Spanish expedition is definitely known to have reached Central Texas (Newcomb 1993). In the middle part of the historic period, remnants of native groups were living in Spanish missions, and the Comanches moved into the area. The nearest Spanish Missions to Fort Hood were along the San Gabriel River. By the mid-19th century, the Comanches, and any other native groups, had all but disappeared from Central Texas, partly as a result of a conscious Texan policy of removing Native Americans from the state.

The later part of the historic period is very well documented for Fort Hood itself. Historical research has been carried out on tracts of land containing recorded historic properties (Stabler 1999; Ward *et al.* 2000). The histories of the properties were based mainly on patent, deed and *ad valorem* tax records, and complete chains of title were constructed for each property. They do not represent exhaustive histories of each tract of land, but have provided information from which general trends and characteristics have been interpreted, and historic contexts for the 1940s acquisition area have been developed, on the themes of agriculture and rural development (Freeman *et al.* 2001). Agriculture was central to the lives of Euroamerican settlers at Fort Hood, and most people were involved in it in one way or another. The pace of change in the late 19th and early 20th century had a dramatic effect on settlement patterns, the landscape, the economy and daily lives. Communities were very abruptly cut off with the establishment of Camp Hood in 1942, and historic activity from then until the present day has been dominated by military and related activity.

Plate 6: Tama Store- – photograph from Fort Hood CRM

3.3.2 Processes of continuity and change (Transitions)

The division between the Late Palaeoindian and Early Archaic periods is a problematic issue considered under this theme. A Pre-archaic transitional period has been postulated, essentially because very little evidence has been found for changes in subsistence strategies between these periods, (McKinney 1981). However, there are few intact deposits and consequently a limited amount of information relating to this period in Central Texas, and the division is largely based on presumed changes in subsistence, and changes in weaponry, which may be associated with environmental conditions. However, there is a growing body of evidence from sites such as the Gault site to indicate that subsistence in the Palaeoindian period did not consist solely of big-game hunting, and evidence of burned rock associated with Palaeoindian material at Fort Hood supports an Archaic-style occupation in that area (Trierweiler 1996b, 658).

The Archaic-Late Prehistoric transition is also a subject of much debate. There is evidence for considerable continuity between the Late Archaic and the Late Prehistoric I (Austin) sub-period, with basic hunter-gatherer subsistence continuing. At Fort Hood, Late Archaic stone tool types and general tool frequencies are similar to the Middle Archaic (Trierweiler 1996b, 675). The terms Neo-archaic or Post-archaic have been used in the past (Prewitt 1981, 83), and Johnson and Goode (1994) and Collins (1995, 385) have suggested that it would be just as acceptable to place the separation of the Archaic and Late Prehistoric periods between the Austin and Toyah sub-periods. There is evidence that drier conditions prevailed, and technology and subsistence strategies of the Toyah have been interpreted as representing a completely different tradition to the preceding Austin sub-period (Mehalchick *et al.* 2000, 13). The fact that the distinctive tool types of the Toyah sub-period and the introduction of pottery appear to represent a distinct horizon has resulted in considerable, unresolved, debate as to whether this constitutes evidence of a spread of people or of ideas (Collins 1995, 385). However, recent work on burned rock middens has provided radiocarbon dating evidence to suggest that some middens, such as at the Honey Creek site, were still in use after AD 1400, challenging the idea that the Toyah culture represents a radical shift to bison hunting (Black *et al.* 1997).

Linked with these transitional issues and the critical question of change, is the status of the bison in Central Texas. It appears that changes in bison exploitation always seem to be linked to changes in movements of people and changes in tool technology (Boyd pers. comm.). There is a need to consider a broader picture to see if this perception is valid for Central Texas, and to examine how work at Fort Hood could elucidate this.

The degree to which practice and custom is socially embedded may be approached by examining processes of continuity and change, and key to this is the examination and understanding of long-term usage of particular places in the landscape and the longevity and significance of traditional technologies including burned rock and its associated features. There is no doubt that the archaeological record for the Archaic period shows distinctive changes, but, as Collins points out (1995, 383) it is not clear how significant these were at the time they occurred. The Archaic period clearly represents a long-term, successful way of life. As stated by Black (1997) "The persistence of burned rock middens for over 5,000 years on and near the Edwards Plateau of Central Texas bespeaks long-term cultural continuity", and at Fort Hood, burned rock constitutes a high proportion of the total cultural assemblage throughout the Archaic and Late Prehistoric periods (Trierweiler 1996b, 697). The evidence for very long term use of individual mounds and middens, and of lithic resource procurement in areas such as site 41CV207 at Fort Hood, which appears to have been utilised for at least 8,000 years (Carlson 1993) suggests that such continuity holds a significance above and beyond convenience and pragmatism. A landscape approach to issues of continuity and change is critical, as landscapes embody not only continuity and sequence but also, potentially, change and transformation (Ashmore and Knapp 1999, 19).

Nowhere are issues of continuity and change more sharply pronounced than in the transition from the prehistoric to the historic period. According to Collins, a direct historical approach to prehistory is of limited use in Central Texas as it was not the long ancestral homeland of any ethnographically documented indigenous group (Collins 1995, 373), and there do not seem to be any well-described contemporary groups who were subject to similar conditions to the prehistoric inhabitants of the area (Newcomb 1993, 50). It is now known that the Jumanos and Tonkawas are not the descendants of Toyah culture (Collins 1995, 373). There are occasional references to indigenous peoples in the literature but these are of doubtful value. For example, mountains identified as the Balcones escarpment and the Edwards Plateau were mentioned by indigenous people to the Spanish in the 16th century (Newcomb 1993, 5), but it is now clear that the Spaniard Cabeza de Vaca, who travelled across Texas and Mexico in the early 16th century, never came into Central Texas, and therefore can say nothing about the people who lived there (Newcomb 1993, 4). Several other expeditions were made by the Spanish in the 16th and 17th centuries, but either they did not reach Central Texas, or made no reference to the indigenous people. Ethnographically-known groups arrived just before or during the first decades of European contact, and as a result, accounts represent a time of drastic change, relating to relocated remnants of earlier groups or very recently arrived groups. The archaeological record for this period is complicated by the fact that some aspects of aboriginal lifestyles continued after the Spanish contact, such as the manufacture of stone tools, and not many settlements associated with indigenous peoples have been examined outside mission sites (Mehalchick *et al.* 2000, 14).

Despite such observations, much work has been done over the last few years to clarify the nature of this hiatus in the record, and to consider the possibility that some indigenous cultural activities may have continued and can be recognised and utilised in the study of earlier periods. Evidence of cultural continuity can be inferred from the presence of Caddoan and Caddoan-style pottery in the Toyah interval and historic accounts of the Hasinai Caddo travelling into Central Texas to hunt bison and camping with indigenous groups (Collins 1995, 386). This is reinforced by the ethnographically documented frequency of large encampments of people with mixed ethnic affiliations, suggesting a long-standing pattern of behaviour (Collins 1995, 386). Newcomb (1993, 49) infers that the widespread use of sign language by historic tribes suggests that the interaction of peoples speaking different languages was a long-standing occurrence. There is potential for these patterns of cultural continuity to be further explored.

Elements of continuity between aboriginal cultures and European settlers are not entirely absent, and it is possible that further examination of the landscape at Fort Hood may highlight such continuity. Despite the fact that aboriginal people had been almost completely removed from Central Texas by the mid-19th century, European settlers did not move into an empty landscape, and there are very few landscapes within which human settlement is undertaken without reference to past land-use or settlement. It is highly probable that there is some continuity in the use of water and other geographic and topographic features. For example, at Fort Hood, the earliest explorers followed trails made by aboriginal peoples and these, in turn, were followed by cattle droves and early roads, and subsequently modern highways (Boyd pers. comm.). The accuracy of the depiction of roads on historic maps may be questionable in some instances, but will provide a baseline for further investigation. There is also evidence of continuity of land-use from the original Spanish land division (Blake and Dase pers. comm.).

3.3.3 Settlement and society

Generally, knowledge of prehistoric settlement and society in the Fort Hood area is very poor. Collins has recognised that archaeological enquiry in Central Texas has concentrated heavily on individual sites, and there has not been enough work at the 'macro scale' (Collins 1995, 372). A statistical analysis of prehistoric and historic site variability was carried out at Fort Hood, resulting in groupings and clusters of sites with respect to archaeological and environmental dimensions (Williams *et al.* 1990a; 1990b). There have been previous syntheses of the data, for example the Fort Hood prehistoric research framework (Ellis *et al.* 1994), but these have tended to concentrate almost solely on subsistence and technology and do not address socio-cultural organisation (Boyd *et al.* 2000, 17). Despite this, the current level of synthesis does allow some consideration of prehistoric settlement and society in and around Fort Hood and across the wider Central Texas area.

Collins (1995, 381) uses the example of the paved floor in the Kincaid rockshelter as evidence that Palaeoindians may have returned to the same places more frequently than might be expected of nomadic, big-game hunters, and the strong evidence for plant processing from the Gault site seems to support this (Collins and Hester 2001). Houses have been identified at a few sites in Central Texas (Boyd pers. comm.), but generally, there is a lack of knowledge regarding the nature and function of prehistoric domestic structures, mainly due to the lack of large-scale excavation aimed at defining intra-site patterning (Boyd *et al.* 2000, 31). A concentration of Early Archaic components has been identified near the eastern and southern margins of the Edwards Plateau (Collins 1995, 383), and Hester suggests that there appears to have been a heavier usage of rockshelters as occupation sites during the Late Prehistoric period along the Balcones escarpment (Hester 1986). Accounts from the early Historic period have demonstrated that groups of indigenous people had considerable contact with other groups (Collins 1995, 386). Patterns of settlement of aboriginal people during this period were changed significantly following the acquisition of horses. During the Middle Historic period, the record essentially consists of records of native groups living in Spanish missions.

The possibility that there is evidence of migration in the Late Prehistoric period is a much-discussed issue in Central Texan archaeology (Collins 1995). It has been suggested that the appearance of distinctive tool types and local and imported ceramics in the Late Prehistoric II (Toyah) sub-period may represent the migration of a distinct ethnic group into the area (Johnson and Goode 1994). Collins (1995, 388) believes there is good evidence that the Toyah interval represents bison hunters migrating into the area. However, this is still an unresolved issue, and the evidence for continued use of burned rock middens in the Edwards Plateau during this period (Black *et al.* 1997; Mehalchick *et al.* 2000, 14) clearly needs to be taken into consideration. Mortuary practices in the Late Prehistoric period display considerable variability, including cremation and inhumation, individual burials and cemeteries. It has been suggested that this variability indicates population movements within the region (Trierweiler 1996b, 40). Beyond Fort Hood there are cemeteries of Late Archaic and Late Prehistoric date with burials providing evidence for violence which indicate tension and perhaps suggesting increased concern with territoriality. Using ethnographic parallels, Newcomb suggests that the Caddoan tribes of East Texas, being technologically more productive and politically better organised, are likely to have exerted considerable influence over their neighbours (Newcomb 1993, 3), and this is supported by the archaeological evidence of Caddoan ceramics and arrow points in burials.

It has been recognised that much archaeological research is undertaken at site-specific scales. However, systematic survey of large heterogeneous terrains is ultimately required to retrieve reliable information on extensive prehistoric settlement patterns, (Blum *et al.* 1992). Wesolowsky has pointed out that settlement patterns could be examined through the use of a regional approach rather than with an 'over concern with specific productive sites' (Wesolowsky *et al.* 1976, 85). Amongst wider regional studies that have occurred is the Texas Clovis fluted point survey (Meltzer 1987; Meltzer and Bever 1995), which recorded data on Clovis points for the whole of Texas. In Texas, the Clovis record is dominated by scattered isolated surface finds, and although there are limitations as to how representative the sample is, the authors concluded that Clovis distribution is not coincident with the distribution of later Palaeoindian remains. Meltzer notes the possibility that despite 10,000 years of erosion, the record accurately reflects the structure of settlement and subsistence strategies, inferring that Clovis groups may not have engaged very frequently in the types of social behaviour and adaptive strategies that produce traditional sites. Landscape approaches to the evidence and off-site methodologies may provide new insights into such situations (Francovich and Patterson 2000).

Some settlement pattern studies have been carried out in and around Fort Hood. Work in the Brazos river basin has provided a basis for the development of regional land use models for different parts of the Brazos river basin and the inner gulf coastal plain, including the Fort Hood area (Thoms 1993, 9). Work at Fort Hood itself includes research into the distribution of projectile points and site components across the Fort Hood landscape (Thoms 1993, 43), the development of a settlement pattern model, applicable to Central Texas, using data on the distribution of stone tools in different environmental zones at Fort Hood (Thoms 1993, 43), and the creation of a model of prehistoric land use for Fort Hood, identifying general trends (Thoms 1993, 61). Investigations were carried out on 119 prehistoric sites at Fort Hood in the early 1990s, and at the time, this was the largest group of prehistoric sites ever excavated in Central Texas within a single research framework (Abbott and Trierweiler 1995; Trierweiler 1996b). Although only a small area of each site was actually examined as part of this programme, a wide range of site types in a variety of depositional environments and landforms were studied. Many questions have been raised by the work at Fort Hood. These include the nature of the relationship between site variability and seasonality, how the low frequency of Perdiz points relative to the high frequency of Scallorn points reflects different use or settlement patterns, and how far the presence of point types that are not key index markers for Central Texas may represent interaction (Trierweiler 1996b, 692).

A number of authors repeatedly stress that efforts to interpret and compare patterns of land use over time in Central Texas are beset with problems related to the small size of available samples. It is also noted that the known archaeological record may not necessarily reflect the original spatial and temporal record, as it is distorted by subsequent cultural and natural formation processes. Johnson and Goode (1994, 18) state that "Black's work from 1989 summarises a number of profusely speculative published statements by regional archaeologists about indigenous settlement patterning, prehistoric social organisation, group mobility and the establishment of group territories". It is clear that sample size is a problematic area, particularly for early sites. There are few excavated components and the paucity of radiocarbon dates in association with diagnostic tools means that there are still unresolved issues regarding basic chronology. In addition, further work needs to include more detailed geomorphological mapping, and targeting of relevant subsurface contexts. Alternative approaches to the data may permit valuable information to be extracted from the archaeological record, even if archaeological sites cannot be precisely and individually dated. For example an apparently abandoned monument still remains part of an active landscape, and can play a major part in how past societies perceived their environment (Bradley 1998). Richard Bradley's work in Europe has demonstrated how much can be gained even from studying abstract carved rock symbols, by examining the relationship between topography and the character of the petroglyphs. Even their organisation in the landscape provides insights into the society that created them (Bradley 1994, 104). A phenomenological landscape approach could be applied to settlement studies and social organisation in the Fort Hood area, potentially, to great effect (Tilley 1994). This may enable research to move beyond basic facts relating to what people ate and what tools they used, to consider issues including social boundaries and frameworks, human and environmental interrelationships and the importance of place in the landscape as opposed to the rather narrow perception of site functionality.

In contrast to earlier periods, a considerable amount is known about settlement and society in and around Fort Hood itself during the Historic period. This situation results from the historical research that has been carried out during the course of assessing significance of sites for inclusion in the National Register (Stabler 1999; Ward *et al.* 2000; Freeman *et al.* 2001). There was little in the way of European settlement in the area from the 16th century until the mid-18th century, as Spanish trade and immigration routes did not penetrate the area that would become Bell and Coryell counties (Freeman *et al.* 2001, 69). Native groups from the early contact period seem to have been characterised by a number of kin-related, politically unstructured entities, rather than tribes. This situation is based on the observation that had group identity been stronger, it would have persisted and these groups would have been in a stronger position to ward-off hostile immigrants (Newcomb 1993, 51).

Historical research has generally involved establishing chains of title for historic properties, revealing information about patterns of land ownership and settlement on specific tracts of land, from which general trends and characteristics have been interpreted (Freeman *et al.* 2001, 2). Initial attempts at settlement were made from 1849-1865. This included the use of slave labour by some settlers, but not on a large-scale, as settlers were unable to reproduce plantation conditions. Rural development was generally slow in Fort Hood lands. Much of the major growth in Bell and Coryell counties took place outside the Fort Hood area (Freeman *et al.* 2001). In the latter part of the 19th century and the early part of the 20th century, hamlets continued to develop as isolated clusters of habitations, but they began to decline from 1914 (Freeman *et al.* 2001, 119). In the 20th century, there were rapid changes and regional shifts, and in years of drought and collapsing markets, there tended to be general population shifts from rural to urban settings.

Plate7: Antelope Home 1908 – photograph from Fort Hood CRM

The earliest land surveys in Bell and Coryell counties and within Fort Hood were carried out along the Leon River and the Cowhouse Creek, and these early surveys had a major influence on subsequent land use patterns (Stabler 1999, 27). The open range conditions meant that fencing and enclosure was not carried out on a large scale, but boundary features were sometimes constructed for crop protection. Early fences were built with crooked poles, brush and rock; there were also hedges, and cedar and oak rails (Freeman *et al.* 2001, 23). The landscape accommodated sheep and cattle ranches, large cash-crop-based farms, and farms that combined aspects of both on a smaller scale (Freeman *et al.* 2001, 48).

3.3.4 Religion and culture

Overall, very little is known about religion and culture in the prehistoric period in the Fort Hood area, and the major body of evidence comes from burials. Two burials of Palaeoindian date from the Wilson-Leonard site and Horn Shelter 2 have produced three relatively well-preserved early human skeletons (Collins 1995, 383). Early Archaic burials from the Eastern Edwards Plateau are uncommon – most that are known come from the Bering sinkhole (Johnson and Goode 1994, 24). Evidence for burial practices for the Middle Archaic on the Edwards plateau is uncertain, and no burials or cemeteries are known from this period at Fort Hood (Trierweiler 1996b, 669).

Most of the dateable cemeteries and isolated burials from Central Texas are assignable to the Late Archaic period and later (Thoms 1993, 56). It is worth noting that no radiocarbon dates are obtained from human remains that are returned to Native American groups for reburial. Probable Late Archaic skeletons have been recovered from the Bering sinkhole, Hitzfelder Cave and the Olmos dam (Johnson and Goode 1994, 39). Late Archaic burials occur at Fort Hood, particularly from within the rockshelters, but also outside them. There is evidence for deposition of single bodies in non-cemetery settings at Fort Hood, but no cemeteries are known from this phase (Trierweiler 1996b, 676). In the Late Archaic period, Johnson and Goode have suggested that exotic material consisting of gulf whelk shells and atlatl weights of exotic stone found in burials on the Edwards Plateau, although not abundant, are representative of the spread of eastern religious influences. Elaborate bone and shell artefacts and atlatl weights found in burials at the Ernest Witte site in Austin County have been interpreted as a regional expression of these religious beliefs (Johnson and Goode 1994, 38). Middle woodland atlatl weights have been interpreted as religious paraphernalia, and the fact that a relatively complex cult with a rich material expression could spread to Late Archaic society in the Edwards Plateau area is of considerable significance. A variety of mortuary practices occur within the Late Prehistoric period in Central Texas, including burials in cemetery and non-cemetery settings, and cremations. At Fort Hood, there is no sign of specialised mortuary practices such as those recorded at the Loeve –Fox site, but it has been suggested that this may be due to sample size (Trierweiler 1996b, 682).

There are not many burials that occur in alluvium within Central Texas. Most are associated with middens, rockshelters or sinkholes. Burials are found in sinkholes from the Early Archaic period through to the Late Prehistoric, and there are indications of differentiation in grave goods from different types of burial, notably those from rockshelters (Boyd pers. comm.). The development of rockshelter cemeteries through time, how and why some became cemeteries or why other natural features, such as sinkholes, attract special treatment is not well-understood (Boyd et al. 2000, 48). However, the transformation of natural places through such associations is an acknowledged area of research in Europe. Bradley's study on the archaeology of natural places indicates the potential value of such research in other areas and this may be particularly applicable to Central Texas where the calcareous bedrock provides many significant natural features which may have possessed an imbued significance in the past (Bradley 2000). At Fort Hood, only four caves and sinkholes are known to contain cultural deposits, and knowledge of these localities is very limited (Boyd et al. 2000, 56). Although there are cemeteries from the historic period, some historic burials also occurred outside cemeteries, and it is not known where these are (Boyd pers. comm.). The army exhumed and removed graves at many of the cemeteries, but they still serve as focal points when former residents return to Fort Hood, and as the scenes of annual gatherings. People are still occasionally buried in the cemeteries on the base. The present-day use of historic cemeteries demonstrates that they continue to be places of considerable importance to local communities. This importance of place can be extrapolated back to the prehistoric cemeteries, and suggests that rockshelters and sinkholes should be regarded as more than simple burial sites.

The significance of rock art in prehistory cannot be determined from Fort Hood, as limestone in wet areas is not good for the preservation of rock art. The handful of rock art sites known in Central Texas are usually late, and occur in areas protected from wet and seepage (Boyd pers. comm.). However, despite the lack of rock art, there is considerable untapped potential at Fort Hood for examining the importance of semi-natural places, including water and sky, to aboriginal peoples, the interconnectedness of relationships to the land, and the importance of place, including places of power, and sacred places.

Alternative approaches to the significance of material objects include the study of structured deposition. Here object deposition may reflect a series of conventions regarding which types of material may be associated or separated. These spatial relations may encompass a series of references to the origins and history of objects, and to the significance of particular places in the landscape (Bradley 2000, 122). The study of burned rock mounds and middens might benefit particularly from such methodologies and throw new light on cultural practices associated with the use of burned rock. In addition, rockshelters provide considerable potential for this type of research. as many are effectively houses with structured spaces within (Shafer pers. comm.).

The potential for alternative research methods is emphasised by studies of ethnographically documented groups such as the Comanches. These groups have a long history of regarding high places, such as mesas, as sacred cultural places (Boyd pers. comm.). It would not be too great an interpretive leap, based on other ethnographic parallels of aboriginal cultures, to extrapolate such belief systems back to the prehistoric inhabitants of the Fort Hood area. This is supported by research carried out as part of the investigations into the Leon River Medicine Wheel at Fort Hood, which has shown that most medicine wheels were constructed in locations with considerable vistas overlooking present or past watercourses (Quigg et al. 1996, 10), clearly demonstrating the importance of the relationship between topography and belief systems. Computerised visualisation studies including viewshed analysis and the study of possible rock alignments from mesas could contribute greatly towards understanding the lives of prehistoric people (Exon et al. 2001). The importance of other natural landscape features such as springs and sinkholes should also be considered. Springs are likely to be a focal point and they require comprehensive mapping, whilst sinkholes could possibly be identified thermally.

In addition, intensively used lithic resource procurement areas (LRPAs) at Fort Hood provide a significant data set through which to study the integration of economic, spiritual and social aspects of life over centuries. So far these sites seem to have been studied solely as evidence of technology and exchange. However, Bradley and Edmonds (1990) have used the Neolithic axe quarries at Great Langdale in the UK to carry out significant research into exchange in its social context, examining the wider context of artefacts, including patterns of association, avoidance and symbolism. The extremely long-term usage of particular places strongly suggests that such places possessed a special significance in their own right (Bradley 2000, 40). Similarly, burned rock mounds and middens also represent long-term, repeated use of places in the landscape, and the repeated centre-orientation of hearths within some burned rock mounds could indicate that aspects of ritual and symbolism are represented here.

3.3.5 Transport

Evidence for, and knowledge of, transport in the prehistoric period appears to be extremely limited. There are references to Native American trails in the ethno-historic literature, but archaeological examination of such features is lacking (Quigg *et al.* 1996). An old Tonkawa trail lay to the east of Gatesville and crossed present-day highway 7 near Cox Springs (Stabler 1999, 12). Although transport-related sites are likely to have low archaeological visibility, there are nonetheless possibilities of improving knowledge of this subject, particularly through exploration of continuity between the prehistoric and historic periods.

Comanches were known to have travelled along specific trails at specific times of the year to carry out raids (Boyd pers. comm.). As mentioned previously, at Fort Hood, the earliest trails followed by explorers almost certainly followed trails made by aboriginal peoples, which would then have been followed by cattle droves, early roads, and subsequently modern highways (Boyd pers. comm.). Early roads on historic maps were often drawn from rough notes made by explorers, but should provide a basic indication of routes followed, which could provide a foundation for further research. Despite the difference in lifestyles, early settlers would have still needed to ford creeks at suitable fording points, and look for the most accessible routes through the terrain. Historical research indicates that the main roads that traversed Fort Hood were in place by 1886, and it is significant that they are described as narrow, graded dirt roads that mainly "wandered between hamlets following topography such as waterways and landforms" (Freeman *et al.* 2001, 104), increasing the likelihood that there could be some correlation between these roads and the routes that prehistoric trails followed.

There may be considerable potential for examining 'travelability' through the landscape through the use of GIS analysis to generate cost paths, based on environmental and topographic information, both in association with, and independently of, known archaeological sites of both the prehistoric and historic periods (Bellavia 2006). It is clear that the rapid changes in transport in the 19th and 20th centuries had a dramatic effect on almost every aspect of everyday life. The construction of railroads in the 1880s prolonged the agricultural and immigration boom and permanently changed not only the economy but the physical appearance of the land (Freeman *et al.* 2001, 95).

3.3.6 Economy and environment

The economy and the environment appear to be the topic which most of the synthetic research in Central Texas has focused on. Although there are gaps in knowledge, a considerable amount is known about subsistence bases and adaptive strategies. Most of this data has been interpreted with reference to analogous Hunter-Gatherer research and Middle Range theory (Binford 1980).

Considerable attention has been paid to changing population densities throughout the prehistoric period, particularly in publications by Prewitt (1981). Such studies have necessarily been closely tied to Palaeoenvironmental studies and climate change, the presence or absence of bison and site formation processes. At Fort Hood, prehistoric site densities are high, which is considered to be partly due to the high surface visibility and erosional upland setting rather than a reflection of population density. These factors also apply to much of Central Texas (Carlson *et al.* 1994, 16).

Evidence for exchange and trade appears to have had a comparatively low level of archaeological visibility within the Fort Hood area. According to Johnson and Goode, the Edwards Plateau was affected by cultural and religious influences from the Coastal Plain and the Eastern Woodlands, and also from the Great Plains during periods of bison presence (Johnson and Goode 1994, 38). Evidence is scarce in the early periods, but appears to be more substantial in the latter part of the Late Archaic, when evidence of more extensive trade patterns starts to emerge. Marine shell is found in cemeteries in Central Texas, and corner tang knives are widely distributed across Texas, although there is little evidence for broad trade networks from this date at Fort Hood (Trierweiler 1996b, 676). There is also evidence for import of obsidian, and burial traditions influenced by Hopewellian burial ceremonialism (Collins 1995, 387), indicating significant population interaction. The most extensive evidence for contact and exchange in Central Texas is in the Late Prehistoric II (Toyah) sub-period. At Fort Hood, there is little to suggest the existence of elaborate trade networks in the Late Prehistoric period, but again this could be a reflection of the sample size. A piece of obsidian found in a burned rock midden at Fort Hood has been sourced to Idaho (Trierweiler 1996b, 701). Central Texas chert occurs in significant frequencies in Caddoan lithic assemblages, suggesting networks developed for exchanging the pre-formed or finished products (Carlson 1993, 54). It has been suggested that Fort Hood was a major lithic resource area. It is therefore likely that little or no raw material was brought to the Fort Hood area; more research is therefore required beyond Fort Hood and Central Texas, to examine patterns of movement of Fort Hood Edwards chert out of the source area (Trierweiler 1996b, 701). It is known that Edwards chert is represented in assemblages from North Colorado and Northeast New Mexico (Trierweiler 1996b, 701). If true, it is necessary to ask what was being imported in exchange for the chert. It seems certain that investigation on trade in the Late Archaic period, and linkages connecting the Gulf Coast with the Fort Hood area could be extremely productive in understanding the broader exchange pattern. Extensive use and exchange of bison products is documented in the Historic period, and Collins expresses doubts that the people of the Edwards Plateau were ever isolated (Collins 1995, 387).

Subsistence strategies have been emphasised heavily in prehistoric archaeological research within the region. Whilst there is a large body of evidence including artefacts, structures and palaeoenvironmental data providing information on prehistoric subsistence strategies, it is clear that this data is by no means comprehensive. The record is notably skewed by poor organic preservation. However, the growing body of more recent evidence relating to the Palaeoindian period, including tools for plant processing at the Gault site (Collins and Hester 2001), indicates that people were exploiting a range of food resources, and were not solely hunting large mammals.

The long time span of the Archaic period appears to represent a successful basic adaptive strategy (Collins 1995, 383), but the fundamental research issue underlying the study of subsistence strategies in the Central Texas Archaic period is the question of burned rock mounds and middens. These were poorly understood for a long time, but considerable progress has been made in recent years and new approaches to investigating these features have been undertaken (Black et al. 1997). It has been suggested that burned rock middens were used to cook plants such as sotol which thrived in dry conditions (Johnson and Goode 1994, 32), and this is supported by evidence of cooked sotol from burned rock middens in West Central Texas. There is also documented recent historic evidence that the Mescalero Apaches pit-baked xerophytic plants (Johnson and Goode 1994, 32). However, as yet, the evidence does not show a clear correlation between the growth of burned rock features and xeric conditions, although there does seem to be a close correlation between mesic conditions and the occurrence of bison remains (Collins 1995, 388). It is also not yet clear whether the presence and use of burned rock middens indicates a greater reliance on plant foods, since the associated tool kits indicate that hunting was still important (Mehalchick et al. 2000, 12). It has been suggested that the hypothetical shift in subsistence strategy in the Middle Archaic, as represented by extensive use of burned rock, may have occurred earlier and lasted longer at Fort Hood, indicating localised variation (Trierweiler 1996b, 38).

Available evidence previously indicated that a radical shift towards bison hunting and group mobility occurred in the Late Prehistoric II (Toyah) period, associated with a corresponding reduction in the use of burned rock middens. However, recent research, supported by radiocarbon dates, has shown that burned rock middens were still important in this period (Black et al. 1997). The evidence from Fort Hood does seem to show a shift in subsistence in the Late Prehistoric II period, with remains of medium to large mammals increasing significantly (Trierweiler 1996b, 686). However, it has not been possible to identify specific cooking features with particular food resources. This may reflect the fact that although large burned rock features might have been constructed for a specific resource, once the effort of construction had been made, any food could then be cooked. Ethnographic parallels have shown that earth ovens are predominantly used in the preparation of plant foods, and it could be that direct evidence for this is minimal due to the relatively low archaeological visibility of plant processing compared to that of animal processing (Ricklis and Collins 1994). There may be many resources that were utilised yet remain archaeologically invisible, for example mesquite beans were used throughout the southwest, yet there is very little evidence for their use, possibly due to the fact that they were ground prior to consumption (Boyd pers. comm.). This could well apply to other plants. There are also questions regarding the importance of fishing, and it is not yet known when, or if, fishing was a significant pursuit. The possibility of culturally significant flora and fauna also needs investigating.

There are therefore many outstanding questions relating to resource exploitation. Little is known about the spatial organisation of individual technologies, movement patterns, seasonality of activities, or the probable range of prehistoric peoples. Evidence from the Historic period may be able to provide insights into prehistoric subsistence strategies, albeit within certain limiting parameters, as historically-observed behaviour would have been affected by the use of horses. The hunting of bison, deer and antelope by aboriginal groups was documented by the Spanish and French, and it appears that much of the behaviour observed was associated with movements of bison (Collins 1995, 386).

Plate 8: Karst feature at Fort Hood – photo from Fort hood CRM

Plate 9: Flooding at the Old Georgetown crossing of the Cowhouse Creek – photo by Gil Eckrich

Plate 10: Historic Black House – photo by Gil Eckrich

Plate 11: Training at Fort Hood – photo by Gil Eckrich

Central Texas was, however, surrounded by areas that adopted agriculture or horticulture in the Late Archaic/Late Prehistoric periods. Migrant Wichita speakers in the area were able to establish productive gardens in the 18th century (Newcomb 1993, 49), indicating that neither natural conditions nor ignorance precluded a shift to such practices within Central Texas itself. Indeed, some basic practices that were not intensive enough to be called agriculture may have been incorporated into hunter-gatherer lifestyles, including the use of mesquite beans from trees that could be owned (Boyd pers. comm.). Despite this, a major shift towards agriculture never occurred. It has been suggested that Apache-type ephemeral gardening could have occurred on the Eastern Edwards plateau during Late Archaic times without leaving a visible archaeological trace (Johnson and Goode 1994, 41). The inference is that in an area where natural resources were abundant and diverse, existing hunter-gatherer lifestyles were efficient enough to continue (Collins 1995, 387). This may also be the reason why ceramics appear so late on the Edwards Plateau.

According to Collins, there has been much sophisticated research into the technology of stone tool manufacture and use, and much descriptive data has been generated. Unfortunately, there has been little regional synthesis of such information (Collins 1995, 372). More research is needed to understand how accurately material culture reflect past economies, and to understand more fully the reasons for changes in point styles (Collins 1995, 382). The Edwards Plateau region is widely known for the excellent quality of its chert, but prior to 1975, studies into lithic resource procurement in Central Texas were restricted as most of the archaeological activity occurred in reservoir salvage projects, where quarry sites do not occur (Carlson 1993, 47). An assessment has been carried out at Fort Hood on the potential for using chert patination as a dating technique (Frederick *et al.* 1994). Studies of lithic resources at Fort Hood have focused on linear reduction models, and research has concluded that lithic assemblages are site specific, and site location or function seems to be the key factor influencing the lithic material use pattern detected. More pronounced patterns may be revealed if further site-specific assemblages are obtained, or assemblages are collected from, for example, sites clustered along a single drainage (Carlson 1993, 49; Trierweiler 1996b, 703).

Of critical significance is the abundance of excellent quality cherts in surface outcrops at Fort Hood, and the extensive utilisation of specific sites for resource procurement, in some cases over c. 8,000 years (Carlson 1993, 51). As mentioned previously (see religion and culture section above), the potential of Lithic Resource Procurement Areas for providing information on the economy in relation to social and cultural processes is enormous. As previously noted (Carlson 1993, 49), if chert was so abundant, why were specific places used so selectively and over such an extensive period? This cannot be explained purely on the basis of the quality of the chert in those locations, and the inference is that these were highly significant places in the landscape. In addition to studying artefacts solely in terms of how they were made and utilised in technology and adaptation, there is a need to study them in new and innovative ways. Stone tools may also carry associations with the places where they were made, and as Bradley has stated, "if the use of particular materials extended outside our normal understanding of technology, then the sites where those materials were obtained call for a more careful analysis" (Bradley 2000, 40).

In the historic period, the practice of agriculture was central to the history of Fort Hood lands, as most of the population was involved in agriculture in one way or another. The main types of agriculture practiced were livestock raising, including horses, cattle, sheep and goats, or raising crops such as grain or cotton (Freeman *et al.* 2001, 54). Not all of this agriculture was practiced on a cash-crop basis, and there were still significant subsistence crops (Blake and Dase pers. comm.). Agriculture at Fort Hood began to decline from the end of the 19th century until the creation of Camp Hood in the 1940s (Freeman *et al.* 2001).

Technological advancements had a considerable effect on agriculture, in ways that may be reflected in the present-day landscape. The use of well drilling equipment and windmills meant that stock farmers and ranchers were freed from a dependency on flowing surface water, thus altering settlement patterns in the landscape (Freeman *et al.* 2001, 24). The introduction of rail transportation made barbed wire readily available, and this tended to replace cedar and oak rails in the landscape. There is potential for useful research to be carried out into how present-day vegetation may reflect historical changes of land use and traditional management regimes.

3.3.7 Military

There is very little knowledge of prehistoric warfare in Central Texas. The most striking evidence is from the Late Prehistoric period; here excavated burials containing arrowheads in contexts indicating they were the cause of death suggest that the introduction of Scallorn and Edwards points was marked by conflict (Prewitt 1981, Mehalchick *et al.* 2000, 13). There is also documentary evidence for warfare and conflict amongst aboriginal peoples following the arrival of Europeans in the region: an event precipitating a chain of events that led to considerable upheaval, turmoil and ultimately the complete disappearance of aboriginal peoples from Central Texas.

Fort Gates was established to the North of the present-day Fort Hood in the 19th century, and a military road was constructed in 1848-49 in the vicinity of Fort Hood. However, the most important military event in the historic period is clearly the establishment of Camp Hood, and ultimately Fort Hood, during the Second World War. This has had a major effect on the present-day landscape and on the level, and nature, of survival of archaeological remains from both the prehistoric and historic periods. For example, the nature and abruptness of the removal of people from the land in the 1940s involved the significant destruction of buildings, but cisterns and wells were left intact in order to provide soldiers with water during training exercises (Stabler 1999, 22). Similarly, military use and public ownership has affected the amount of archaeological and historic recording and research carried out across the base. The existing prehistoric archaeological database for the Eastern Edwards Plateau and adjacent areas derives mainly from federally mandated cultural resource studies (Thoms 1993, 10). In addition, the unique military use of the land is significant in its own right as a type of historic land use that is now embodied in the fabric of the present-day visible landscape, and should therefore be afforded due value and significance.

3.3.8 Palaeoenvironment and Geomorphology

In order to be able to interpret the archaeological record in a meaningful way, it is necessary to understand the geological processes that have affected it. The Late Quaternary stratigraphic framework has had a profound effect on the spatial and temporal pattern of the archaeological record (Waters and Kuehn 1996). Furthermore, the Edwards Plateau is a climatic and vegetational borderland, and as a result has been subject to considerable fluctuations in precipitation (Johnson and Goode 1994, 42). In such an area, climate change is seen as a central issue to hunter-gatherer adaptive strategies. A number of palaeoenvironmental records have been produced for Central Texas, including those by Collins (1995) and Johnson and Goode (1994). A geomorphological study of the major drainages at Fort Hood has also been carried out (Nordt 1992), and Toomey has produced a climatic history based on radiocarbon dated faunal remains and the stratigraphic sequence from Hall's Cave. This work was described by Collins (1995, 379) as a "Landmark contribution to Quaternary studies". The various different palaeoenvironmental records do not agree entirely with each other, but all recognise a period of extreme aridity in the Archaic period in Central Texas, often represented by stream incision (Collins 1995, 379). There also seems to be a general correlation between bison occurrences and mesic conditions.

Nordt's geomorphological study now enables comparison between the depositional sequence at Fort Hood and other areas such as the Brazos river, Colorado River and Medina River. The study provides an assessment of the recovery and period potential from eight major drainages at Fort Hood. It has provided a greater understanding of how processes have non-randomly altered, buried and destroyed sites, for example, Nordt suggests that there is a marked contrast in the stratigraphic contexts of sites in the valleys compared to sites on landform surfaces. In the valleys, rapid rates of aggradation through the Middle and Late Holocene precluded the formation and burial of long-term occupation surfaces, so buried sites in the valleys tend to be within stratigraphically discrete sedimentary contexts. This is not the case on landform surfaces, where sites tend to contain mixed cultural assemblages spanning long time periods (Nordt 1992). The study confirmed that the evidence from surface survey of an apparent increase in the number of sites between 1200 and 2600 years old was a significant cultural pattern and not the result of depositional factors. It also indicated that the preserved surface cultural record in the alluvial valleys at Fort Hood is biased towards sites dating from the Middle Archaic to the present.

The geomorphological investigation of the Henson Creek drainage basin, which was supplementary to Nordt's 1992 study, substantially refined the Holocene terrace sequence for this drainage and indicated that the potential for buried sites for most of the Holocene is low due to the active deposition and erosion taking place (Carlson 1993). There has been increasing attention paid to the identification and analysis of stratigraphically discrete site components in order to refine chronological sequences, and Collins has assessed the gisements reported in Central Texas in terms of their stratigraphic integrity (Collins 1995, 376). A study of amino acid racemization of land snail shells from a variety of sites in a variety of positions at Fort Hood suggested that there was re-deposited material in a large number of proveniences as a result of sedimentary processes involved in site burial and later disturbance, and most showed evidence of mixed-age land snail assemblages (Black *et al.* 1997).

Existing palaeoenvironmental studies have provided a useful outline of prevailing trends, but further work is still required. Collins has pointed out that Central Texas environments are not uniform and understanding is more likely to emerge locally (Collins 1995, 388). Generally, future research needs to determine whether archaeological scarcity reflects cultural reality or gaps in the record. The integration of cultural history and past climatic conditions is still a problem area as neither record has been consistent (Collins 1995, 373). There is some evidence of conflict in different records, for example the results of bison bone analysis in relation to Nordt's work (Trierweiler 1996b, 694). Unfortunately, organic preservation is generally very poor in Central Texas, although there is sometimes better pollen preservation from rockshelters (Boyd pers. comm.).

In terms of Palaeoindian sites, there is a need to relate locations of Clovis material to palaeotopography and palaeoenvironments, as many issues are only likely to be resolved through the discovery and excavation of more sites (Meltzer 1987, 59). Focusing on deeper deposits may locate Palaeoindian sites with stratigraphic integrity. Collins (1995, 388) outlines the need for locating and comprehensively analysing gisements with a fully integrated palaeoenvironmental approach, as such a small percentage of the archaeological database derives from well-stratified contexts. Further research needs to be carried out into the relationship between geomorphology and particular site types. For example, the geographic and geomorphic distribution of caves and sinkholes with archaeological potential is not known (Boyd et al. 2000, 19), and the question of whether long-term camps would have been located in areas of potential flood remains unresolved. There are several areas of research with potential for further exploration. Severe erosion and stripping of soils in the Mid-Holocene created pockets of survival, and there may be potential for locating and investigating these pockets (Boyd pers. comm.). Open campsites in alluvial and/or colluvial settings at Fort Hood have high potential for containing stratigraphically discrete components.

At Fort Hood, the Leon River palaeosol has been identified since Nordt's study, and represents a critical horizon for cultural and environmental change in the Late Prehistoric I (Austin) interval. The general distribution of palaeosols could be mapped from Nordt's study - this could be very informative as Fort Hood stream chronologies are very consistent, so palaeosols can be precisely dated (Boyd pers. comm.). Abundant snail shells are available, which are valuable for chronological control and evidence of past environments (Trierweiler 1996b, 692).

Vegetation in the live fire zone at Fort Hood is different to elsewhere on the installation, and it has been theorised that this may be due to periodic fires caused during training keeping the vegetation healthy. Elsewhere, overgrazing has led to inroads by invasive species (Boyd pers. comm.). There may be potential for useful studies to be carried out on present day and historically documented vegetation in relation to past land use.

There has been some site-based research at Fort Hood into the occurrence of different types of site in relation to particular landforms, and to each other, for example it has been noted that there is a fairly common association between burned rock middens/mounds and rockshelters (Boyd pers. comm.). It is not yet clear whether differences between burned rock features represent different sets of activities occurring on particular parts of the landscape (Boyd et al. 2000, 42). A large number have now been radiocarbon dated, and there is considerable potential for further study at a landscape level (Boyd pers. comm.).

3.3.9 Landscape

One of the recurring issues that is raised in any discussion of archaeology in Central Texas is that of the need to locate and excavate sites which contain buried occupation layers that can be separately and closely dated (gisements). However, many of the known sites are palimpsest accumulations that cannot be securely dated and assigned to one of the intervals or sub-periods within the chronological framework that has been developed. However, whilst recognising that knowledge needs to be built on the basis of excavating coherent components, the importance and significance of palimpsest accumulations should not be overlooked, as they may yield very different, but equally important information. The fact that places in the landscape are continually re-used for the same, or different activities over hundreds and sometimes thousands of years is extremely significant. Similarly, places that were not being used at all need to be considered in the light of systems of avoidance and taboo. Since landscapes embody multiple times as well as multiple places (Ashmore and Knapp 1999, 19), they provide a completely different means of studying how places in the landscape were used. These issues are particularly pertinent to the study of burned rock mounds and middens, which often represent very long-term usage of places in the landscape and by inference must have assumed a significance above and beyond the practicalities of cooking food. Furthermore, the preparation of food may itself have had a larger social significance (Bray 2003).

Site-based approaches do not recognise, or enable the study of, particular activities that may have occurred away from sites. It is possible that there will be entire phases that are primarily represented by non-site activity. Similarly, site-based approaches do not deal adequately with areas which exceeded the usual parameters of what is perceived of as a site, for example extensive lithic procurement resource areas or very large, dispersed encampments such as those observed in the historic period (Collins 1995, 386).

At Fort Hood, the present-day visible landscape represents a land-use history that included both hunter-gatherer societies and settled agricultural communities. Both these types of society interacted very differently with the landscape. Mobile groups interact with their landscapes by projecting ideas and emotions onto the world as they find it, whereas sedentary people often structure their landscapes more obtrusively, constructing buildings and dividing the land with physical boundaries (Ashmore and Knapp 1999, 10).

No landscape is either exclusively natural or totally cultural, but somewhere in between. It is known from ethnographic studies that aboriginal people had a holistic relationship with the landscape in which they lived, and natural features were of considerable significance to them, for example the Western Apache recognised a moral landscape where ethical lessons were associated with natural features (Ashmore and Knapp 1999, 16). Tacon has identified four types of places about which aboriginal people have subjective feelings (Tacon 1999, 37). These are:

1. Results of great natural events such as raised mountain ranges, volcanoes, steep valleys or gorges
2. Points of change between geology, hydrology and vegetation or some combination of all three, such as sudden changes in elevation or waterfalls
3. Unusual landscape features such as a prominent peaks, caves or a sudden hole in the ground
4. Places providing panoramic views or large vistas

A question that may be raised concerning aboriginal cultural landscapes is how feasible it may be to analyse the role and significance of entirely unaltered features of the natural landscape, and whether any useful results can be gained from studying areas where monuments are absent. Research carried out by Bradley (2000, 43) has demonstrated that, provided there is associated archaeological material, then extremely valuable results can be obtained.

The Fort Hood area has clear potential for the examination of special places in the landscape. Hundreds of caves and sinkholes have been documented for environmental purposes, but only a few have been considered as potential archaeological sites (Boyd et al. 2000, 19). Of 281 springs documented for Texas, 49% (139) are in Central Texas (Collins 1995, 366). As mentioned previously (see religion and culture section) the tops of mesas represent prominent high places that are known from ethno-historic accounts to have been regarded as sacred cultural places (Boyd pers. comm.). Similarly, in terms of historic archaeology, different ways of approaching the evidence may provide new insights, perhaps by considering the active role that landscape plays in shaping economic and political systems as opposed to perceiving it as a passive backdrop (Kealhofer 1999, 77), or by exploring the role of landscape in expressions of individual, as well as group identity. Furthermore, contemporary landscapes can be imbued with memories that can contribute significantly to an understanding of the complexity and antiquity of local traditions (Ashmore and Knapp 1999, 14).

There is clearly a need for phenomenological landscape approaches to understanding the significance of archaeology at Fort Hood. Research carried out as part of the investigation of the Leon River Medicine Wheel demonstrated this clearly. Here it was observed that "Native American traditional elders rely as much on the sensual aspects in the delineation of sacred sites as they do on the physical manifestations" (Quigg et al. 1996, 172). It has been pointed out that as federal law is presently structured, archaeologists are required to recognise the importance of religious sites on the basis of physical morphological attributes, but, as Wilson states, "we cannot dig up ideas" (Quigg et al. 1996, 18).

3.3.10 Oral traditions and documentary accounts

It has already been stressed that there are no substantive ethnographic accounts of prehistoric indigenous groups in the Fort Hood area. By the time Europeans arrived in Central Texas, large-scale displacements and movements of people had already occurred as a result of the arrival of Europeans in other areas. It was long assumed that the Tonkawa tribe were direct descendants of Late Prehistoric groups in Central Texas, but the testimony of a Native American from 1601 indicates that the tribe originally came from Oklahoma (Newcomb 1993, 26). There are oral traditions from the historic period relating to the Native American groups who subsequently inhabited Central Texas and adjacent regions, but there are no remaining oral histories from these Native groups that relate to any specific feature. This may be due in large part to the systematic removal of Native Americans from Texas in the 19th century (Quigg et al. 1996, 115). However, there may be useful information to be gained from more general oral traditions from Native groups who inhabited the area in the historical period, particularly in relation to perceptions of the natural and cultural landscape. Oral histories from the later historic period have been utilised in developing historic contexts for Fort Hood (Freeman et al. 2001).

Although there is Native American placename evidence from other parts of Texas, there is none from the Fort Hood area, undoubtedly due to the fact that there was no long period of co-existence between aboriginal groups and European farmers. The only placename evidence continuity is that for Clear Creek (Blake and Dase pers. comm.).

3.3.11 Specific regional issues

Fort Hood is particularly important in a regional context for a number of reasons. Significant elements of the prehistory and history of present-day Texas are well-represented in the Fort Hood area, and the size of the installation allows large contiguous blocks to be surveyed, providing a broader perspective on archaeological resources than can normally be obtained. Also, much of the archaeological work carried out in Central Texas has been in reservoir basins which are almost always located in floodplains, whereas at Fort Hood, most of the terrain is defined as upland or intermediate upland environmental zones, often located well away from permanent water sources (Carlson 1993, 16).

Fort Hood has the largest well-documented group of lithic resource procurement areas (LRPA) in Texas (Boyd et al. 2000, 20), and it is particularly important as a study area since past archaeological activity in Central Texas has been concentrated in reservoir areas where quarries did not occur (Carlson 1993, 47). The potential for LRPAs to inform on a whole range of themes from raw material acquisition, manufacture, trade and transport through to settlement pattern studies, socially embedded customs and sacred landscapes has been outlined in previous sections. However, these areas are problematical in terms of recording and management, in large part due to their enormous size. The full potential of these sites is not known, and it is not necessarily true that a decision to preserve any specific part of such a site is a truly representative act (Carlson 1993, 57). Analysis, understanding and ultimately management of areas such as these can only be progressed through integrated landscape studies.

Plate 12: View from within the live fire zone – photo from Fort Hood CRM

Plate 13: Cave in the Karst area – photo from Fort Hood CRM

Plate 14: Smith Mountain – photo by Gil Eckrich

Plate 15: A rockshelter at Fort Hood – photo from Fort Hood CRM

Burned rock mounds and middens have been extensively researched and written about by many Central Texas archaeologists who are experts on the subject, including Hester (1991) and Black *et al.* (1997), and a detailed discussion of this subject is therefore not attempted here. However, it is necessary to highlight burned rock mounds and middens thematically as they are clearly fundamental to the understanding of Central Texas prehistory, and Fort Hood provides a unique opportunity to study these monuments in their landscape context. Burned rock use in Central Texas was very poorly understood for a long time, but in recent years, fundamental advances have been made in approaches and understanding, including not only inquiry into their form and function, but also their behavioural significance (Collins 1995, 373; Hodder and Barfield 1991). Recent approaches have taken their direction from Middle Range theory and from detailed scientific analysis of material remains. However, there is still considerable debate over the interpretation of these enigmatic features (Black *et al.* 1997, Boyd *et al.* 2000).

Burned rock middens and mounds appear to be concentrated within the oak savannah and limestone country of Central Texas. They have been interpreted as settlement-related features used for plant-processing and, to a lesser extent, animal processing (Black *et al.* 1997). Very few were radiocarbon dated until the last 10-15 years; prior to this they were dated on the basis of projectile points. A note of caution has been raised regarding the possibility that earlier time markers from middens may represent recycled remains from pre-midden deposits rather than earlier midden-use (Black *et al.* 1997). Recent radiocarbon dates suggest that burned rock midden accumulation in Central Texas spanned the period from before 3300 B.C. to the end of the Prehistoric era, which has led to serious re-examination of the interpretation that Late Prehistoric II (Toyah) culture represents a radical shift in subsistence to bison hunting (Black *et al.* 1997).

It has been suggested that there is a clear structural and material differentiation between middens and mounds at Fort Hood (Boyd *et al.* 2000, 40) and that they form distinct classes of features representing different types of prehistoric behaviour in different geomorphic settings. However, no mound or midden at Fort Hood has been fully excavated, so detailed information is lacking.

It is certainly true that much progress has been made in the understanding of the structure of burned rock mounds and middens. However, it is also true to say that research questions have tended to concentrate on cultural affiliations, chronological issues, what the precise formation processes of the structures were, what resources were being cooked, and how the considerable variability in size and morphology can be explained through adaptive strategies. The focus of research has been almost entirely site-based. Beyond this it is important to note that the burned rock middens of the Edwards Plateau "represent historically unique intersections of time, place, resource, process, and prehistoric Native American life" (Black *et al.* 1997). Consequently, the overall context of these features may not be well explained by previous research. Certainly, some of these monuments were highly visible landscape features, clearly representing special places in the landscape, and have vast potential for providing information on aboriginal peoples perspectives and attitudes to the landscape in which they lived. Landscape approaches could potentially provide different types of information to that yielded from site-based investigations, providing valuable new insights on social and cultural organisation.

Sites lying on Paluxy sand formations also form a significant area of research at Fort Hood and are threatened by current land use activities. Evidence of prehistoric activity on this formation appears to be quantitatively and qualitatively different (Kleinbach *et al.* 1999, 39) and there is a need to more fully understand what attracted people to these areas, and what resources they were exploiting. Sites on Paluxy sands are likely to have provided a unique combination of well-drained soil, and diverse and abundant floral resources not found in other settings (Kleinbach *et al.* 1999, 389).

Fort Hood contains the last cluster of relatively well-preserved rockshelters in Central Texas, and has the greatest potential for the identification of unexcavated deposits of Early and Middle Archaic date (Shafer pers com), although looting is a very serious problem for these sites (see managing the resource). They are confined primarily to the northern and eastern half of Fort Hood and are a particularly valuable resource for the Late Archaic and Late Prehistoric I periods. There is very little evidence for rockshelter occupation in the Palaeoindian period at Fort Hood, although this may be due to collapse within shelters. Rockshelters are rich in occupation and burial deposits and have high potential for palaeoenvironmental research. The areas that lie down-slope from rockshelters are relatively unexplored. Such areas may contain valuable information relating to the occupation of rockshelters and are less subject to vandalism. Rockshelters may also provide an unparalleled opportunity to explore themes of households, spatial organisation and structured deposition, and the significance of natural places in the landscape in association with mortuary practices and stratified archaeological remains. Viewshed analysis integrated with studies of past climate change and changes in vegetation could provide valuable information on the use of rockshelters through time.

Fort Hood has also been identified as important in terms of providing information on the Post-Archaic Caddoan culture. Caddoan materials have been recognised along eastern tributaries of the Leon River, and a site in the Belton reservoir area was identified as a potentially intact Caddoan site 20 years ago (Shafer pers. comm.).

In the historic period, the development and abrupt cut-off of historic communities offers opportunities to examine the archaeological evidence for communities in the landscape in a way that would not be possible had these communities continued in existence. Some work has already been done on this theme in the form of using exploratory data analysis to classify and analyse historic communities (Williams *et al.* 1990a; 1990b), but this study used a site rather than a landscape-based approach.

3.3.12 Methodological and technical development

It has been recognised by Texas archaeologists, in common with archaeologists the world over, that in the past, through lack of understanding, there was a tendency to preserve the wrong kinds of materials from excavated sites (Collins 1999), whilst advancement of knowledge was slow due to duplication of data recovery. However, considerable progress has been made in Central Texas archaeology over the last few years towards obtaining representative samples of assemblages that can be securely-dated (Collins 1995, 389). In addition, it has been recognised that fuller use needs to be made of more sophisticated techniques of dating and archaeometry using data from contexts of high integrity. The problem of the lack of suitable organic material for radiocarbon dating can be overcome to a certain extent by the use of AMS and newer scientific dating techniques. Furthermore, wide area excavations are increasingly being carried out in recognition of the need to examine evidence of human behaviour as opposed to concentrating so heavily on chronology and artefact types.

The study of site-formation processes, taphonomy and residuality is relatively well-developed in some areas of research, particularly in relation to geomorphological processes, for example it is recognised that interpreting the depositional context of caves and sinkholes is very important, as they tend to collect colluvial and/or alluvial runoff, trapping sediments that may contain cultural materials (Boyd *et al.* 2000, 56).

Effective field evaluation of archaeological sites can be difficult to achieve without missing aspects that are hard to detect. There is now a considerable body of literature relating to field evaluation techniques, both methodologically and conceptually (Hey and Lacey 2001). A consideration of more sophisticated approaches, using combinations of techniques and alternative methods for sites and groups of sites, may help to address some of the sampling and significance issues that have adversely affected understanding in the past.

There has been very little large-scale geophysical survey carried out in the Fort Hood area. Proton magnetometer investigations were carried out on four burned rock middens in West Central Texas, in the Stacy reservoir area. This represented a new approach to burned rock midden investigation, and the results provided support for the idea that different cultural formation processes were responsible for different middens (Abbott and Frederick 1990; Frederick and Abbott 1992). Geophysical survey was carried out at the Leon River Medicine Wheel to see if the missing Eastern half of the medicine wheel was buried, but the results proved to be negative (Quigg *et al.*, 1996). However, continuing developments in geo-prospection techniques means that there is enormous potential for many different applications of such technology at a local landscape level (Dockerill 1991; Gaffney and Gater 2003; Hunter and Dockerill 1990). Similarly, large-scale image processing and analysis of remotely sensed data such as aerial photography and satellite imagery holds great promise for the development of landscape methodologies. Air based laser scanning (LiDAR) may, under favourable conditions, also offer significant opportunities for mound or other landscape feature detection (Challis and Howard, in press).

There have been some attempts at site patterning and predictive modelling in the past, for example the exploratory data analysis carried out on prehistoric and historic sites at Fort Hood (Williams *et al.* 1990a; 1990b). Predictive models for Fort Hood were developed in the 1980s and subsequently revised for prehistoric and historic site locations at Fort Hood (Carlson *et al.* 1994). On the basis of this, a model for prehistoric land use was developed that identified general trends and focused on the increasing use through time of food sources with comparatively lower cost benefit ratios (Thoms 1993, 61). Possibly the use of geophysical survey and analysis of remotely sensed data could also be usefully applied to the formation of predictive models, although it will be necessary to consider what sites are likely to have surfaces that will be responsive to detection through predictive modelling.

The development of an agreed regional standardised monument classification system should be considered as a matter of urgency. It has been acknowledged that much of the confusion surrounding burned rock middens in Texas is down to terminology, as several distinctly different types of feature have been aggregated under the term 'midden' (Trierweiler 1996b, 582). Prewitt & Associates Inc. have begun this process by defining a series of site types for prehistoric and historic sites (Boyd *et al.* 2000; Freeman *et al.* 2001). Although there may not be enough data at present to provide generally accepted, definitive types, standardisation at the present level of knowledge would provide the foundation on which to build, as and when further information becomes available. Some progress has already been made on classifying types of burned mounds and middens, and the possibility of subdividing generalised lithic procurement areas and open campsites into subclasses representing different areas of activity should be explored

3.3.13 Managing the resource

There are several known problem areas in terms of managing the resource at Fort Hood. Many would agree that one of the most urgent problems is that of vandalism and looting, particularly of midden sites and rockshelters. Rockshelters are perhaps the most important, and at the same time most threatened, resource at Fort Hood. Although measures taken so far have greatly reduced the looting problem, there may be a role here, in tandem with punitive and preventative measures, for more active engagement with the wider community through the use of innovative dissemination of information about the archaeological resource, as it is far easier to protect resources that are valued by the local community.

Much has already been achieved on the base in terms of the participation of living communities, including Native and Euro-American groups through the production of a popular history, and the holding of annual reunions. Significant achievements include the recognition of the Leon River Medicine Wheel as a Native American Traditional Cultural Place and the establishment of the Comanche National Cemetery. Landscape approaches may provide further potential for such participation. Associated peoples do not necessarily have to be current occupiers or users of the land, but may have a historic relationship that is still significant to their culture or family history.

Another major difficulty in managing prehistoric sites at Fort Hood is the enormous size of some of the sites. One Lithic Resource Procurement Area covers a square kilometre (Carlson 1993, 55). This type of problem may be addressed through detailed landscape characterisation and the potential for development of different management strategies for different landscape zones. Easier integration with other environmental disciplines through landscape characterisation may also assist with other problematic issues, such as the vulnerability of sites on Paluxy formations, and increased attention focused on archaeologically significant natural sites such as springs, caves and sinkholes. Landscape characterisation will also facilitate the targeting of resources for data recovery programs, helping to ensure that the most significant sites in the most significant and representative landscape areas can be investigated should they come under threat of destruction.

3.3.14 Dissemination

Education and dissemination of information should be central to any research programme. Rights to data are not restricted to academics and many interested groups may wish to have significant access to information from the base for a variety of cultural or other reasons. Central to this is the fact that the enhancement of the archaeological record will be paralleled by the development of a digital environment capable of storing, retrieving, manipulating and displaying the data. Recent convergence of key technologies, most notably through GIS and the WEB suggests that this has a significant role in enhancing public access to data and interpretation and facilitating educational initiatives (Chapman 2006; Lake and Conolly 2006). Although it is probably not desirable to provide unfettered access to all archive data much may be made available through local and regional data hubs. At an organisational level the introduction of map server technologies will permit better use of the data at base level and allow filtered access to the database to remote users across the web. Other initiatives could be promoted. Interactive web sites can allow active participation in the creation of local histories. Such sites might encourage the directed use of Fort Hood resources by local schools. Alternatively members of local communities (past or present, civilian and military) could be encouraged to record past and current historical development through the a web site by depositing documents, images, video and sound clips within reserved web areas. These technologies could be used to create a living history for the base which will extend and develop with the communities of Fort Hood.

Plate 16: The Leon River Medicine Wheel and the Comanche National Cemetery – photo from Fort Hood CRM

4. The Fort Hood archaeological database

"In the 21st century, this data base may prove very important to archaeologists as a conserved, well documented archaeological record that may be made available for focussed research efforts."
Stephen L. Black (1995, 37), (Texas) Archaeology 1995.

When an archaeologist records any information, that data should be both available and capable of use in the future. To achieve this data records need to be consistent, not only within an individual inventory, but also with inventories compiled by other people or organisations. As stated in chapter 2, historic landscape characterisation (HLC) is intended as a framework for integrated resource management, and therefore it should not be regarded as a stand-alone data set, but should be used in conjunction with other datasets to inform management decisions and research priorities. During the appraisal of existing data that was carried out as part of the Fort Hood landscape characterisation project, it became apparent that if the HLC data was to be properly utilised in the future as part of an integrated management process, a consistent, baseline dataset of recorded archaeological sites was needed, in a structure that would facilitate the consideration of sites within a landscape context. With this aim in mind, a new database structure was designed and implemented as part of the characterisation project, which could be built-on and enhanced in the future.

4.1 Database structures and the Event-Monument-Archive model

When the project commenced, the primary archaeological site inventory in use at Fort Hood was a flat-file database stored in Microsoft Access, and a set of GIS polygons. The database records and the GIS polygons could be correlated via the primary record number known as the TARL number (Texas Archaeological Research Laboratory number), but there was no dynamic link between the database and the GIS data. There were also a number of other data sets from external organisations containing management and interpretive information. These data sets are listed in detail in section 4.3.1. The new Fort Hood database design aims to draw together information from all the different existing data sets into a relational database structure, recording descriptive information about archaeological sites, features and objects, and their management, and draws heavily on data standards developed in the UK, mainly by English Heritage. In the UK, the primary sources of information on the archaeological and historic environment are the county Sites and Monuments Records (SMRs), or Historic Environment Records (HERs), archaeological inventories which are generally maintained by local authorities. These databases:

- underpin the archaeological conservation and management processes
- provide a starting point for fieldwork and research
- form a basis for resource audits in formulating research frameworks
- provide an information context for archaeological intervention
- are an increasingly valuable resource for education and public understanding of heritage resources

In England, work was undertaken in the 1990s to produce a data standard for the SMRs, facilitated by the Royal Commission on the Historical Monuments of England (RCHME - now English Heritage's National Monument Record) and the Association of Local Government Archaeological Officers (ALGAO). It was recognised that in order to successfully manage the archaeological and historic environment at a landscape level, it is necessary to record not just archaeological and historic features and finds, but also the activities of the people involved in investigating the resource, and the sources of information used, as well as information about the management process.

The aim of this work was to develop a framework for modelling the dynamic nature of the archaeological process as it moves from the information gathering event, to the supporting data, and finally the interpretation of the site or monument. The standard that was developed is called the Data Standard for Monument Inventories, usually referred to as MIDAS (English Heritage 1998). It should be emphasised that the main objective of MIDAS is to provide a framework to encourage consistency in recording, and not to specify use of a particular data model, indexing terminology or IT system. However, MIDAS does identify a set of information schemes and recommended units of information that should be present in a monument inventory. The philosophy underlying MIDAS is summarised in the MIDAS documentation as follows:

> - To enhance *retrieval* of information (particularly automated retrieval) from inventories.
> - To provide a *common format* for site-related inventories, ensuring that important information is recorded.
> - To promote *consistency* within a given inventory and between site type inventories.
> - To facilitate the *exchange* of information between inventories.
> - To assist in the *migration* of inventories from old information systems to new.
> - To increase the opportunities for the *evolution* of inventories, ensuring their survival and relevance as technologies change.
>
> (English Heritage 1998, 5)

The UK SMRs that are based on the MIDAS standard usually model the process of recording and interpreting the historic landscape via the concepts of *'events'* and *'monuments'*, utilising what is generally known as the *'event-monument-archive'* data model. Such a flexible structure allows sites to be considered not just in isolation but within a broader context, relating sites to sites and sites to landscape. Some monuments survive in visible form, some are buried, and some are interpreted from place name or other evidence from maps and historic documents. Information about how they were recorded sets the monuments within the context of the pattern of investigation and discovery. Monuments can be defined as "any feature of the modern landscape that, by its nature, imparts knowledge about the past" (English Heritage 1997). Using an *event-monument-archive* model for an archaeological database can help this process by:

- identifying areas where new work is required
- filling apparent gaps in the distribution of recorded archaeological sites and landscapes
- informing new understanding
- suggesting appropriate investigative techniques

Event records
An *'event'* can be defined as "a single exercise in the collection of primary data over a distinct and measurable area of the cultural landscape using one or more investigative techniques" (English Heritage 1997). Events can include:

- Chance finds of single artefacts
- Systematic surface artefact collection (field walking)
- Site condition monitoring visits and reports
- Shovel testing
- Watching briefs
- Geophysical survey
- Aerial Photograph Interpretation
- Large scale excavation
- Historic document research
- Environmental sampling

The word event implies a fixed period of time during which a specific body of evidence is collected. The result is an unchangeable record and archive that might include artefacts, drawings, photographs or other information on paper and other media. A new date assigned to an artefact as a result of, for example, a new advance in science would be a separate event, which would result in a new event record being created in the database. An event, therefore, by definition, is inherently static as the data that results from it is recorded and archived, and is never overwritten. Although an event may not result in any data, e.g. failure to recover artefacts during field walking or a negative watching brief, it is still an important step in the interpretation of the historic landscape. This data structure allows negative evidence to be recorded.

The event is the basic building block in the archaeological recording and interpretation process. It enables synthesis and interpretation of the historic landscape, and provides the framework for building models of the past.

Monument records
The defining characteristics of *'monuments'* (referred to as *'sites'* in the context of the Fort Hood database) are that they form part of the landscape and need to be examined *in situ* (as opposed to e.g. a museum collection), and are subject to continuous change, either man-made or natural. A site record is a dynamic interpretation of recorded archaeological data that is constantly subject to re-interpretation from new data as a result of new events, e.g. a re-dating of an artefact as a result of an advance in scientific techniques. A site record should be preceded by some sort of activity that results in the collection and understanding of archaeological data, i.e. an event such as a site survey, excavation, chance find etc. The data from events can be combined to form new site interpretations at any time, as an existing interpretation is scrapped and a new one created.

Separating the recording of events and site character has the key advantage that the information on which an interpretation is based (the event) is made clearly distinct from the interpretation itself (site character). New relationships between events and sites can be made whenever required. This approach is particularly appropriate for inventories of archaeological sites, where the existing information is characteristically uncertain. For this reason, a model that divides events and site character information has gained much support amongst local authorities maintaining historic inventories.

A site cannot exist in its own right without some sort of previous archaeological activity (i.e. an event), so theoretically every site record should have at least one associated event record. However, in practice, most British inventories existed long before the *event-monument-archive* model was conceived, so a pragmatic approach is taken to the recording of events. General practice seems to be that event records are created for new monument records, and where time and resources allow, they are created retrospectively for existing monument records, but most, if not all, British registers do not have comprehensive event records for all of their recorded monuments. This will also be the situation at Fort Hood, but the important point is that the *structure* should be in place to enable the event data to be consistently recorded whenever possible.

Archive records
The MIDAS data standard also identifies a *'Resources'* information scheme for recording sources of information used or referred to by the inventory (English Heritage 1998, 18), for example publications, maps, photographs or museum collections. There was neither sufficient time within the project, nor sufficient information within the existing data sets, to create useful sources and archive information, but this should be a high priority during any future database development.

4.2 The new Fort Hood database structure

As a preliminary task in the Fort Hood characterisation, therefore, the existing Fort Hood archaeological database was re-cast into an *event-monument* data structure, to enable the modelling of the dynamic nature of the archaeological process as it moves from the activity (event), to the record (the supporting data), and finally the interpretation (the site type). The proposal that a distinction should be made between site data and event data leads to two logically distinct groups of data: one containing information about sites including site types, features and objects, and the other about event and administrative data.

Although the logical design splits the data into two separate groups, there is within the site group a hierarchy of site, feature and object. This hierarchy allows for sites to be classified according to a series of types, which may also be associated with one or more features or objects, thus allowing multiple site type indexing, in accordance with the MIDAS standard. The hierarchical structure also allows the recording of multi-period sites, where sufficient data exists to assign periods. This has an impact on the physical design and implementation of the database. It must be implemented in such a way as to maintain the logical separation of sites from events, and to accommodate the fact that for some sites there will be multiple features per site and multiple objects per feature. Conceptually, the initial design is as follows:

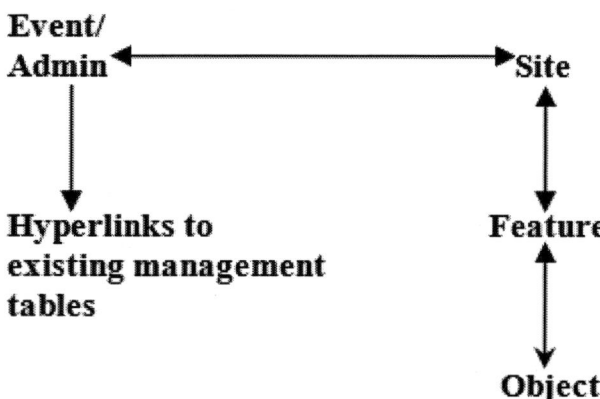

Figure 13: Data model for the new Fort Hood database

The hierarchy needs to be flexible as objects or features could be components of features or sites, or sites in their own right. The concept of a hierarchy of site type, feature and object hinges on the presence or absence of other data within the site and the way that data is associated with other data in the same site. If, for example, a site consists of a cemetery, it would be recorded with cemetery as the site type, a human burial as an associated feature and human remains and any other associated finds as the objects. If, on the other hand, a site consists of a stray find only, e.g. an arrowhead, then the site type will be recorded as an arrowhead because there is no other data associated with the arrowhead. However, the interpretation of this arrowhead as a site may change in the light of further work, for example, it may prove to be part of a lithic scatter, in which case it will no longer be a site in its own right, but an associated object.

It can be seen, therefore, that the boundary between object and feature, and feature and site type is sometimes variable and requires an understanding of the archaeological record before an interpretative leap can be made. This is why the interpretation is recorded, so that others can follow the process of organising the data in a hierarchy. The experience of others who have used this type of hierarchical structure has shown that flexibility is an important element. Although the hierarchy permits a sophisticated way of recording data, there is a risk that it may not be flexible enough if it is applied too rigorously.

The initial database implementation results in a separate table for event and administrative data, and one for site types, features and objects. At Fort Hood, in some cases it is clear that archaeological remains currently recorded under one TARL number and digitised in the GIS as one polygon, are actually multiple sites and/or features. Such records need to be broken down to reflect this, and the structure is designed to allow for this breakdown. For example, in the case of TARL number 41BL0877, this is actually three different sites - a cave/sinkhole, a burned rock mound and a burned rock midden. In the new database, three site records would be created, each with a new site number, and the TARL number would be maintained as a separate field in each record so that the records can always be grouped together as and when required. All records are allocated either a site number, a feature number or an object number. Feature numbers are sub-divisions of the site number, and object numbers are sub-divisions of the feature or site number, so that they can always be related to the relevant site within the database. Site and feature association fields are created for each record. These will allow for bottom-up association of objects and features with sites, thus enabling utilisation of the concepts of group value and spatial relationships at a landscape level.

An important aspect that is encompassed by the new database is the recording of multi-period sites, as many sites will cover more than one period. Where sufficient data exists, for each record (site, feature or object) a primary period should be assigned, and then other periods encompassed should be recorded as present or absent. The primary period can be recorded as a general period, and also recorded with a more specific date where possible. This is in accordance with the MIDAS standard, as it allows the recording of the phases within the development of a site, and enables more sophisticated and consistent period-based data retrieval. Event data is recorded at the site level of the hierarchy. The event record contains the TARL number and the site number so that a site record can be linked to its corresponding event record. There should be one separate record for each different event.

Field Name	Field Description
TARL	Admin number
UTM East	Map Co-ordinate
UTM North	Map Co-ordinate
Site Number	Primary number – empty if record is a feature or object
Site Type	Glossary list – empty if record is a feature or object
Feature Number	Subdivision of site number – empty if record is a site or object
Feature Type	Glossary list – empty if record is a site or object
Object Number	Subdivision of feature number – empty if record is a site or feature
Object Type	Glossary list (?) – empty if record is a site or feature
Site Association	Glossary list – completed only if record is a feature or object
Feature Association	Glossary list – completed only if record is an object
Primary Period General	Glossary list
Paleoindian	Also Present/Absent
Early Archaic	Also Present/Absent
Middle Archaic	Also Present/Absent
Late Archaic	Also Present/Absent
Late Prehistoric	Also Present/Absent
Historic C16	Also Present/Absent
Historic C17	Also Present/Absent
Historic C18	Also Present/Absent
Historic C19	Also Present/Absent
Historic C20	Also Present/Absent
Specific Date	Input mask e.g. 3000-2000 or 1850-1860
Description	Free format text: initially loaded with text from AllSites

Table 3: New Fort Hood database - site data structure

Field Name	Field Description
TARL	Admin number
Site Number	Primary number of site
Organisation	e.g. Prewitt, Fort Hood Archaeology Society
Date	e.g. February 1979 to May 1987
Type of Event	e.g. Field Evaluation, Test-pit survey
Hypertext link to event file	
Description	Free format text

Table 4: New Fort Hood database - event data structure

4.3 Implementation of the Fort Hood database

4.3.1 Existing datasets

Below is a list of all the datasets that were assessed and utilised during the design and implementation of the new Fort Hood database. The list excludes the data created by the Arkansas Archaeological Survey (Williams *et al.* 1990a), as this could not be obtained during the project, but includes data collected by Prewitt & Associates Inc., the archaeological company that have undertaken most of the contracted archaeological work on the base in the 1990s, and data held at the Texas Historic Commission.

- Fort Hood Allsites database (MS Access database)
- Prewitt historic site data (MS Excel file)
- Prewitt prehistoric planning document Tables A, B and C (MS Excel files)
- Prewitt prehistoric sites (MS Access database – six tables)
    1. Archaeological Site Form – 152 records
    2. Cultural Material – 96 Records
    3. Features Description – 219 Records
    4. Photographs – 4 Records
    5. Previous Investigations and References – 289 Records
    6. Samples – 4 Records
- Texas Historic Commission data (MS Excel files – nine files)
    1. Fort Hood Archaeological Site Monitoring Form: the observation dates fall between February 1979 and May 1987.
    2. Fort Hood Archaeological Site Survey: this data was recorded early in 1979.
    3. Fort Hood Site Survey: this data was recorded over a fairly long period between April 1984 and Dec 1991.
    4. Fort Hood Archaeology Society Site Form: this data was recorded during 1979.
    5. Fort Hood Archaeology Survey V4: this data was recorded between Dec 1978 and May 1979.
    6. Fort Hood Site Survey Form V3: this data was recorded between May 1973 and Oct 1977.
    7. Fort Hood Historic Site Survey Form: this data was recorded between May 1973 and Oct 1977.
    8. Fort Hood Historic Archaeological Site Survey Form: this data was recorded between Oct 1979 and March 1987.
    9. Fort Hood Monitoring Form: the observation dates fall between January 1976 and July 1985.

4.3.2 Standardisation of terminology

A critical task that needed to be accomplished before any data could be migrated into the new database structure was to create standard wordlists for recording the character of archaeological sites. At the time of the landscape characterisation project, there were no standard lists of site types in existence. There were 50 different site types in the Allsites database, recorded in the field called 'label'. These are listed in Table 5 below.

Value in the field LABEL	Number of Records	Value in the field LABEL	Number of Records
Spaces	12	LRPA	5
Artefact Scatt	262	Medicine Wheel	1
Artefact Scatte	2	Midden	108
BR Scatter	2	Midden?	2
Bridge Footing	3	Mound	58
BRM	1	Mound?	2
BRMs 2	1	Mult. Bldg Foun	1
Burned Rock Scatter	323	Open Camp	1
Buried Hearth	1	Other features	56
Buried Site	14	Other structure	1
Burned Rock	2	Quarry	65
Burned Rock Sca	1	Quarry LPRA	1
Campsite	1	Quarry?	2
Cemetery	22	Rock Art	2
Cistern	1	Rock Pile	1
Domestic	636	Rock Shelter	145
Domestic?	2	Scatter	1
Dump	4	Scatter – L&BR	1
Elephant Bones	1	Sheep Dip	1
Farmstead	1	Shell Midden	2
Foundation	2	Show Buried Cam	1
Hist/Prehist	1	Structural	122
Lithic Scatter	342	Structural?	1
Lithic/BR Scatter	1	Unknown	11
LRP	1	WP A Roadside BBQ	1

Table 5: Prehistoric and Historic site types recorded in the Fort Hood Allsites database (12 records did not have a label)

This is an issue of paramount importance because unless site character is recorded consistently, it is virtually impossible to retrieve meaningful data from the database. The use of consistent terminology limits the possibility of two similar sites being categorised differently and facilitates a common and easily understood interpretation of the archaeological landscape. A vast amount of work has been undertaken in England on standardisation of terminology by English Heritage's Data Standards Unit, particularly on creating a thesaurus of monument types (English Heritage 1999). It was not possible during the course of the project to try and emulate this as it is the product of years of work, not only by English Heritage, but also by the wider UK archaeological community. Furthermore, it is a task that should really be undertaken by those archaeologists who work in the central Texas landscape and have a more intimate knowledge of the character of the archaeology. However, the aim for the purposes of this project was to at least provide a foundation on which to start building. To this end, preliminary lists of site/feature types for the prehistoric and historic periods have been created, which can be enhanced to create comprehensive glossaries of agreed terms, with accompanying scope notes. The new database structure already enforces standardised recording of period. Prewitt & Associates Inc. suggested a series of site types for both prehistoric and historic sites as described in the next two sections.

Prehistoric Site Types

The Prewitt study assigned one of ten different site types to each NRHP eligible site as follows:

Cave/sinkhole	Open camp	Lithic scatter
Open camp/midden	Medicine wheel	Paluxy
Midden	Rock art	Mound
Rockshelter		

They also provided a list of site types and feature types as follows:

Site Type	Feature Type
Lithic procurement area	Burned Rock Midden
Lithic scatter	Burned Rock Mound
Rock art	Human Burial
Open campsite	
Paluxy site	
Rockshelter	
Cave/sinkhole	

The following glossary of site types is proposed for the Fort Hood prehistoric sites and has been adopted for the implementation of the new database.

Possible Site Types	Description
Lithic procurement area	A site which has produced evidence of in situ working of stone for the manufacture of tools, weapons or other objects. Usually located where natural outcrops of chert are exposed. The lithic source can be primary outcrops (i.e. cherts embedded in limestone) or secondary deposits (i.e. lag gravels on uplands, exposed alluvial gravels).
Lithic scatter	A surface scatter of lithic artefacts. Found in areas where no natural cherts crop out. Burned rock features are absent. A lithic scatter differs from an open campsite in that it exhibits a small range of cultural activities relating only to the manufacture or use of chipped stone tools.
Rock art	Locations where an image was carved (petroglyphs) or painted onto rock surfaces by Native Americans.
Open campsite	An occupation site, excluding occupations of caves and rockshelters. Contains a diversity of artefacts along with burned rock features and/or scattered burned rocks indicating heating/cooking activities. Features and artefacts indicate a range of different types of prehistoric activities.
Rockshelter	The area beneath a natural overhang at the base of a cliff or crag. This may have been used for occupation, burial, etc. Rockshelters contain cultural materials and features buried in sediment.
Cave	A subterranean feature entered from a hillside, cliff face, etc. A cave is a naturally occurring cavity at least 5 metres in length or depth. It differs from a rockshelter in that the dimension of the entrance is smaller than its length or depth. A cave may have been used for occupation, storage, burial, refuse, or as a hide-away.
Sinkhole	A solution cavity: a depression in the ground surface and/or a cavity below the ground surface formed by solution processes. May have been used for occupation, storage, refuse, or as a hide-away.
Burned rock midden	An accumulation of fire-cracked stones thought to be related to cooking/processing of plant remains. Extremely variable in terms of associated artefact assemblages. Large burned rocks for which no morphology is discerned are classified as middens. A completely buried burned rock mound would be classified as a burned rock midden until its morphology was revealed through test excavations.
Burned rock mound	An accumulation of fire-cracked stones with a distinctive dome-shaped or rounded morphology. The shape appears to be related to formation, with a mass of fractured burned rock representing debris discarded out of a central earth oven feature. Assumed to be locations where heated stones were used to boil water primarily for cooking purposes.
Burial	A grave in which human remains and other associated materials were intentionally interred by Native Americans.
Medicine Wheel	Leon river medicine wheel

Table 6: Proposed prehistoric site types

In accordance with the flexible nature of the hierarchical structure as described in section 4.2, these site types may also be used as feature types in association with a site, for example, a burned rock midden may be a feature within an open campsite.

The new list contains 11 site types and varies very little from the Prewitt study site types. The need for a separate site type for a Paluxy site type is possibly arguable. The only difference between an open campsite and a Paluxy site is that the latter is found on predominantly sandy sediments from the Cretaceous-age Paluxy formation. As this is a geological difference only, and not one relating to human activities as far as we can tell, it is suggested that a Paluxy site should not be a separate site type.

If required there could be a field within the site data table to indicate whether or not an open campsite is located on a Paluxy formation. It should be noted that this information could be derived from an environmental layer within the GIS, but for this to be an option, it may be necessary to carry out an assessment of the adequacy of the mapping of Paluxy sands. From an archaeological perspective, open campsites and Paluxy sites would still be classified in the same way.

The list of site types defined so far is a preliminary baseline list. More site types will almost certainly be defined as and when new archaeological and other data emerges. This is one of the main reasons for proposing a database structure and a data hierarchy that models the dynamic nature of the archaeological process.

Historic Site Types

There were 1123 historic records on the Allsites database at the time of the characterisation project. The labels, i.e. site types, assigned to these records are shown below:

Labels on Allsites Database	No. of Occurrences	Labels on Allsites Database	No. of Occurrences
Artefact Scatter	263	Mult. Bldg Foun	1
Bridge Footing	3	Other Features	56
Cemetery	22	Other Structure	1
Cistern	1	Rock Art	1
Domestic	638	Rock Pile	1
Dump	4	Sheep Dip	1
Farmstead	1	Structural	123
Foundation	2	Unknown	1
Hist/Prehist	1	WP A Roadside BBQ	1
Midden	1	Spaces	1

Table 7: Historic site types recorded in the Fort Hood Allsites database

Between 1996 and 1999 Prewitt & Associates Inc. assessed 1120 historic sites. With the exception of the 85 sites revisited in 1996, the remaining 625 sites acquired in the 1940s and the 410 sites acquired in the 1950s were assessed using information from previous investigations.

Sometimes the Prewitt study could only give a tentative site type classification to a site. All the military sites, for example, have a provisional classification. When features such as foundations, root cellars, cisterns and so on were recorded together, the Prewitt study classified the site as a farm/ranch.

Similarly, the Prewitt study used the site type livestock feature to denote isolated structures such as dip vats, corrals etc. used exclusively for activities associated with livestock ranching. The Prewitt study's site type 'water feature' refers to any isolated feature specifically designed to capture or channel water for human or animal use, including windmills, troughs, wells, cisterns and water tanks.

A community consists of multiple independent habitations on one site. A dump is a site where there are no features and consisting mostly of artefacts such as cans, bottles, car parts: probably intentional. A Farm/Ranch is a catchall term for habitation or habitation related sites. All military site types are queried. The Prewitt study sometimes classified some sites as combinations of more than one site type, e.g. school and cemetery.

The 1120 sites were classified into site type categories shown overleaf in table 8:

Site Types Used by Prewitt study	No. of Occurrences	Site Types Used by Prewitt study	No. of Occurrences
Artefact Scatter	453	**Quarry?**	1
Bridge	18	**Railroad**	1
Cemetery	18	**Rockshelter with Historic Rock Art**	2
Cemetery & Farm/ranch	5	**Rock Wall**	2
Church & Cemetery	2	**School**	10
Culvert	1	School & Bridge	1
Demolished Building	1	School & Cemetery	1
Dump	20	School?	1
Dump & Livestock Feature	1	**Structure**	2
Farm/Ranch	897	**Unknown**	25
Historic Graffiti	1	**Unknown Others**	14
Livestock Feature	43	**Water Feature**	132
Military or Farm/ranch?	1	Spaces	6
Military?	13		

Table 8: Historic site types defined by the Prewitt study

The Prewitt study originally defined 17 site types. These are shown in Table 8 in bold, except for community. The Prewitt study did not specifically classify any sites as community, although four are classified as "unknown: community".

The Prewitt historic site data contains many variations of the same term. Some examples are listed in Table 9 below.

Enclosure	Pen	Compound
Enclosure	Pen	Compound
Livestock Enclosure	Livestock Pen	Livestock Compound
Barbed Wire Enclosure	Barbed Wire Pen	
Wire Enclosure	Wire Pen	
Hog Wire Enclosure	Hog Wire Pen	
Hog Wire Animal Enclosure		
Fenced Enclosure	Log Pen	
Stone Enclosure	Stone Fence Pen	
Stone Wall Enclosure		
Limestone Enclosure		
Limestone Rock Enclosure		
Rock Wall Enclosure		
Enclosure Walls		
Yard Enclosure		
	Stock Pen	
	Animal Pen	
	Sorting Pen	
	Corral Pen	

Table 9: Variations of historic site type terms used in the Prewitt study's historic site data

The proposed preliminary list standardises the different terms for what appear to be the same features. Two examples may help to explain why. The use of the term dump (or trash if preferred) is suggested rather than trash dump, trash scatter, recent trash, trash, domestic trash, trash concentration, trash pile, historic trash or metal trash, and the use of the term pen rather than enclosure or compound. The term pen is a broad definition. Within pen there are two narrower definitions, namely, stock pen and sorting pen.

Some of the terms used in the current historic data are synonymous. Take for example, sidewalk and pavement. It is suggested that one of these should be the preferred term. Walkway and path tend to be used interchangeably, and another example is gravestone, where it is suggested that this should encompass headstone, footstone and tombstone.

Table 10 below shows a list compiled from the various historic data sources of some terms that have been used interchangeably to describe the same site or feature, and shows the standard term that should be used.

Term previously used	Preferred standard term
Animal Pen	Use Stock Pen.
Burial Plot	Use Grave.
Compound	Use Pen.
Domestic Dwelling	Use House.
Domestic Trash	Use Dump.
Enclosure	Use Pen.
Foot Stone	Use Gravestone.
Headstone	Use Gravestone.
Habitation Site	Use House.
Latrine	Use Privy.
Livestock Compound	Use Stock Pen.
Log Cabin	Use Cabin.
Outhouse	Use Outbuilding.
Pistol Range	Use Firing Range.
Refuse Scatter	Use Dump.
Residence	Use House.
Retaining Wall	Use Revetment.
Rifle Range	Use Firing Range.
Rock Alignment	Use Stone Alignment.
Tombstone	Use Gravestone.
Trash	Use Dump.
Trash Dump	Use Dump.
Trash Scatter	Use Dump.
Well Shaft	Use Well.

Table 10: List of historic terms used and preferred terms

Features should be defined by their function rather than the material from which they are made although the hierarchy of site, feature and object makes it possible to sub-divide pen into cattle pen, sheep pen, barbed wire pen, wire pen, hog wire pen, stone pen and so on. The use of the material from which the pen is built could, however, lead to the loss of the functional description, e.g. stock pen. The same could apply to corral. The difference between corral and pen is assumed to be that of size rather than function: a corral is a larger enclosure than a pen.

In the absence of any other data, a feature can be a site, but some site types cannot be feature types as they are always at the top of the hierarchy. Table 11 gives a preliminary list of proposed site types only, whilst Table 12 contains a preliminary list of proposed site/feature types for the Fort Hood historic data. The lists of types have been compiled from the data sources listed in section 4.3.1 above.

The list was also compiled with reference to English Heritage terminology (English Heritage 1999), and this was adhered to as far as possible. Where there was no equivalent term provided by English Heritage, e.g. Stoop, the definition as given in the Hypertext Webster Gateway was used (see http://work.ucsd.edu:5141/cgi-bin/http_webster/).

Possible Site Types	Description
Army Camp	Use Military Camp.
Blacksmith	Place where a smith works iron. May be for small-scale local use or within a larger industrial complex.
Bridge	A structure of wood, stone, iron, brick or concrete, etc, with one or more intervals under it to span a river or other space.
Cemetery	An area of ground set apart for the burial of the dead.
Church	A building used for public Christian worship.
Dirt Road	A road without a made surface.
Farm/Ranch	A tract of land, often including a farmhouse and ancillary buildings, used for the purpose of cultivation and the rearing of livestock, etc.
Farmstead	A farmhouse, the adjoining land and ancillary farm buildings forming a group.
Firing Range (Military)	A piece of ground over which small arms or large artillery may be fired at targets.
Ford	A shallow place in a river, creek or other stretch of water, where people, animals and vehicles may cross.
Graveyard	Use Cemetery.
Hamlet	Small settlement usually without a church or any other administrative function.
Homestead	A small settlement, usually consisting of one dwelling with ancillary buildings.
Military Camp	Use Military Site.
Military Depot	A building or group of buildings, often enclosed by a system of fortifications, used by an armed force for the storage and distribution of military equipment.
Military Road	Road used primarily, but not exclusively, for the rapid transport of military vehicles, equipment and personnel.
Military Site	A site where a body of troops has been temporarily or permanently lodged, with or without entrenchments, fortifications or buildings.
Military Training Site	Buildings, structures and sites for the training of military personnel.
Parsonage	The residence of a parson, rector or vicar.
Pistol Range	Use Firing Range.
Quarry	An excavation from which stone for building and other functions, is obtained by cutting, blasting, etc.
Railroad	A line or track consisting of iron or steel rails, on which passenger carriages or goods wagons are moved, usually by a locomotive engine.
Ranch	A large tract of land used for the raising of livestock, especially cattle.
Rifle Range	Use Firing Range.
Road	A way between different places, used by horses, travellers on foot and vehicles.
School	An establishment in which people, usually children, are taught.
Settlement	A small concentration of independent dwellings. (Used instead of community.)
Slaughter House	A building where animals are slaughtered.
Trail	A track or pathway, not necessarily designed as such, beaten down by the feet of travellers.
Weapons Pit	Usually a small, two or three man trench, dug as an isolated fieldwork rather than as part of a defensive system. Fox hole.

Table 11: Proposed historic site types

Possible Feature/Site Types	Description
Agricultural Building	A building used for an agricultural and/or subsistence purpose. Use more specific type where known.
Animal Dip Tank	A place or building where animals can be washed. Often in the form of a pool with a walled funnel-like structure enabling animals to be guided into the pool.
Artefact Scatter	An artefact scatter is a spatially discrete scatter of mixed artefactual material recovered from the surface, e.g. During fieldwalking, rather than from a particular archaeological context. The site consists of artefacts only with no associated features.
Barbecue	A frame or spit to hold meat that is cooked over an open fire or cured by exposure to smoke. Usually out of doors.
Barn	A building used primarily for storing hay, grain, and farm equipment or as a shelter for livestock.
Berm	A ledge at the bottom of a bank or cutting designed to catch earth that could roll down the slope, or to strengthen the bank.
Bomb Crater	A depression in the ground caused by the explosion of a mine or bombshell.
Brick Rubble	Waste fragments of brick from a house or wall or other structure.
Building	A structure with a roof to provide shelter from the weather for occupants or contents. Use specific type where known.
Building Platform	A site where a building once stood as identified by a level area of ground, often compacted or made from man-made materials.
Cabin	A small house usually built out of rough logs.
Cable Trench	A long, narrow, covered ditch used as a means of concealing and protecting cables.
Cattle Dip Tank	A place or building where cattle can be washed.
Cattle Guard	A trench under a railroad track and alongside a crossing, e.g. a public highway, designed to prevent cattle from getting on the track.
Cattle Tank	Large vessel, usually made of metal, wood or concrete containing water for cattle.
Cattle Trough	A long metal or stone vessel usually where food or water for cattle is put.
Cellar	A room or group of rooms usually below the ground level and usually under a building, often used for storing fuel, provisions etc.
Cess Pool	A covered pit into which raw sewage is discharged.
Cistern	A covered tank in which rainwater is stored for use when required.
Chicken Coop	Usually a small henhouse with a cage over the run. Can be moved frequently.
Chimney	A channel, built from brick or stone, which carries off smoke from an internal domestic fire.
Concrete Rubble	Waste fragments of concrete from a house or other structure.
Cooking Pit (Barbecue Pit)	A pit that shows evidence for having been used for cooking. Often contains charcoal, burnt bone fragments etc.
Corral	A large enclosure for horses, cattle and other livestock.
Culvert	A drainage structure that extends across and beneath roadways, canals or embankments.
Dam	A barrier of concrete or earth, etc, built across a river to create a reservoir of water for domestic, agricultural or industrial usage.
Depression	A hollow on the ground surface where a building may once have stood.
Ditch	A long and narrow hollow or trench dug in the ground, often used to carry water though it may be dry for much of the year.
Domestic Vegetation	Flowers, herbs, vegetables, bushes, fruit and other trees grown in a domestic environment.
Drainpipe	A pipe used for carrying off surplus water.

Drainage Ditch	A long, narrow ditch designed to carry water away from a waterlogged area.
Dump	A site that consists exclusively of artefacts such as whole cans, bottles, car parts and other large debris. The term implies intentional dumping of refuse. There are no other features on the site.
Electrical Hookups	A device that connects a user to a source of electricity.
Electricity Power Line	A cable providing electricity.
Electricity Power Pole	A tall wooden pole used to support overhead electricity cables.
Farm Building	A building or structure of unknown function found on a farm. Use more specific type where known.
Farmhouse	The main dwelling house attached to a farm.
Fence	A construction used to enclose an area of land, a building, etc. can be made of wood, wire, stone, rock or metal.
Fence Line	The original line or course of a fence.
Fence Post	An upright post usually made from timber, but other materials also, to which the fence is attached.
Field	An area of land, often enclosed, used for cultivation or the grazing of livestock.
Fireplace	An open recess in a wall at the base of a chimney where a fire can be built.
Firing Range	A piece of ground over which small arms or large artillery may be fired at targets.
Floor	A layer of stone, brick or boards, etc, on which people tread. Use broader site type where known.
Flower Bed	A plot of earth used for the raising of flowers and shrubs.
Foot Post	A hole dug to provide a firm base for an upright post.
Footings	Projecting course at foot of wall that supports building. See Foundation.
Foundation	Solid ground or base, natural or artificial, on which building rests.
Fox Hole	Usually a small, two or three man trench, dug as an isolated military fieldwork rather than as part of a defensive system
Garage	A building that houses motor vehicles. Includes garages for vehicle repair.
Garden	An enclosed piece of ground, normally attached to a house, devoted to the cultivation of herbs, flowers, fruit or vegetables and/or recreational purposes.
Garden Feature	Unspecified garden feature. Use more specific type where known.
Gas Pipe	A conduit for conveying gas.
Gate	A movable structure which enables or prevents entrance to be gained. Usually situated in a wall or similar barrier and supported by gateposts.
Gate Post	A pier of brick, masonry, stone, rock etc, to which the hinges of a gate are attached.
Granary	A storehouse for grain, especially after it has been threshed or husked.
Grave	A place of burial.
Gravestone	A stone placed over or at the head or foot of a grave, or at the entrance of a tomb. (This term is used for headstone, footstone and tombstone).
Headstone	Use Gravestone.
Hearth	A slab, usually stone or concrete, on which a fire is made.
Historic Graffiti	Casual scribbles, drawings or carvings on walls, stones or other surfaces. Often applied to humourous, satiric or obscene writings or drawings or name carvings executed anonymously in public places.
House	A building for human habitation, especially a dwelling place. Use more specific type where known.

Ice House	A structure, partly underground, for the preservation of ice for use during warmer weather.
Incinerator	An apparatus for burning refuse to ashes.
Kitchen	A building or room where food is prepared and cooked.
Military Building	A building of unknown purpose found at a military site. Use more specific type where known.
Military Dump	A site that consists exclusively of discarded military artefacts. The term implies intentional dumping of refuse. There are no other features on the site.
Military Earthwork	A usually temporary earthwork or fortification, the latter constructed by military forces operating in the field. Use more specific type where known.
Mill Dam	A dam constructed across a stream to raise its water-level and make it available to power a mill wheel.
Mill Pond	The area of water retained above a mill dam for driving a mill.
Natural Gas Tank	Large receptacle for storing natural gas.
Outbuilding	A detached subordinate building.
Oven	A brick, stone or iron receptacle for baking bread or other food in.
Path	A way made for pedestrians, especially one merely made by walking (often not specially constructed).
Patio	A small paved area attached to a building.
Pavement	A path for pedestrians, beside a street or roadway, laid or beaten in with stones or other materials.
Pen	A small enclosure for cattle, sheep, hogs, horses, poultry, etc.
Piling	A column of wood, steel or concrete that is driven into the ground to support a structure.
Privy	A small building housing a lavatory.
Porch	A covered and enclosed entrance to a building. It is either an internal vestibule next to the front door or an external structure, with a separate roof, attached to the building often forming a covered entrance. Sometimes the porch is large enough to serve as a covered walk or a veranda.
Post Hole	A hole dug to provide a firm base for an upright post, often with stone packing.
Quarry	An excavation from which stone for building and other functions, is obtained by cutting, blasting, etc.
Pump House	A small building where a machine is used to raise water from an underground source.
Revetment	A facing of wood, stone or other material to support an embankment when it receives a slope steeper than the natural slope. A retaining wall built to retain a bank of earth.
Roadbed	A foundation of earth or rock supporting a road.
Rockshelter	An area beneath a natural overhang at the base of a cliff or crag.
Rock Wall	A wall made from rock or rubble possibly indicating a property line.
Root Cellar	A room or group of rooms below the ground level or built into the side of a slope, often used for storing vegetables and fruit during the winter months.
Septic Tank	A watertight reservoir or tank that receives sewage, and by sedimentation and bacterial action effects a process of partial purification.
Shed	A slight structure built for shelter or storage, or for use as a workshop, either attached as a lean-to to a permanent building or separate. Use more specific type where known.
Sheep Dip Tank	A place where sheep are washed to clean the wool and combat diseases. Often in the form of a pool or through with a walled funnel-like structure enabling sheep to be guided into the pool.
Shelter	A structure that protects an area of ground from the weather.
Sidewalk	A paved area for pedestrians beside a street or roadway. A pavement.

Sluice	A dam that can be raised or lowered to regulate the flow of water.
Sluicegate	The gate of a sluice that can be opened or shut to let out or retain water.
Smoke House	A building used to smoke fish or meat.
Sorting Pen	A pen where livestock can be separated.
Spillway	A passage for surplus water from a dam.
Spring	A point where water issues naturally from the rock or soil onto the ground or into a body of surface water.
Spring House	Small building enclosing a natural spring.
Stable	A building in which horses and sometimes other animals are accommodated.
Staircase	A flight of stairs with a supporting framework of balusters, handrail etc.
Stairs	A means of access to another level consisting of a set of fixed indoor steps
Steps	A series of flat-topped structures, usually made of stone, wood, brick or concrete used to facilitate a person's movement from one level to another.
Stock Pen	An enclosure used for containing cattle, sheep, hogs, goats or poultry.
Stock Pond	A body of still water, often artificially formed, providing water for livestock.
Stock Tank	Large vessel, usually made of metal, wood or concrete containing water for livestock.
Stone Alignment	A single line, or two or more roughly parallel lines, of standing stones set at intervals along a common axis or series of axes.
Storage Pit	A pit dug in the ground used to store meat, grain and other foodstuffs.
Storm Cellar	A room usually below the ground level in which people take refuge from tornadoes, thunderstorms and high winds.
Storehouse	A building in which goods or other items are stored.
Stoop	An out of door flight of stairs consisting of seven to fourteen steps, with platform and parapets, leading to an entrance door.
Telephone Pole	A tall wooden pole used to support telephone wires.
Terrace	A series of raised level areas formed on a slope and used for cultivation. An alternative meaning is a paved outdoor area adjoining a house, for which use patio.
Tree House	Small building constructed within the branches of trees.
Trough	A narrow, open container, usually where food or water for livestock is put.
Underground Structure	A constructed space beneath the surface of the ground. Use specific type where known.
Vault	An underground room or building with an arched roof.
Walkway	A path set aside for walking.
Wall	An enclosing structure composed of bricks, stones or similar materials, laid in courses. Use specific type where known, e.g. revetment, garden wall etc.
Water Pipe	A pipe, made from metal, concrete etc. through which water is conducted.
Water Tank	A receptacle for the storage of water.
Water Tower	A tower serving as a reservoir to deliver water at a required point.
Water Trough	A narrow, open container, where water for livestock is put.
Well	A shaft or pit dug in the ground over a supply of spring-water.
Well Cover	A lid for a well. Well covers can be made of various materials.
Well Head	The structure at the top of a draw well.
Well House	Small building enclosing a well.

Windmill	A tower-like structure of wood or brick with a wooden cap and sails that are driven around by the wind producing power to work the internal machinery.
Windmill Base	A platform or artificial mound of earth indicating either the former site of a windmill or built as the base of a post windmill.
Yard	Usually a small enclosed area of land in front of, or around, a house.

Table 12: Proposed historic site/feature types

It should be emphasised that site types are never definitive, and need to be flexible. New site types can be added whenever new archaeological and other data leads to a different understanding of a site's character. It is the presence or absence of other data associated with the site that helps the archaeologist and others to understand the site and to interpret it.

If a site consists of a well and nothing else, the site type should be "well" and not water feature. The same applies to corral, cistern, troughs, dip vat and so on. Yet the hierarchical system of classification is flexible enough to allow, for example, a dip vat with no other features present to be regarded as evidence for a farm/ranch and classified accordingly. If new data emerges a new interpretation is possible.

4.3.3 Site Data

The existing Fort Hood Allsites database was used to create the initial records in the new Fort Hood database. This database was used to populate the following fields in the site table:

- TARL
- UTM East
- UTM West
- Site Type
- Primary Period General*
- Primary Period Specific**

*initially Prehistoric or Historic in the absence of any other information
**where possible – very little data existed for this field

Once the initial records were created from the Allsites database, the additional datasets from the Prewitt study and the Texas Historic Commission were used to enhance and update the site type and period fields, and where required create feature records. Also, some of the records in the Allsites database had been identified as being multiple sites, and had therefore been divided into 'sub-areas'. These were examined and where appropriate, new site and feature records were created for them. Where more than one event had occurred for a site, it was assumed that the last event was the most up-to-date and this was used to update the site type and date fields on the site record.

4.3.4 Event Data

There are a large number of different datasets in existence for Fort Hood (see section 4.3.1), recording various assessment and management information, each of which reflects an event. It was not possible within the timescale of the project to create comprehensive event data for every record, but the framework to do this as and when resources allow is now in place. The event data sources have been left as standalone data sets, without changing any of the data or the format in which it is held.

The event table contains a hyperlink to the relevant data source, effectively providing an index to all the different events that have been carried out, and preserving the integrity of the original site event. Any future database development should prioritise integrating all the separate data sources into one single event table that should then be used to record any further event data. Administrative data that will not change should initially be recorded in the event table, but the task of moving this into a separate administrative table could be part of future database development work.

Field Name	Field Value
TARL	41BL0158
UTM East	3431
UTM North	4610
Site Number	e.g. 000100
Site Type	Farm/Ranch
Feature Number	Spaces
Feature Type	Spaces
Object Number	Spaces
Object Type	Spaces
Site Association	Spaces
Feature Association	Spaces
Primary Period General	Historic C19
Paleoindian	Spaces
Early Archaic	Spaces
Middle Archaic	Spaces
Late Archaic	Spaces
Late Prehistoric	Spaces
Historic C16	Spaces
Historic C17	Spaces
Historic C18	Spaces
Historic C19	Y
Historic C20	Spaces
Specific Date	1860-1880
Description	VANDALIZED, EXHUMED GRAVES?-POOR COND.

Table 13: New Fort Hood database – example of a site record

Field Name	Field Value
TARL	41BL0158
UTM East	3432
UTM North	4611
Site Number	Spaces
Site Type	Spaces
Feature Number	000100.001
Feature Type	Foundation
Object Number	Spaces
Object Type	Spaces
Site Association	Farm/Ranch
Feature Association	Spaces
Primary Period General	Historic C19
Paleoindian	Spaces
Early Archaic	Spaces
Middle Archaic	Spaces
Late Archaic	Spaces
Late Prehistoric	Spaces
Historic C16	Spaces
Historic C17	Spaces
Historic C18	Spaces
Historic C19	Y
Historic C20	Spaces
Specific Date	1860-1880
Description	Free format text

Table 14: New Fort Hood database – example of a feature record

Field Name	Field Value
TARL	41BL0158
UTM East	3432
UTM North	4611
Site Number	Spaces
Site Type	Spaces
Feature Number	Spaces
Feature Type	Spaces
Object Number	00100.001.001
Object Type	Coin
Site Association	Farm/Ranch
Feature Association	Foundation
Primary Period General	Historic C19
Paleoindian	Spaces
Early Archaic	Spaces
Middle Archaic	Spaces
Late Archaic	Spaces
Late Prehistoric	Spaces
Historic C16	Spaces
Historic C17	Spaces
Historic C18	Spaces
Historic C19	Y
Historic C20	Spaces
Specific Date	1860-1870
Description	Free format text

Table 15: New Fort Hood database – example of an object record

4.4 Future database developments

The new Fort Hood database should be considered as a foundation on which to build, and there is much work that can be done to expand the scope and functionality of the database. Possibilities for future development that have already been mentioned are:

- The addition of related sources and archives data
- Creation of comprehensive event records
- Creation of a separate table for administrative data

Other possibilities include:

- Links to databases of artefacts
  There is already provision in the new database for recording objects, which can include artefact scatters that constitute a site, single artefacts that are the only evidence for a site and therefore also constitute a site (i.e. 'stray finds'), or artefacts that have been recovered in association with a site. In accordance with MIDAS, the database is not intended to be an artefact inventory, and only provides for recording of basic artefact information. However, it may be useful to provide cross-referencing functionality to specialised artefact inventories, particularly given the quantity and fundamental significance of projectile points and other stone artefacts within the archaeology of Central Texas.

- Integrated GIS linkage
  Although the database records and the GIS polygons can be correlated on the basis of the TARL number, there is no dynamic linkage between the two. This means that they have to be separately maintained and updated, and data retrieval and analysis is more complicated and more limited. Providing an integrated GIS link would combine the sophisticated querying and retrieval capabilities of a relational database with the spatial analysis capabilities of a GIS, creating a very powerful tool for management and research. This would greatly facilitate the integration of the HLC data with the archaeological sites inventory. This type of integrated GIS linkage is already in widespread use in UK Sites and Monuments Records via, for example, the exeGesIS HBSMR software package (www.esdm.co.uk/HBSMR.asp), and is being used to great effect for both SMR data and HLC data.

5. The historic landscape characterisation project

The Fort Hood HLC project largely utilised an 'attribute-based' approach to characterisation, as outlined in chapter 2, whereby the landscape was divided into base polygons, attributes were assigned to these polygons, and then GIS analysis was carried out to determine the HLC types to which each polygon should be allocated. This approach was thought to be the most objective approach, and also the most appropriate for characterising a landscape which was not already organised into easily accessible landscape units, and where no detailed mapping was available. As the characterisation progressed, a considerable amount of experimentation and testing was undertaken, and the methodology was continually being adapted and refined on the basis of the results obtained. It was considered vital to use such a responsive approach in a project that was breaking new ground, and this experimentation and adaptability has turned out to be one of the greatest strengths of the Fort Hood HLC project.

5.1 Creation of the historic landscape polygons

The most fundamental task of the characterisation project was to establish what the landscape units would be, and what core data sources would be used to map these units. British based studies have shown that the process of historic landscape assessment is primarily desk-based, using maps as *Core Sources'*, providing a 'vertical' birds-eye perspective. In England, implementation of Historic Landscape Characterisation has therefore relied heavily on the interpretation of available mapping to identify the basic Landscape Types, and the core data sources have almost universally been Ordnance Survey mapping (http://www.ordnancesurvey.co.uk/oswebsite/). Initially the chosen scale of representation adopted has been that of 1:25,000. Characteristically this map series provides a comprehensive coverage of the current environment, sufficiently detailed to allow the desired *'broad brush'* approach necessary for characterisation, but sufficiently rationalised to avoid becoming overwhelmed with an over-complication of detail. Sufficient particular aspects can be interpreted (e.g. grassland, heathland, woodland habitat) to establish the necessary landscape types (Aldred and Fairclough 2002, 26).

This approach works well in the UK, where successive land use is often frozen into the landscape in the form of, for example, distinctive enclosure forms or boundary types. When W.G. Hoskins wrote The Making of the English Landscape in 1955 he stated "The English Landscape itself to those who know how to read it right, is the richest historical record we possess" (Hoskins 1955, 14). To that, perhaps, could be added that 200 years of detailed cartographic record have chronicled that landscape, providing a ready-made set of building blocks as a basis for contemporary landscape characterisation. More recent characterisation projects have turned to a wider range of cartographic products, primarily digital in format and including scales of 1:1250, 1:2500, 1:10,000 and 1:25,000, the choice of scale being dependant on the grain of the characterisation (Aldred and Fairclough 2003). The forms present within such a record may or may not be ancient, but even when of comparatively recent origin, often provide secondary evidence of earlier land use, for example when early parliamentary enclosure field boundaries follow even earlier medieval furlong boundaries, displaying the characteristic 'reversed-S' shape of medieval ploughing.

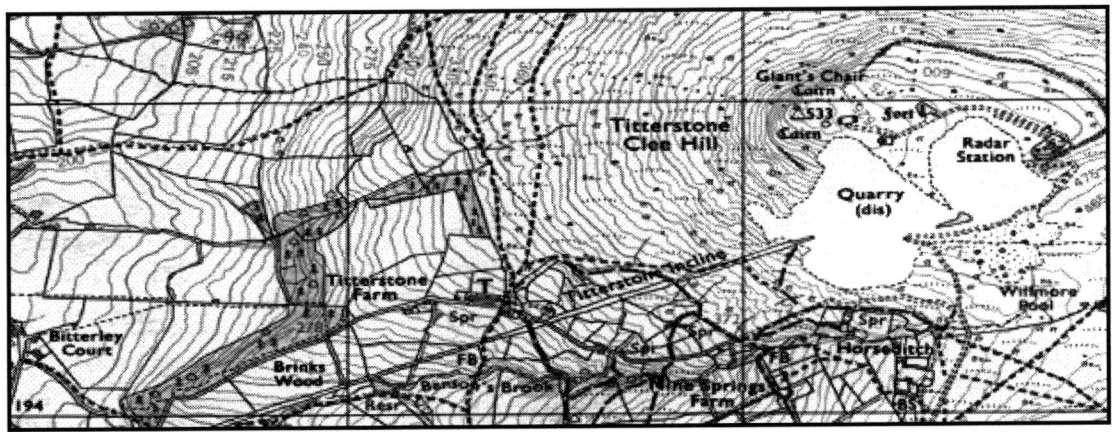

Figure 14: Extract from Ordnance Survey 1:25000 mapping. © Crown Copyright/database right 2007. An Ordnance Survey/EDINA supplied service.

In the case of Fort Hood, this depth of cartographic record was not available as the basis for characterisation, and neither were the fieldscapes which were the fundamental building blocks of most English characterisation work. The Fort Hood HLC project therefore needed to find an alternative set of primary building blocks, and after careful consideration, Landsat TM satellite imagery was selected as the base source of spatial data from which to begin the characterisation. Landsat imagery, as well as fulfilling the essential criterion for a core HLC data source in that it provides comprehensive coverage of the study area, is readily available, comparatively inexpensive and compares favourably in terms of resolution to the 1:25,000 base mapping used as a base in English characterisation (Aldred and Fairclough 2002, 26). It is of sufficiently broad-brush resolution (30m pixel size) to give the desired level of detail while providing a sensing system specifically designed for observation of earth resources, including subtle changes in vegetation, forestry cover, water bodies, land use and minerals. Satellite sensors offer several advantages over aerial photography in such a context. They provide a synoptic view offering complete cover of the extensive target area within one scene, sufficiently fine detail and if necessary a systematic repeat coverage.

Comprehensive, high resolution aerial photography was available for the whole of Fort Hood, and this was also identified as a core data source for the initial mapping of landscape polygons. In addition, the characterisation was to be informed by:

Supporting sources: these directly assist or refine mapping and interpretation. These sources also provide comprehensive coverage but tend to provide more tangential information, which assists interpretation less directly than the core sources (e.g. geology and soils, additional photographic cover, earlier map coverage, elevation information, vegetation cover etc).

Indicative sources: these are available sources which assist the definition of landscape types rather than facilitate their mapping. Often these sources are limited in area or selective in their coverage or in the nature of the record. Specific surveys, site records or environmental designations are all valuable data sets within this context.

Within the characterisation process, the use of available archaeological inventory information is consciously avoided to prevent the danger of the characterisation becoming no more than a self-fulfilling backdrop to the existing archaeological record. Such independence strengthens the potential later uses of the characterisation.

5.1.1 Classification of Landsat Data

Two Landsat scenes were initially selected as fulfilling the requirements of the Fort Hood HLC project, one from the Spring of 2000 and one from the Autumn. The scene captured in May 2000 was chosen as the most appropriate core data source, and it offered a largely cloud-free view of the area of the Fort Hood base. The image was obtained in the form of raw data from the UK imaging provider Infoterra, based at Leicester and Farnborough

The seven georeferenced raw data bands of the Landsat satellite image were imported into 'ERDAS Imagine' software, a well established image processing software which offers a usefully wide variety of import and export formats and facilities. Once successfully visualised within 'Imagine', each separate band was saved into the generic Imagine format (.img files). The area of the Fort Hood base was limited to the southeast quadrant of the scene, so a rectangular subset of each of the image bands was extracted from the scene and exported in GeoTiff Format.

During the export, the following band combinations were chosen as being appropriate for subsequent analysis:

- Bands 1-5-6: A preferred combination to target potential changes in soils.
- Bands 2-3-4: A preferred combination for the recording of vegetated and urban areas
- Bands 3-4-5: A further combination of vegetation/urban band types (useful for vegetation discrimination.)

The transferred GeoTiffs were then imported into ESRI's GIS ArcView which was to be used as the main processing software. Once within ArcView, each of the selected image band combinations were georegistered using the ArcView Image Analyst extension. The original Landsat data was supplied in correct coordinate space, making registration a simple process. After a comparison between a rectification using 25 points and one using only four points, the four-point registration was deemed more useful due to the extremely accurate correlation with the existing aerial photography and the vector data set. The registered images were then re-imported into ERDAS Imagine to check for any possible errors created in the file transfer and exportation processes, for example any data corruption or cross-compatibility problems. Comparison of the images in ArcView Image Analyst and in ERDAS Imagine, perhaps surprisingly, showed better definition at the same given scale within ArcView, and as a result this software was used for most of the subsequent image-processing work.

The original Landsat image was also imported and georegistered as individual bands using the same methodology, to provide additional datasets for inclusion as necessary in any subsequent image analysis.

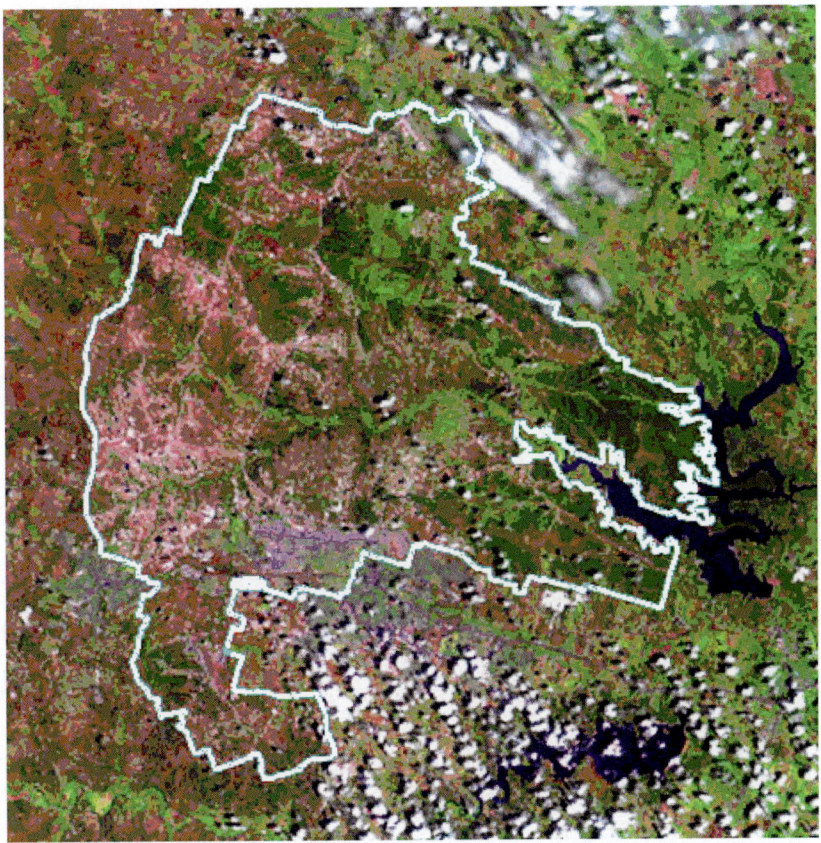

Figure 15: Subset of Landsat Scene covering the extent of Fort Hood

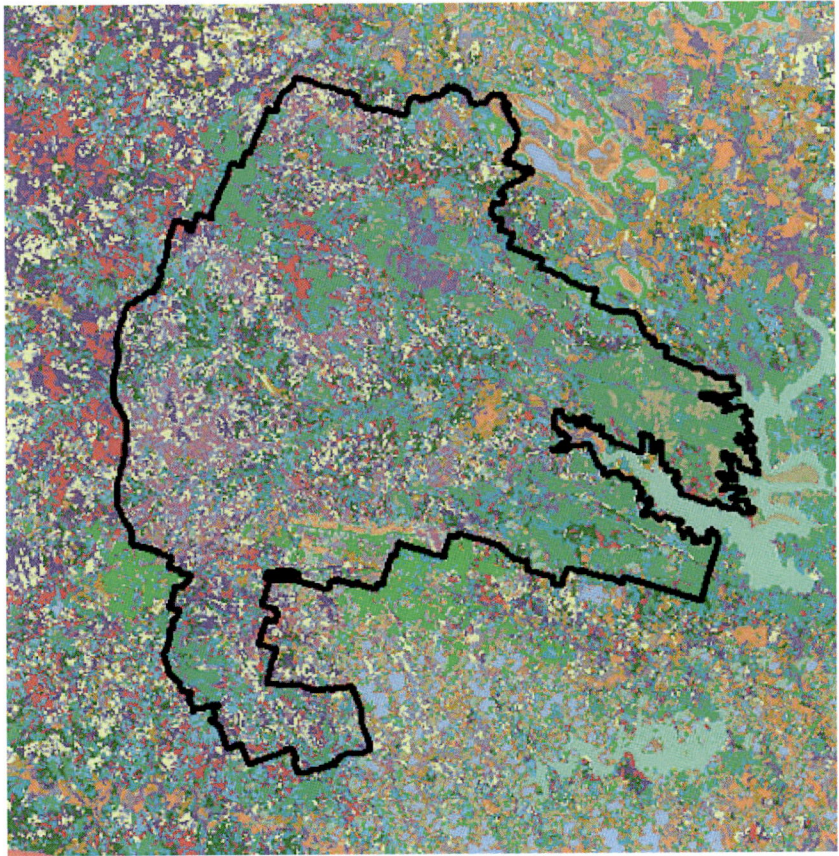

Figure 16: Initial unsupervised classification of Landsat sub-scene.

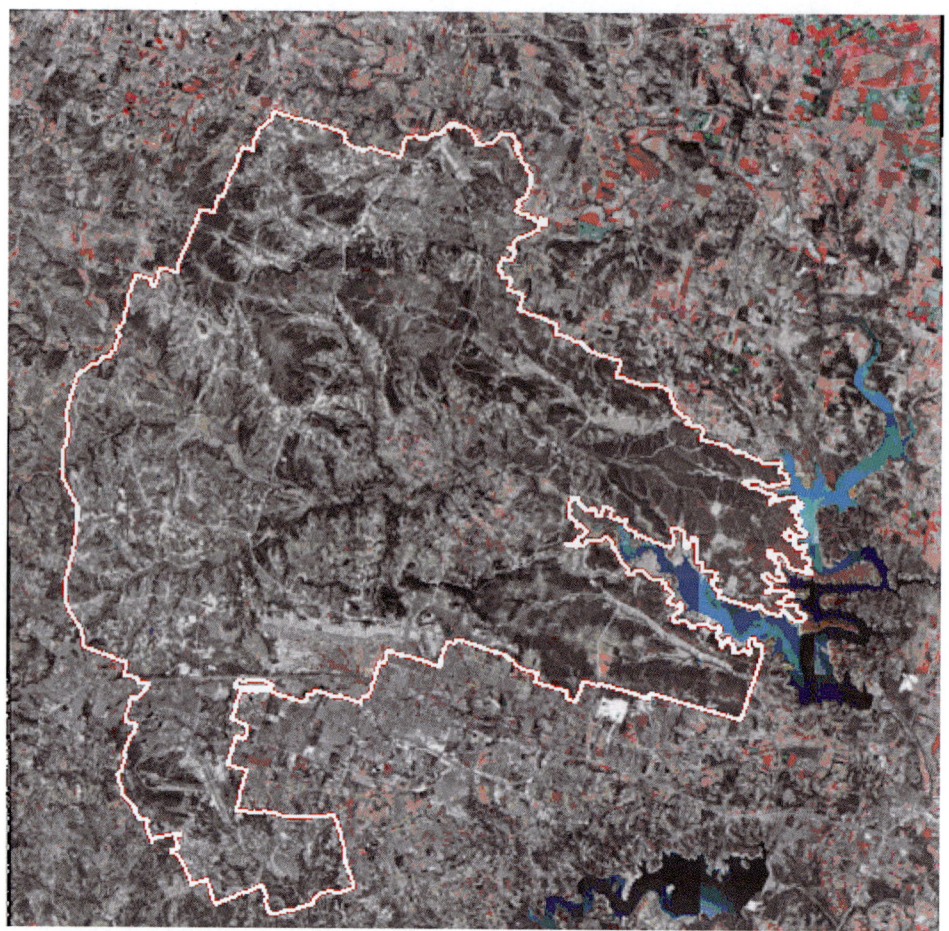

Figure 17: The false colour infra-red aerial photography composite image of Fort Hood

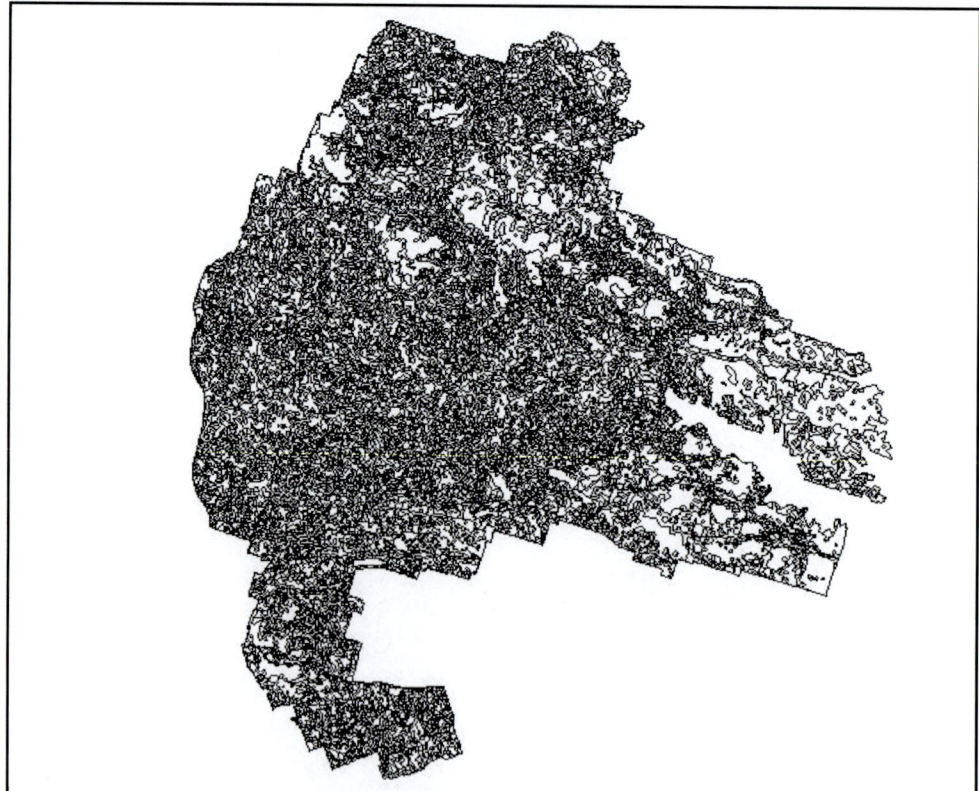

Figure 18: Initial polygons derived from classification

The selected satellite imagery was then processed using unsupervised classification to create a set of base polygons, which formed the starting point for dividing the landscape into units for analysis and interpretation. Image classification can be defined as the process of assigning pixels to classes, and is a valuable tool within the field of remote sensing and image analysis. Each pixel is treated as an individual unit and by comparing pixels to one another it is possible to assemble groups of similar pixels into classes. These classes form regions so that after classification, the digital image is presented as a mosaic of uniform parcels, each identified by a separate colour. In principle, these classes are composed of homogeneous pixels which are more similar to each other than to pixels within other classes.

In practice each class will display some internal diversity. Classification may form an end in itself, as in the case of land use classification, or may form an intermediate step within a more elaborate analysis. Classification can be split into supervised classification and unsupervised classification. The former requires the interaction of the analyst to guide the classification based on known characteristics of an area within the image, often termed a training set. The latter is a more automated process, requiring a minimum of interaction with the analyst to group the pixels within the image into their natural classes.

The unsupervised classification of the Fort Hood Landsat image was carried out using the 'categorize' command in ArcView Image Analyst. This ArcView extension provides the facility to categorise multi-band continuous data into a selected number of classes. The classification process is based on the values of the pixels that make up the image, and the pixels are assigned to classes based on their value. The values of pixels correspond to their brightness or darkness, which designates different elements like land and water, so typically the classes represent land cover types. The 'categorize' command uses the ESRI ISODATA algorithm to perform unsupervised classification. ISODATA stands for "Iterative Self-Organizing Data Analysis Technique". It is iterative in that it repeatedly performs an entire classification (outputting a thematic raster layer) and recalculates statistics. "Self-Organizing" refers to the way in which it locates the clusters that are inherent in the data. The ISODATA clustering method uses the minimum spectral distance formula to form clusters. It begins with either arbitrary cluster means or means of an existing signature set, and each time the clustering repeats, the means of these clusters are shifted. The new cluster means are used for the next iteration.

A variety of methods and variables were tested in order to determine the most appropriate methodology and achieve results that fitted the purpose of the characterisation project. To establish the optimum class size, the images were classified into 10, 20 and 30 classes. Several combinations of bands were experimented with, and the 3-4-5 band combination proved to be the most successful.

The images were also classified in ERDAS Imagine, to see if the classification produced different results to those produced in ArcView. The 3-4-5-band combination, which proved to be the most successful combination in ArcView, was chosen as a test and classified using the Imagine Classifier Module's 'unsupervised classification' function. Class sizes of 10, 20 and 30 were again used. When these images were compared with those produced by ArcView Image Analyst, no discernible differences were observed.

After systematic observation of the results of all these classifications, it was clear that the 3-4-5-band image had the best contrast and resolution, whilst largely avoiding the major hindrance of cloud cover. Therefore, on the basis of clarity and sensitivity to changes in the landscape, the 3-4-5 image, classified into 20 classes, was selected as the base data source for the creation of the landscape characterisation polygons.

5.1.2 Classifying aerial photography and merging satellite images

Although the Landsat data was chosen as the primary data set for creation of the characterisation polygons, tests were also carried out to establish the suitability of the false colour infra-red aerial photography composite image of the base that was provided by the U.S. army. Although aerial photography is used less often for landscape classification in this way, it was felt that it was an avenue worth pursuing with some experimentation. Accordingly the aerial photographic mosaic (Doqq99), which covered the area of the base and offered a potential resolution of 1m was classified into 20 classes using the same methodology as that used for the satellite imagery. However, perhaps not unsurprisingly, this experiment produced unsatisfactory results as the high resolution of the image split up any major blocks of colour, so limiting its usefulness for any broad-brush landscape characterisation.

A similarly experimental attempt was made to merge the satellite imagery and aerial photography, to try and enhance the resolution of the satellite imagery. This was tested using both ArcView and ERDAS Imagine, but proved impossible in the latter due to file and image spatial incompatibles. The ArcView "Stack" Function was used to merge the images together, but the results were unsatisfactory as the output image was produced at the same resolution as the satellite image. Therefore, it was decided to limit the aerial photography to the role of a supporting data source, and to use the satellite data alone to produce the initial base polygons for the landscape characterisation.

5.1.3 Vectorisation of the classified images

The next step in the processing was to use the classified satellite data to create base polygons for the whole of the area of Fort hood. The 20 classifications of the 3-4-5 band satellite image were smoothed in ArcView Image Analyst ten times prior to vectorisation, in an attempt to reduce and simplify the number of potential polygons. The resultant image was then clipped to the Fort Hood boundary and vectorised by converting it to a shapefile. The ArcView 'quality control' extension was used to highlight 'sliver' polygons below 0.5 hectares in size, which were then manually edited out.

Three 5km x 5km areas were then clipped out from the overall image as sample areas for the testing of procedures and methodology. The extents of the areas are as follows, denoted by their respective Upper Left X and Y coordinates and their Lower Right X and Y coordinates:

- **Area 1** (Northern)   UL – 610929.42,3463054.29
  LR – 616078.52,3457959.06

- **Area 2** (Eastern)   UL – 630935.90,3458012.52
  LR – 635977.67,3452970.82

- **Area 3** (Southwestern) UL – 606960.36,3451039.75
  LR – 612055.86,3446105.22

5.1.4 Creation and integration of slope data

An important part of landscape character, in terms of both the natural and the human-influenced landscape, is the relative slope of the land parcels. Within the context of the Fort Hood characterisation, this was considered to be a key supporting data source, and it was therefore decided to refine the polygons that had been created from the classified Landsat data by integrating slope data with them. This process, as with most of the data processing undertaken for the characterisation, necessitated a considerable amount of testing and experimentation of software, methodology and datasets in order to achieve the best possible results.

The first step in this process was to generate a digital elevation model (DEM) from contour data supplied by the U.S. army. Three digital contour plots had been provided at vertical intervals of 1m, 5m and 10m. As these data sets were provided from a military source, it was not possible to ascertain how, or at what level of resolution, the original height data from which the plots were derived had been collected. Digital elevation models were created for the whole of the study area from each of the 1m, 5m and 10m contour layers, in order to see which data set produced the best results. The 1m contour data proved to be too detailed, as it incorporated features such as tree canopies into the elevation model, suggesting that the original data source was aerial, possibly uncorrected LiDAR. The 10m data, while not suffering the same information overload, did not provide enough detail at a more localised level. The 5m contour data provided a practical compromise and was therefore used to create the DEM that was eventually used in the final analysis.

The model was created initially within ArcView as a TIN (Triangulated Irregular Network). A TIN partitions a surface into a set of contiguous, non-overlapping, triangles. A height value is recorded for each triangle node. Heights between nodes can be interpolated thus allowing for the definition of a continuous surface. TINs can accommodate irregularly distributed as well as selective data sets. This makes it possible to represent a complex and irregular surface with a small data set.. The next step in the process was to convert the TIN within ArcView into a grid, in this case with a selected cell resolution of 5m.

At this point the possibility of carrying out a single step geomorphological modelling using Idrisi GIS software was explored. Idrisi provided a comparatively new tool called 'toposhape', and this was tested extensively. The output of 'toposhape' is a surface shape classification consisting of 11 possible topographic features: peak, ridge, saddle, flat, ravine, pit, convex hillside, saddle hillside, slope hillside, concave hillside, and inflection hillside. Any pixels not assigned to these classes are assigned to the 'unclassified' class. The procedure is performed on either a DEM, or on a DEM that has been transformed, filtered, and back-transformed with FOURIER and its companion modules.

This was tried with each of the three different resolution DEMs. The data was imported into Idrisi both as a TIN which was then converted to a raster grid within Idrisi, and as a raster grid created within ArcView, and each method of import was tested with 'toposhape'. However, although this was tried at various resolutions and using different variables, the results were very poor. The 1m resolution DEM proved too complex for Idrisi to process, resulting in a meaningless myriad of geomorphological forms. A similar result was obtained from the 5m resolution DEM. The 10m resolution data initially appeared to be more promising, but when compared visually with both the contour data and the aerial photography, there were significant errors and inconsistencies which rendered the results unusable. The cause of the lack of success within Idrisi could not be ascertained, and as processing of such large datasets took up substantial amounts of time, further experimentation was not deemed to be the most effective way forward and was therefore abandoned.

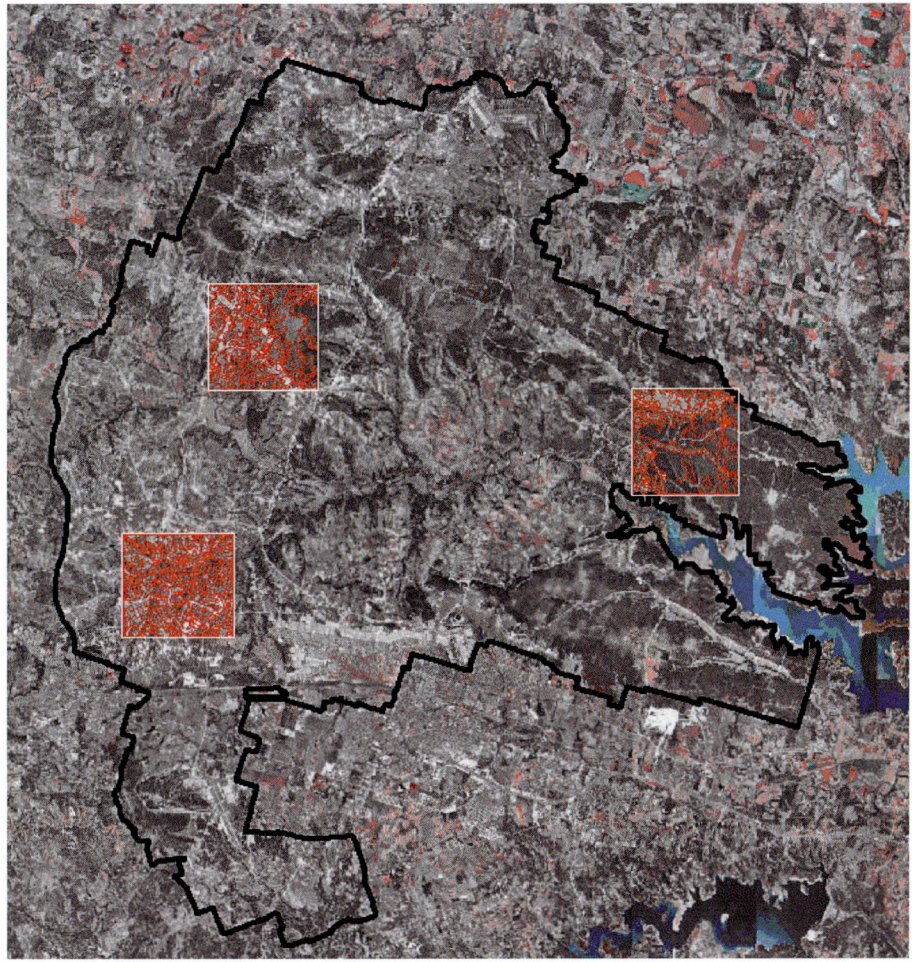

Figure19: Location and extent of 5km sample areas

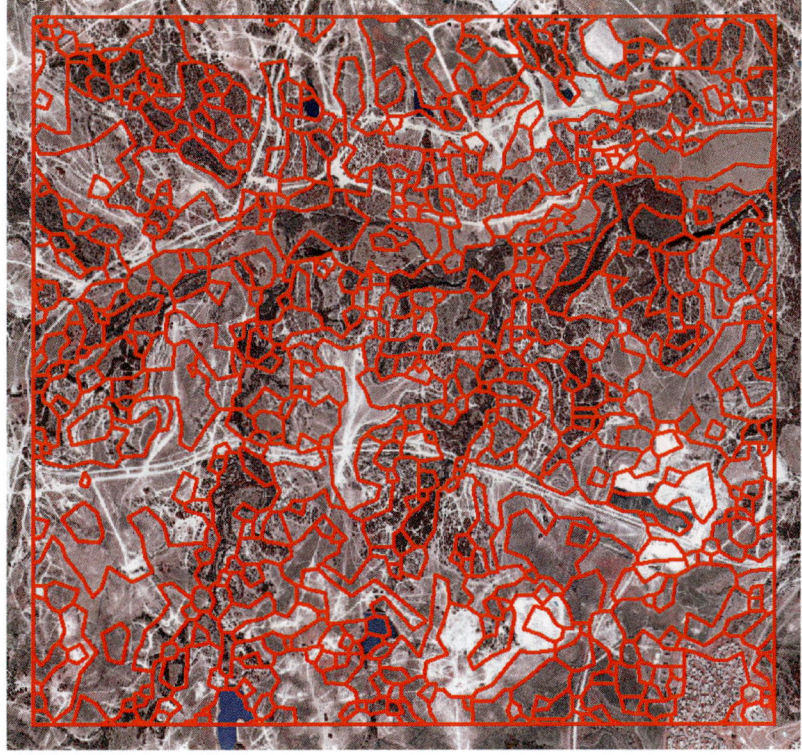

Figure 20: Detail of south-western square sample area

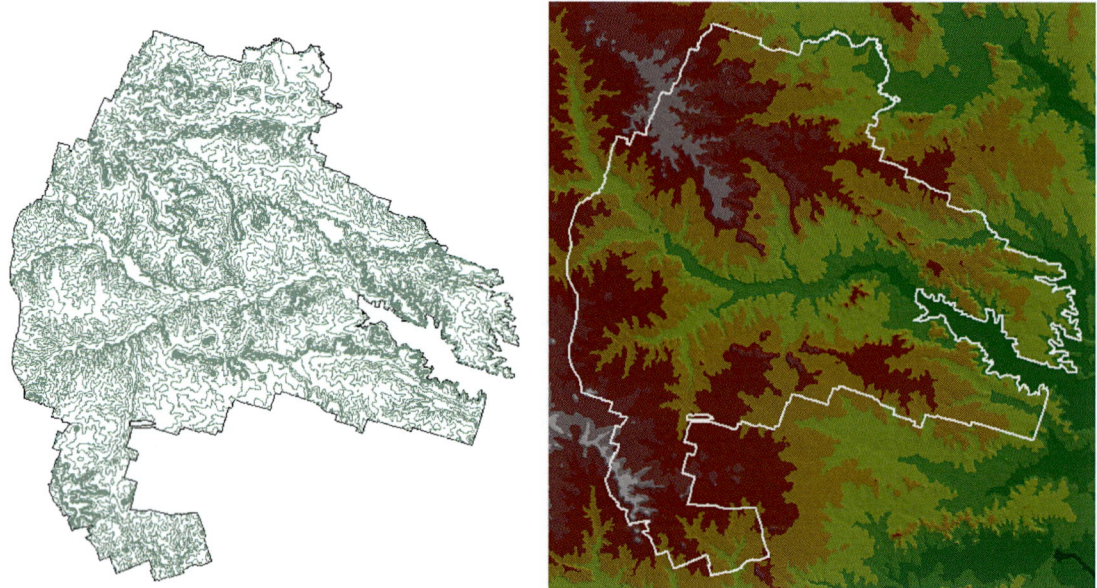

Figure 21: 5m contour model and derived TIN (Triangulated Irregular Network).

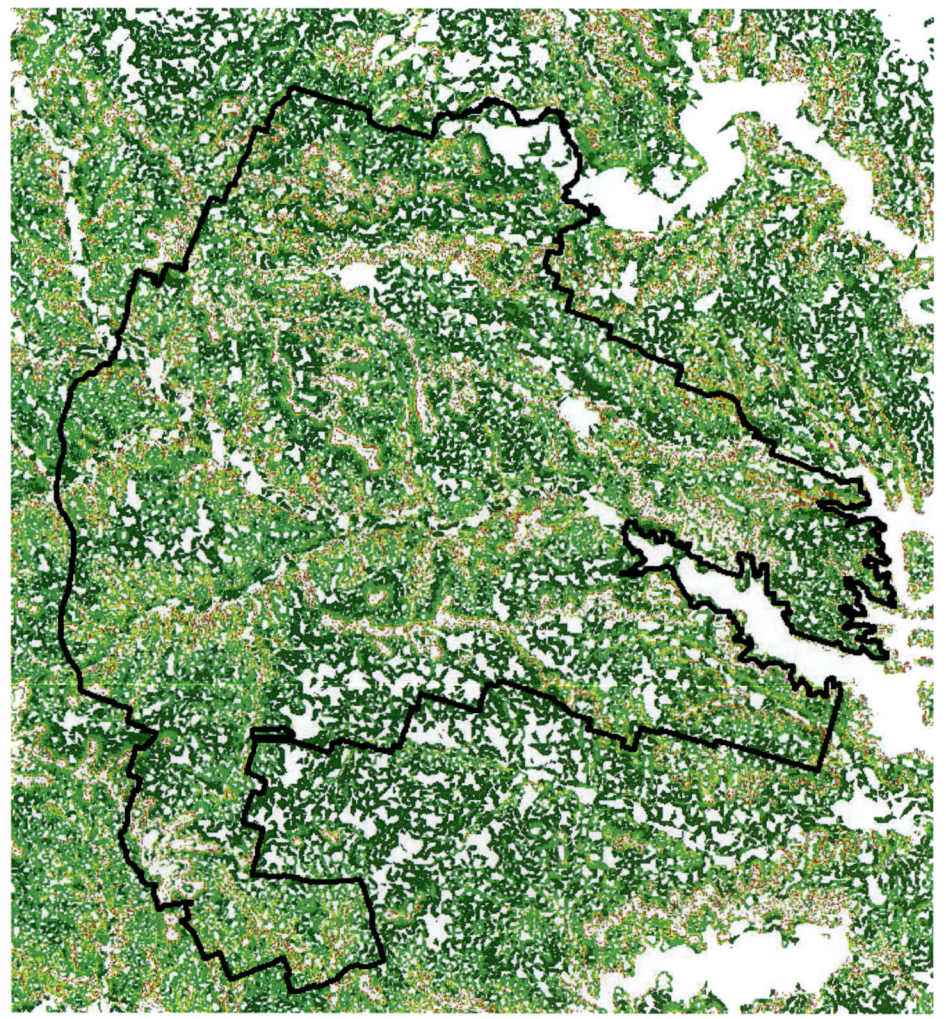

Figure 22: Slope derived from TIN

With the failure to obtain a satisfactory product within Idrisi, further processing and data was undertaken in ArcView using the 5m resolution DEM. The 'derive slope' function was used to create a raster model of the slope information for the study area. Numerous map query tests were carried out in order to establish the most appropriate categories of slope, and as a result it was decided to classify the study area into three slope classes - flat (<1% slope), gentle slope (>1% and <10% slope) and steep slope (>10% slope). These classes were then vectorised into 'slope' polygons, saved as individual shapefiles, and all 'sliver' polygons of less than 0.5ha in size were identified and removed.

The slope polygons were then integrated with the polygons created from the satellite imagery through a successive series of union and dissolve operations. The integration process was an extremely time-consuming process, mainly due to the very large data sets involved, but also because the methodology had to be carefully developed and thoroughly tested on sample data sets. In total it involved nine successive steps of dissolve, union and clean procedures on a very large dataset, which took considerable processing time and power, and often the processes had to be left to run overnight. The resulting dataset consists of more than 18,000 polygons.

Firstly, the original landclass polygons were subject to a dissolve operation using the "dissolve adjacent polygons" script (obtained from the ESRI website, script by Jeff Jenness) whereby all polygons less than 1ha in area were dissolved into the adjacent largest polygon. Choice of polygon-size is an important consideration when considering the 'grain' of historic landscape data and incorporates the perception scale at which landscape character may be perceived and the digitisation scale of the database (Aldred and Fairclough 2002, 26). Although there are arguments for using relatively larger polygons, the selection of 1ha as a minimum for land units is based on the testing of methodology carried out in various English landscape characterisation projects such as that in Devon, where it was demonstrated that areas below this size are too small to determine character at a landscape level (Wigley 2002, 7). A union operation was then carried out between the Landsat classified polygons and the polygons from the 'steep slope' shapefile. The resulting polygons were again dissolved using the same 1ha criteria, and a union operation was carried out between the dissolved polygons and the polygons from the 'flat' shapefile. A final dissolve operation was followed by cleaning and building of topology in ERDAS Imagine, to produce the final landscape units to be used for the characterisation. The data sets created by the various dissolve and union operations were saved at each stage, to allow future users of the HLC data to see how the building blocks of the characterisation were created, thus ensuring transparency of the methodology.

The result of this extensive processing of satellite imagery and contour data was a set of contiguous polygons covering the whole of the military base, that could be used as the basic landscape units for historic landscape characterisation. It was inevitable that some subjective decisions had to be made, for example deciding which Landsat combination to use, how many classes the satellite imagery should be divided into, which slope categories should be used etc, but overall, the division of the landscape in this way was a completely transparent and highly objective process.

5.1.5 Adding attribute data

The next step in the characterisation process was to add attribute data to the landscape polygons. Adding attribute data enabled the definition of different historic landscape character types through database analysis of the occurrence of different attribute combinations, following a similar methodology to a number of the more recent English characterisation projects such as Shropshire (Wigley 2002). Using a range of digital spatial data sources, a GIS database of attributes was built up and populated for each landscape polygon. Some of these attribute values were added directly from supplied digital spatial data sources, and some were derived from GIS analysis of existing data sources, or from the creation of new digital spatial data sources. The data sources include:

- environmental data such as vegetation, geology, soils, geomorphology, topography
- land-use data such as transport routes, live fire zone, cantonment area
- cultural data such as historic land divisions, ritual areas, archaeological sites, major chert outcrops, visibility

Although archaeological data does not provide seamless, continuous coverage over the base, and thus can only be used as an 'indicative' data source, and, as previously stated, the use of available archaeological inventory information is consciously avoided within the characterisation process, the archaeological sites data set was used to assign a primary period value to each landscape polygon. It was decided that this was a necessary step in order to add time-depth to the characterisation data, as there was so little historic mapping available. In accordance with the principles of HLC, the primary period attribute was not used for determining HLC type, but it could potentially be used in the future, in combination with other attributes, to assign polygons, wherever possible or appropriate, to a 'previous' HLC type. Previous HLC types have been used fairly widely in English characterisations to provide increased time-depth and understanding of cause and process (English Heritage 2002, 29). The ritual areas data encompasses recorded prehistoric sacred areas, such as the Leon River medicine wheel, and recorded historic cemeteries. However, it should be noted that this data set does not include burials that occurred outside cemeteries, from either the prehistoric or historic period.

The GIS polygon data set containing the final landscape polygons and associated attribute data is called 'final_characterisation.shp'. Table 16 below provides details of all the attribute fields in the GIS database associated with the landscape polygons. The first column lists the name of the field in the GIS database table. The second column describes how the values for the field were obtained or derived, for example the origin of the data source used, or what method was used to derive the values. The third column lists the data type of the field, for example text, numerical or Boolean. The fourth column lists, where applicable, the source file that was used either for populating the field or for deriving values which were then used for populating the field. The fifth column lists, again where applicable, the topology type of the source file i.e. point, line or polygon.

Field name	Obtained/Created/derived	Field data type	Source file name	Source file topology
poly_id	Unique polygon identifier created as autonumber field	Consecutive number	N/A	N/A
Area	Automatically derived by ArcView	Actual numerical value	N/A	N/A
dslv_area	Automatically derived by ArcView	Actual numerical value	N/A	N/A
perimeter	Automatically derived by ArcView	Actual numerical value	N/A	N/A
histogram	Automatically derived by ArcView	Actual numerical value	N/A	N/A
X_coord	Easting of polygon centroid - derived from final_characterisation.shp using ArcView script	Actual numerical value	N/A	N/A
Y_coord	Northing of polygon centroid - derived from final_characterisation.shp using ArcView script	Actual numerical value	N/A	N/A
Height	Height of polygon centroid - derived from final_characterisation.shp using ArcView script	Actual numerical value	N/A	N/A
lsat_gcode	Landsat classification code number, indicating one of 20 classes from classification of original Landsat image	Number from set range	10x_smoothed_20cat_of_3-4-5_landsat_bands.img	polygon
av_slope	Slope derived from 5m DEM and classified into 3 - flat (<1% slope), gentle(>1%and <10% slope) and steep (>10% slope) and vectorised	Text value from set range	Flatclip.shp Steepclip.shp	polygon
av_aspct	Aspect derived from 5m DEM and vectorised	Text value from set range	Aspectmerge.shp	polygon
soils_name*	Soil type from soils shapefile provided by Fort Hood	Text value from set range	soils.shp	polygon
soils_bulk*	Soil characteristic from soils shapefile provided by Fort Hood	Text value from set range	soils.shp	polygon
soils_hydr*	Soil characteristic from soils shapefile provided by Fort Hood	Text value from set range	soils.shp	polygon
soils_d_no*	Soil characteristic from soils shapefile provided by Fort Hood	Text value from set range	soils.shp	polygon
veget_cat*	Vegetation class from vegetation shapefile provided by Fort Hood	Text value from set range	Vegetation.shp	polygon
Geomorph*	Geomorphology type from geomorphology shapefile provided by Fort Hood	Text value from set range	Geomorphology.shp	polygon

Drainage*	Drainage area from drainage shapefile provided by Fort Hood	Text value from set range	Water_sheds_small.shp	polygon
riverprox	Land classed as close to a river - derived by creating a 500m buffer around the major rivers, a shapefile newly created from rivers and rivers_large shapefiles provided by Fort Hood.	Boolean	maj_rivers.shp	polygon
valleybott	Land classed as flat valley bottom - derived by creating an elevation buffer encompassing all land with an elevation change of less than 5m up to 500m away from major rivers	Boolean	Valleybottoms.shp	polygon
Terrace**	Created from MA student original desk-based and field research. Not comprehensive base coverage - only from specific study areas	Text value from set range	Simons_terraces.shp	Polygon
geol_perio**	Created from MA student original desk-based and field research. Not comprehensive base coverage - only from specific study areas	Text value from set range	Simons_terraces.shp	Polygon
Upland	Land over 280m - derived from DEM	Boolean	Upland280.shp	Polygon
Mesa	Prominent high places - point data created by identifying sub-circular areas of steep slope (>15%) from slope grid and contour data and cross-checking with Fort Hood ITAM training map	Boolean	Mesas.shp	Point
Cave*	Cave locations from caves shapefile provided by Fort Hood	Boolean	Caves.shp	Point
Karst*	Karst areas from karst shapefile provided by Fort Hood	Boolean	karst.shp	Point
Chert	Major chert outcrops created by digitising from paper map (ref)	Boolean	chert.shp	Polygon
Lake	Major lakes created by digitising from Fort hood ITAM training map	Boolean	Lakes_new.shp	Polygon
Lakeside	Land classed as close to a lake - derived by creating a 100m buffer around lakes	Boolean	Lakes_new.shp	Polygon
roadprox	Land classed as close to a major road - derived by creating a 100m buffer around major roads shapefile provided by Fort Hood	Boolean	Roads.shp	Polygon
Airfield	Land classed as in use as an airfield - created by digitising from doqq99 aerial photograph, with reference to	Boolean	Airfieldsnew.shp	Polygon

		Fort Hood ITAM training map			
urban_type	Land classed as one of a range of urban types - created by digitising from doqq99 aerial photograph, with reference to Fort Hood ITAM training map	Text value from set range	Urban_new.shp	polygon	
field_patt	Land showing landscape features (roads, tracks, boundaries) orientated on historic land divisions - created by digitising from doqq99 aerial photograph and georectified historic maps, with reference to Fort Hood ITAM training map	Boolean	Fieldsunion.shp	polygon	
ritual_type	Land comprising historic cemeteries or native ritual areas	Text value from set range	ritual.shp	polygon	
Ranges*	Land classed as in use as ranges from ranges shapefile provided by Fort Hood	Boolean	Ranges.shp	polygon	
Livefire*	Land classed as in use as live fire zone from ranges shapefile provided by Fort Hood	Boolean	Livefire.shp	polygon	
impact_are*	Land classed as in use as impact area from impact areas shapefile provided by Fort Hood	Boolean	Impact_area.shp	polygon	
vis_actual***	Visibility measure created from cumulative viewsheds from mesa tops (see separate section on viewsheds). Figure based on polygon modal average - the higher the figure the greater the visibility.	Text value from set range	Cumulative	grid	
vis_reclas***	Visibility measure reclassed into 5 categories	Text value from set range	cum_reclass	polygon	
prim_per	Derived from new database created by Birmingham Archaeology for Fort Hood - primary period allocated to each site polygon of each site.	Text value from set range	site_periods.shp	polygon	
Clc_type	Cultural Landscape Characterisation Type - assigned from analysis of other attributes (see section 5.2 for detailed description of how types are assigned)	Text value from set range	N/A	N/A	
Clc_subtype	Cultural Landscape Characterisation Sub-type - assigned from analysis of other attributes (see section 5.2 for detailed description of how types are assigned)	Text value from set range	N/A	N/A	

Table 16: List of fields in the landscape polygon GIS database table

*Values for these fields were obtained directly from digital data supplied by Fort Hood. All other fields were populated with values derived either from GIS analysis of existing digital data carried out during the project, or from digital data newly created as part of the project.

**The data sources for these attributes did not cover the whole base, and therefore it was not possible to use these attributes for determining HLC types.

***The creation of the visibility data is described in detail in section 5.1.6

Since adding attributes to such a large dataset involved a considerable investment in time and processing power, a significant amount of time was spent in developing and testing the methodology before implementing it. 'Attribute-led' landscape characterisation is based on assigning landscape character types on the basis of predominant characteristics.

It was decided, therefore, that in most cases a particular attribute value would only be assigned to a landscape polygon if the characteristic it represented was present over more than 50% of the polygon area. Exceptions to this general rule are explained below. Attributes from a range of different digital data sources were attached to the landscape polygons using a function called "transfer attributes" from an ArcView extension called "EditTools 3.6 demo version" (obtained from the ESRI website, extension by Ianko Tchoukanski). This script allows the user to transfer attributes from a source polygon data set to the target polygon data set (in this case the landscape polygons) based on spatial associations. Using the geomorphology dataset as an example, each landscape polygon was assigned the geomorphological type that comprised the majority of the area of the polygon. The mathematical principles behind the type (majority) option are shown below:

$$area\_a / (area\_a + area\_b) > area\_b / (area\_a + area\_b) \Longrightarrow type\_A$$

$$area\_b / (area\_a + area\_b) > area\_a / (area\_a + area\_b) \Longrightarrow type\_B$$

(Script by Ianko Tchoukanski)

The script only works for text string values, so any numeric values had to be changed to text strings using the ArcView field calculator. This method was relatively straightforward where the source data set consisted of a range of values covering the entire study area, such as geomorphology, vegetation, soils, drainage, slope or aspect. However, some source data sets did not contain values covering the entire study area, consisting instead of one or more polygons representing a Boolean value for a particular type of land use (e.g. airfield, urban areas, communications etc). In such cases, the required attribute value to be attached to the landscape polygons was not one of a range of types, but a yes or no value. With this type of data source, a number of procedures had to be implemented before attribute transfer took place, otherwise the script would transfer an attribute wherever features in the source data set intersected with features in the target data set, regardless of whether the intersection comprised more than 50% of the polygon area in the target data set or not. This would mean that, for example, if an airfield polygon intersected with a landscape polygon, then the 'yes' value would be transferred to the landscape polygon, even if the area of intersection comprised only 1% of the total area of the landscape polygon. This would be incorrect in landscape characterisation terms, as the effect of the airfield on that polygon would actually be very minor.

To counteract this problem, a new field was created in the source data set, with a relevant title, which was populated with a text string value of 'yes'. A separate data set was created containing a single polygon representing the bounding polygon of the study area. A union operation was then carried out between the source data set and the boundary polygon, and all records within the resulting union theme that did not contain a 'yes' value under the relevant field name (i.e. null values) were updated to 'no' using the ArcView field calculator. This allowed the script to establish whether the yes or no attribute comprised the greatest area of any landscape polygon, and transfer the correct value accordingly. In this way, to return to the airfield example, once the transfer attributes operation was carried out, the 'yes' value would only be transferred if an airfield polygon intersected with more than 50% of the area of a particular landscape polygon. The only polygon data sources that were treated differently in terms of attribute transfer were archaeology and lakes. Lakes were treated differently because several of them covered just under half of a landscape polygon, but after testing the transfer attributes script, it did not adequately reflect the influence of many of the lakes on the landscape character. Therefore, a different function from the ArcView edit tools menu was used to transfer attributes, called "attributes from polygon", whereby an attribute was transferred from the source polygon data set to the target polygon data set on the basis of a spatial relationship (inside, centre, inside, intersect). In the case of the lakes source data set, all the relationships were tested, and the relationship that gave the best results was the "centre inside" relationship.

The archaeology inventory data was also treated differently to the other data sources. This is because after carrying out tests using the same methodology as applied to the other data sets, the results were so diluted as to be rendered meaningless. As this data is such an important source for time-depth, it was decided that the influence of archaeological sites on landscape character had to be treated differently. The same "transfer attributes" script that was used for all of the other source data sets (apart from lakes) was used, but without carrying out the union operation with the boundary polygon and updating null values. This meant that a landscape polygon intersecting with any part of an archaeological site or sites was assigned the relevant period attribute (either prehistoric, historic C19 or historic C20). Where sites of more than one period were present within the same landscape polygon, the script assigned the spatially dominant period. Where a landscape polygon did not intersect with any archaeological site, the script did not transfer an attribute at all, but the resulting null values were subsequently updated to 'N/A' using the ArcView field calculator.

Transferring attribute data from point data sources (including karst, caves and sink holes) was achieved by carrying out an intersect operation on the landscape polygons data set and the point source data set, and updating the resulting selected polygon records to 'yes' using the ArcView field calculator.

5.1.6 Creating visibility attributes

Embracing intangible aspects of the historic landscape, particularly in relation to indigenous people's perception of the landscape, was one of the key challenges of the project. As described in the review of the archaeology of Fort Hood in Chapter 3, high points in a landscape are often themselves culturally significant to the communities living in their shadow. A prime example (as quoted in section 3.4.8) is of the Western Apache who recognise a moral landscape where ethical lessons were associated with natural features such as places providing panoramic views or vistas.

Such associations with natural phenomena are problematic in terms of modelling them into any landscape characterisation. However an attempt can be made by considering the visibility potential of potentially significant locations, in effect employing viewshed analysis which identifies the areas on a surface that are visible from one or more observation points. This answers the question, 'What can I see from these locations?' or 'Which locations can I be seen from?'.

Experimental cumulative viewshed analysis, using ArcView, was therefore carried out from prominent high points within the study area – the tops of the mesas – and the results were used to populate visibility fields within the GIS database (vis_actual and vis_reclas in table 16).

To carry out cumulative viewshed analysis, a set of observation points and a digital elevation model (DEM) of the landscape are required. First of all, the prominent high places were defined by identifying sub-circular areas of steep slope (>15%) from the contour data and the derived slope grid, and then cross-checking the identified areas with the Fort Hood ITAM training map. A shapefile of point data, one for each mesa top, was then created, to be used as the observation points. A viewshed was produced for each observation point in the file, based on the DEM, but also correcting for earth curvature and light refraction. The formula used to do this is a standard formula, and was taken from the web pages of the University of Melbourne as follows.

$$Z_{actual} = Z_{surface} - (DISTANCE^2 / DIAMETER_{Earth}) + 0.13 * (DISTANCE^2 / DIAMETER_{Earth})$$

where DISTANCE is the planimetric distance between the observation point and the observed point.
The third term accounts for the refraction of visible light.
The value used for the diameter of the Earth is 12,740,000 meters.
(Formula from University of Melbourne http://www.sli.unimelb.edu.au/cgism/GISA/visibility_files/frame.htm)

This meant that a separate DEM had to be created for each mesa top, in order to calculate the effects of curvature from that particular point. It was decided to create the new DEMs at a resolution of 10m rather than 5m, as the processing time required for such large datasets was considerable, and the benefit gained from using 5m resolution grids would not have been enough to justify the time investment needed. For each observation point, the ArcView 'find distance' function was used to create a grid showing the planimetric distance between the observation point and every other possible point within the study area. This grid, and the DEM, were then used in the formula to create a new DEM for that observation point. The ArcView 'visibility' request was then applied using the observation point, the newly-created DEM, and offsets of 1.8m for the elevation of the observer and the objects to be observed, to generate the viewshed. This resulted in a grid with values of 1 for the cells that were visible from the observation point, and 0 for those that weren't. Once this had been carried out for every mesa top, the grids were added together to create a cumulative viewshed grid (figure 23), where the highest values represented those cells that were visible from the most mesas, and vice versa. The ArcView 'getgridvalue' extension (obtained from the ESRI website, script by Jeremy Davies) was used to transfer the underlying cell value from this cumulative grid to the landscape polygon GIS database ('vis_actual' in table 16), based on the value of the underlying grid cell at each polygon's centroid. In order to provide a more coherent visual representation of the data, the cumulative viewshed grid was also reclassified into five classes and the underlying grid value was transferred to the polygon theme in the same way (figure 24).

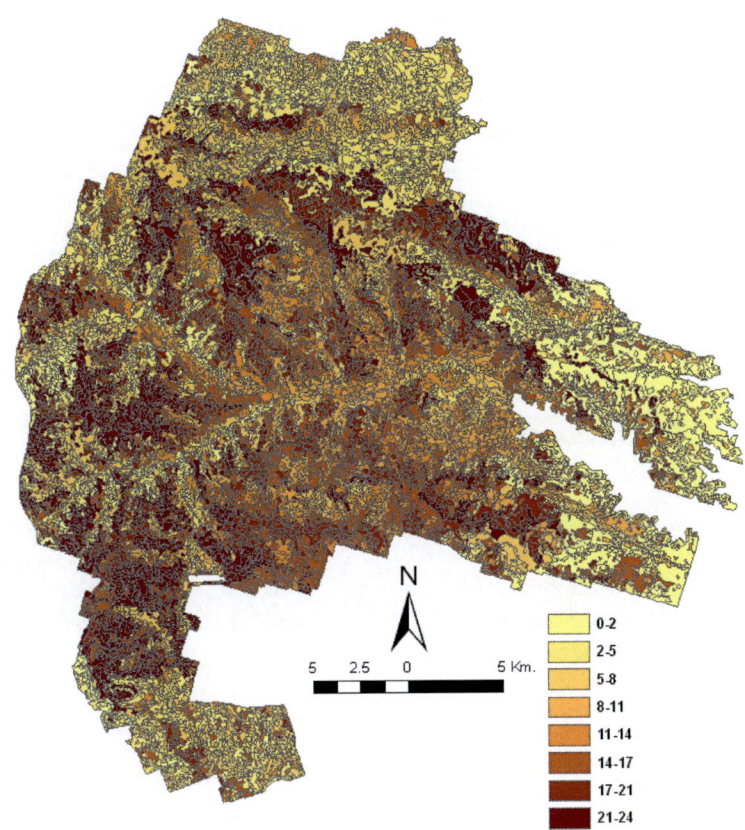

Figure 23: Actual viewshed values displayed by HLC polygon

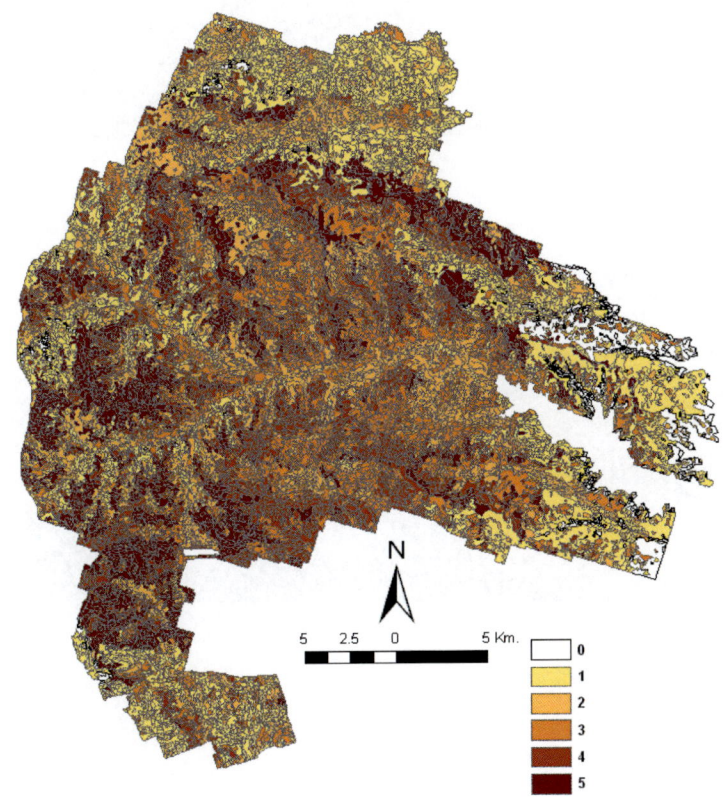

Figure 24: Reclassed viewshed values displayed by HLC polygon

Castle Mountain

Jackson's Knob

Lone Mountain

Stampede Mountain

Plates 17 – 20: Panoramic Photo Mosaics from sample view points

5.2 Definition of the historic landscape characterisation types

5.2.1 Experimental raster data analysis

Initially, an attempt was made to define the historic landscape characterisation types (HLC types) through an almost entirely objective, raster-based methodology. In this method, the landscape polygon data set was converted into a series of raster grids and allocated different cell values for each conversion. As an example, the polygon data set was converted to a raster grid once, and the cells were allocated values on the basis of the vegetation attribute. Then the original polygon data set was again converted in exactly the same way, creating a second raster grid, but this time the cells were allocated values based on the visibility attribute.

In this way, a whole series of 'attribute' grids with different numerical values were created. Experiments were then undertaken by adding the grids together in various different combinations in order to try and observe patterns, and establish whether or not areas of landscape could be grouped together in meaningful ways.

Different ways of allocating cell values to grids were explored, and it was decided that three different allocation methods should be tested to see which, if any, yielded the best results. These allocation methods were as follows:

- Cells in a grid allocated consecutive numerical values.

- Cells in a grid allocated consecutive numerical values which were then normalised into ranges of 1-10.

- Cells in a grid allocated consecutive numerical values, but in a range which lay far apart numerically from any of the other grids.

Three sets of tests were undertaken for each cell value allocation method. In each set, grids based on different attributes were added together in various combinations and the results analysed. The same combinations of grids were tested in each set so that the results could be compared.

Unfortunately, the results proved to be disappointing. Although groups of cells with similar values were visually apparent, there was no discernible trend in the attributes that produced these patterns, and no meaningful interpretations could be made. It was felt by the project team that although this method of defining HLC types would be very objective, transparent and repeatable, the project would be in danger of becoming too technology-led, with the results obscured by abstract classifications that did not reflect known historical processes. It was also felt that this is a subject that could be explored more thoroughly as part of a separate, more statistically-based research project. However, the experimentation proved to be a very valuable exercise, and there now exists a large dataset which provides considerable potential for powerful statistical analysis, which may allow future development of new and exciting methodologies in landscape characterisation.

5.2.2 Polygon attribute-based analysis

Although the highly objective raster-grid methodology for defining HLC types was abandoned, it was also felt that imposing pre-defined HLC types on the landscape without explicit evidence should be avoided, so an approach was sought that lay somewhere between these two methods.

The first step was to define initial broad HLC types with reference to categories that had been defined in English HLC projects, whilst taking into account the differences between the landscapes involved (table 17). This was considered to be a valid method, since there are still common points of reference in terms of both the natural environment and human activity within it.

The next step was to establish a set of attribute combinations within each broad type that could be used to break down each type into a more closely-defined sub-type. Table 18 shows the attribute groups that were defined for each broad type.

HLC sub-types were then defined for each broad type, based on values occurring within the respective attribute groups. The sub-type definitions are shown in table 19. This enabled a systematic analysis of the landscape polygon database to be carried out, whereby each and every polygon was assigned to a sub-type by matching its attribute values against the sub-type definitions. It was possible for a particular polygon to match more than one sub-type, and it was necessary to make a decision as to which sub-type the polygon should be assigned to.

A rule-base for order of priority was therefore established for the sub-types, to ensure consistency (shown in the text below table 19). Of necessity, this order of priority was relatively subjective in that some sub-types were considered to be more influential on the landscape than others. However, this reflects the interpretive nature of HLC, and by utilising a rule-base, the level of interpretation and subjectivity is made explicit, and can therefore be defended (or contested !).

HLC broad type	HLC broad type code
WOODLAND-RELATED	WD
FIELD PATTERNS	FP
OPEN LAND	OP
NATURAL LANDSCAPE	NL
WATER-RELATED	WR
URBAN	UR
DEFENCE	DF
COMMUNICATIONS	CM
RITUAL	RT

Table 17: Broad HLC types

HLC broad type	Attribute group
WOODLAND-RELATED (WD)	Woodland type (coniferous, deciduous, mixed, scrub)
	Slope
	Valley Bottom
	Elevation
FIELD PATTERNS (FP)	Field pattern
OPEN LAND (OP)	Vegetation type (short grass, tall grass, barren area)
	Slope
	Elevation
	Valley Bottom
NATURAL LANDSCAPE (NL)	Geomorphology
	Cave
	Karst
WATER RELATED (WR)	Lake
	Lakeside
	River Proximity
	Valley Bottom
URBAN (UR)	Urban Type
DEFENCE (DF)	Impact zone
	Live fire Zone
COMMUNICATIONS (CM)	Airfield
	Road Proximity
RITUAL (RT)	Ritual Type

Table 18: Attribute groups defined for each broad type

HLC broad type	HLC sub-type	HLC sub-type code	HLC sub-type definition
WOODLAND-RELATED	WOODED UPLAND	WDUP*	Land above 280m that is predominantly covered by deciduous, coniferous or mixed woodland or scrub*
WOODLAND-RELATED	WOODED VALLEY BOTTOMS	WDVB	Land within 500m of a river with an elevation change of less than 5m that is that is predominantly covered by deciduous, coniferous or mixed woodland or scrub
WOODLAND-RELATED	WOODED LOWLAND SLOPES	WDLS*	Land below 280m, with a slope of <10%, that is predominantly covered by deciduous, coniferous or mixed woodland or scrub*
WOODLAND-RELATED	WOODED LOWLAND FLAT AREAS	WDLF*	Flat land below 280m that is predominantly covered by deciduous, coniferous or mixed woodland or scrub*

OPEN LAND	OPEN UPLAND	OPUP*	Land above 280m that is predominantly covered by short grass, tall grass or barren areas*
OPEN LAND	OPEN VALLEY BOTTOMS	OPVB	Land within 500m of a river with an elevation change of less than 5m that is that is predominantly covered by short grass, tall grass or barren areas
OPEN LAND	OPEN LOWLAND SLOPES	OPLS*	Land below 280m, with a slope of <10%, that is predominantly covered by short grass, tall grass or barren areas*
OPEN LAND	OPEN LOWLAND FLAT AREAS	OPLF*	Flat land below 280m that is predominantly covered by short grass, tall grass or barren areas*
FIELD PATTERNS	ENCLOSED FIELD PATTERNS	FPEN	Land showing boundaries, roads and other linear features orientated on the same pattern as land divisions displayed on historic maps and on the AP
NATURAL LANDSCAPES	KARST LANDSCAPE	NLKA	Areas of Edwards limestone containing caves or other Karst features+
WATER-RELATED	LAKE	WRLK	Areas comprised of a body of water, either artificial or natural+
WATER-RELATED	LAKESIDE	WRLS	Land within 100m of a lake
WATER-RELATED	RIVER BORDER	WRRB	Land within 500m of a river, other than that categorised as valley bottom
URBAN	CANTONMENT	URCA	Built-up area, predominantly cantonment
URBAN	RESIDENTIAL	URRS	Built-up area, predominantly residential
URBAN	RECREATIONAL GOLF COURSE	URGC	Recreational golf course
DEFENCE	IMPACT ZONE	DFIM*	Impact zone*
COMMUNICATIONS	AIRFIELD	CMAF	Airfield, including buildings and landing strips+
COMMUNICATIONS	MAJOR ROAD	CMMR	Land comprised of, or within 100m of, a major road+
RITUAL	HISTORIC CEMETERY	RTHC	European settler cemeteries+
RITUAL	NATIVE RITUAL AREA	RTNA	Areas of ritual importance to aboriginal groups, whether historic or prehistoric, including the medicine wheel and the Comanche National Cemetery+

Table 19: HLC sub-type definitions

*These types comprise land that does not otherwise fall into any of the more diagnostic types

Rule-base for order of priority of sub-types (1=high, 9=low):
1. NLKA/RTHC/RTNA/WRLK
2. CMAF/CMMR/URCA/URRS/URGC
3. WRLS
4. FPEN
5. WRVB/OPVB
6. WDRB
7. WDUP/OPUP
8. MIIM
9. WDLS/OPLS/WDLF/OPLF

5.3 Truthing of the historic landscape characterisation data

5.3.1 Desk-based truthing

Desk-based testing of the characterisation was undertaken within selected pilot areas, comparing the selected classifications visually with the high-resolution aerial photography and with the contour mapping. This suggested a good correlation between the characterisation and actuality.

The tables below show the quantifications of HLC broad types and sub-types for the pilot areas.

HLC broad type	Area 1	Area 2	Area 3
Communications (CM)	23	7	44
Field Patterns (FP)		106	
Natural Landscape (NL)	2	16	
Open Land (OP)	187	48	240
Urban (UR)			16
Woodland-Related (WD)	335	231	304
Water-Related (WR)	4	56	20

Table 20: Count of polygons in pilot areas by HLC broad type

HLC broad type	Area 1	Area 2	Area 3
Communications (CM)	1028572	232265	2297945
Field Patterns (FP)		6857306	
Natural Landscape (NL)	5584840	15403278	
Open Land (OP)	12506272	1936749	15901018
Urban (UR)			916467
Woodland-Related (WD)	14316605	9726853	11725453
Water-Related (WR)	63757	1649024	469791

Table 21: Sum of area of polygons in pilot areas by HLC broad type (square metres)

HLC sub-type	Area 1	Area 2	Area 3
CMMR	23	7	44
FPEN		106	
NLKA	2	16	
OPLF	31	4	5
OPLS	57	27	57
OPUP	98	1	162
OPVB	1	16	16
WDLF	29	86	24
WDLS	88	130	169
WDUP	218	12	47
WDVB		3	64
WRLK	1		5
WRLS	2		15
WRRB	1	56	

Table 22: Count of polygons in pilot areas by HLC sub type

Figure 25: Site polygons superimposed on the terrain model draped with aerial photography

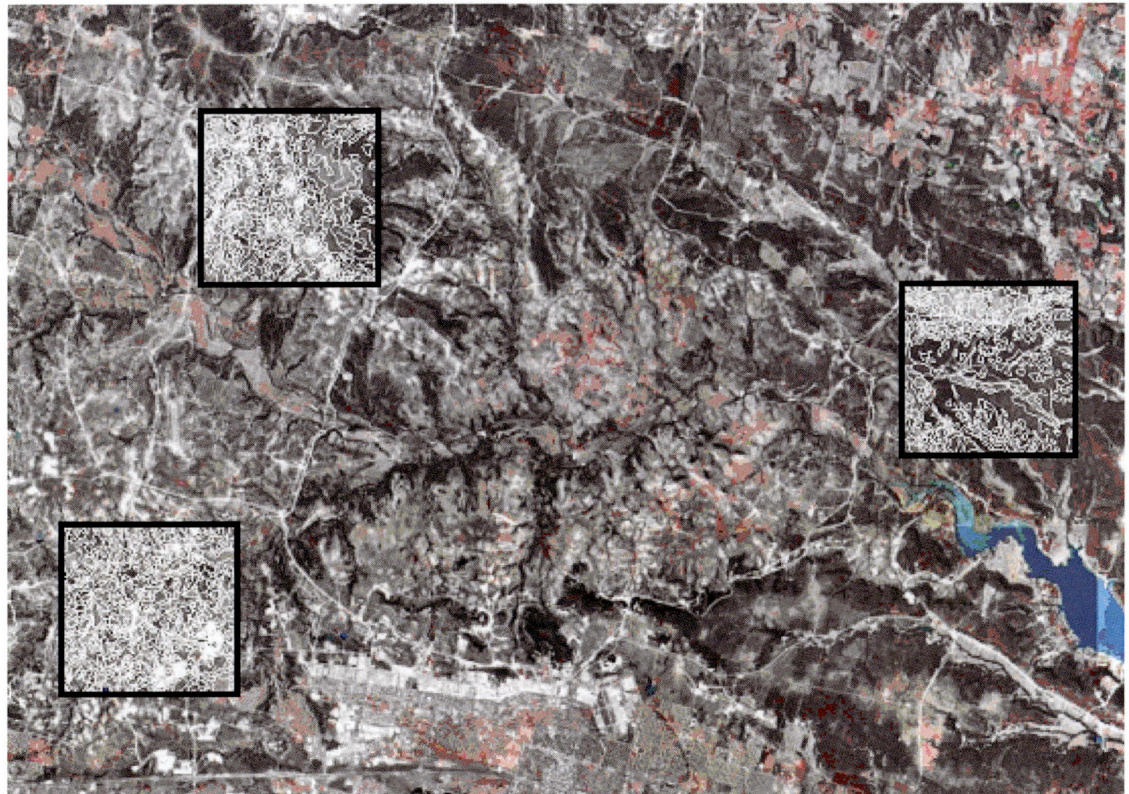

Figure 26: Characterisation pilot areas overlaid on the infra-red false colour AP

Figure 27: Detail of eastern pilot area (area 2)

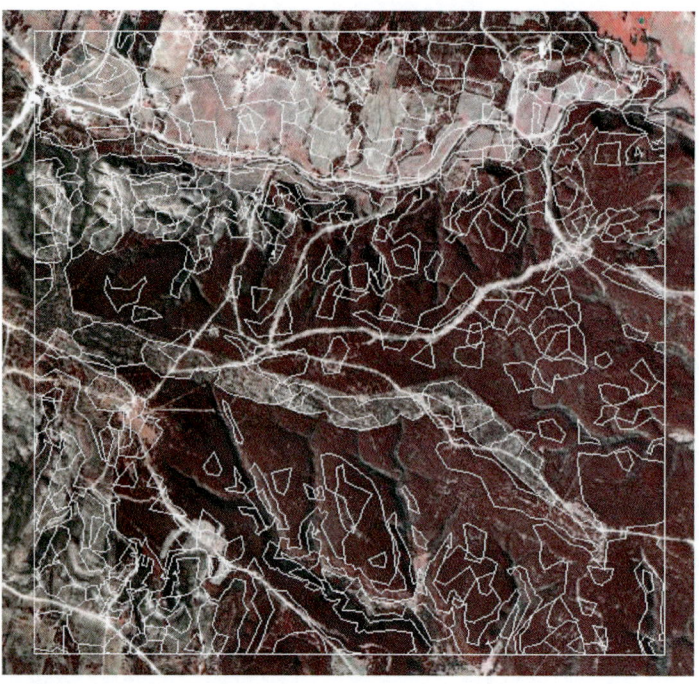

- CMMR
- FPEN
- OPVB
- WRRB
- WRLS
- OPLS
- NLKA
- WRUP
- OPUP
- OPLF

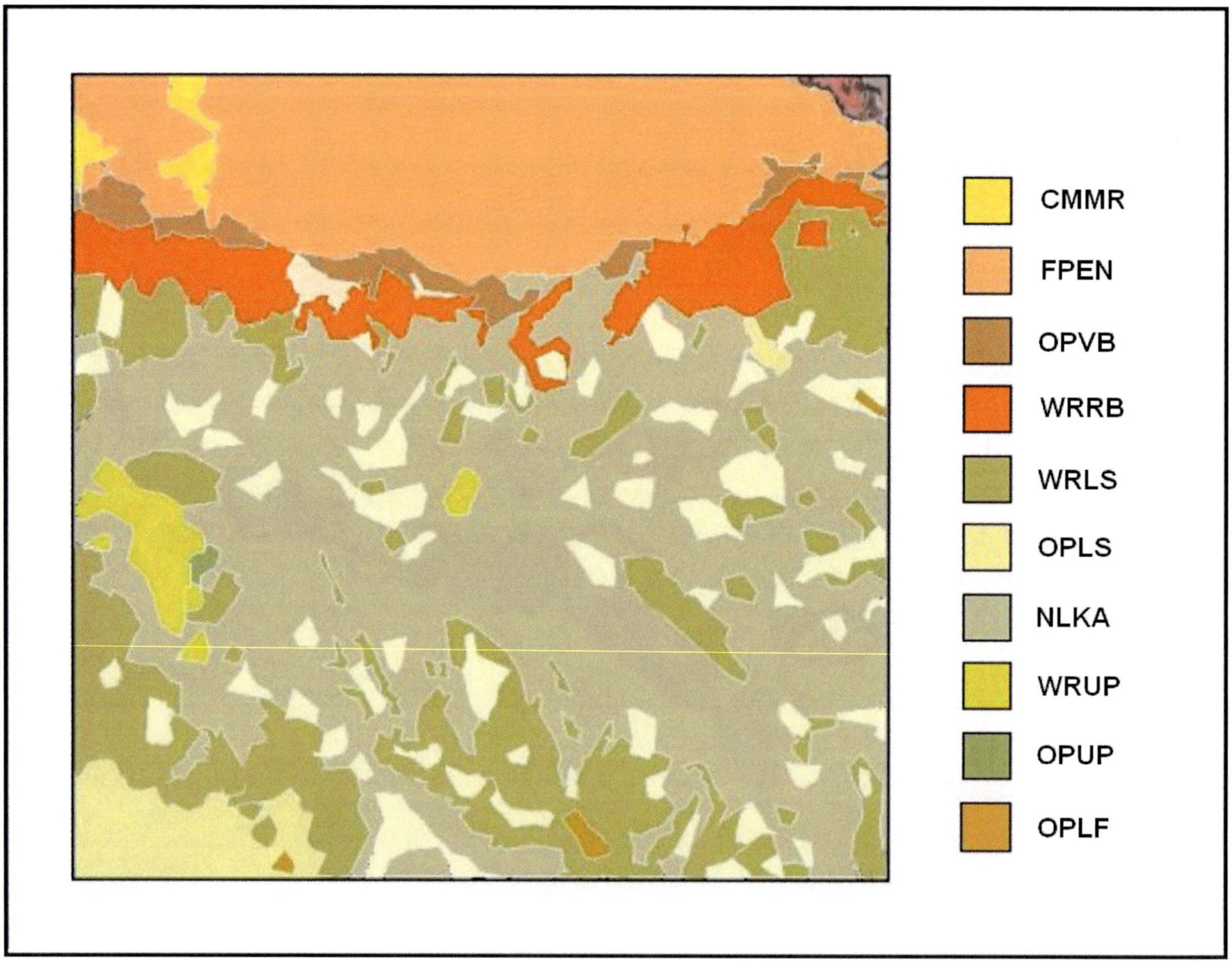

Figure 28: Eastern pilot area (area 2) HLC sub-type polygons

Sum of Area of Polygons in Pilot Areas by CLC Sub-Type (square metres)

CLC_SUBTYP	Area1	Area2	Area3
CMMR	1028572	232265	2297945
FPEN		6857306	
NLKA	5584840	15403278	
OPLF	1008543	88359	64939
OPLS	5342922	1227431	3267013
OPUP	6133454	29212	11931884
OPVB	21353	591747	637183
URGC			297405
URRS			619062
WDLF	496812	2196098	524536
WDLS	4918106	7018572	7312811
WDUP	8901687	429027	1776920
WDVB		83156	2111186
WRLK	18386		117453
WRLS	27716		352338
WRRB	17656	1649024	

Table 23: Sum of area of polygons in pilot areas by HLC sub-type (square metres)

5.3.2 Ground truthing

There was clearly also a need for a program of ground-truthing of the HLC data. The ground-truthing was undertaken by a post-graduate student as part of an MA internship program arranged between the University of Birmingham and Fort Hood (Fitch 2002a), and built upon work already completed by that student as part of an MA course in Landscape Archaeology and Geomatics at the University of Birmingham (Fitch 2002b).

The aim of the ground-truthing was to take the desk-based HLC data and assess its validity on the ground. A major part of the ground-truthing program was to acquire more accurate GIS data than was previously available, and to correlate this to the survey of sections of eight streams and seven upland creeks undertaken by Nordt (1992). The survey by Nordt was useful but did not cover the entire area of the base and the information was not available in a GIS format. The ground-truthing program, therefore, aimed to work not only in a compatible manner to the 1992 survey, but also to digitally record other river terraces in different areas of the base. The data provided by this exercise was to be used to inform further, more detailed characterisation of the drainage terrace system.

The program also provided an opportunity to field test the potential for recording supporting information from the available high-resolution aerial photography, and for observing features that were not highlighted by the relatively coarse-grained characterisation data. The opportunity was also taken to evaluate the usefulness of a pocket GIS system and PA computer in the field, which allowed the possible benefit of direct digital capture of map information in the field, effectively providing a one-person self-contained mapping unit. All field investigations were to be non-destructive, using observation and survey based techniques, and requiring no physical disturbance of the landscape. It should be noted that the HLC data is intentionally coarse-grained, and any results base on this should data be regarded within these constraints.

Specific objectives were:
- A systematic walkover of selected landscape areas, to observe and record any human activity of archaeological significance related to the terraces. Combined with this, any exposures of stratigraphy would be recorded, drawn and photographed. All recorded data would be directly integrated into the project GIS.
- A CA GPS (Coarse Acquisition – Global Position System) survey of the river terraces in the selected areas, to verify the digitised data and to place the field investigation into its proper spatial alignment.
- An inspection to validate the significance of he river terraces highlighted by the characterisation
- Evaluation of the high-resolution aerial photography. This would consist of investigations of the features observed during the survey, and would test the assumptions of their provenance, through direct observation.

The following text describes the ground-truthing of the areas targeted for investigation and is largely taken from the resulting project report (Fitch 2002a).

Areas for ground investigation were targeted in advance of the fieldwork by interrogating the characterisation GIS database to identify a series of river terraces with potential for occupation. The HLC polygon attributes of proximity to rivers and minimum slope were used to identify the areas for field investigation. The relevant subset of landscape polygons was extracted by a query as follows:

areas of flatland: [Av_slope] = 'Flat'
proximity to rivers: [Riverprox] = 'yes'

This selected all those polygons which contained flat areas lying within 500m of a river. Figures 29-31 below illustrate the procedure for extracting potential river terraces from the HLC polygons.

As it was not practical to investigate all of the selected terrace sites, the ground-truthing set out to record the terraces in three selected areas. These areas were chosen because of their character, which demonstrated a range of the terraces on the base. The three chosen test sites were: -

- North Nolan Creek – chosen due to the relatively small size of the terraces and therefore the potential ease of data capture
- House Creek – chosen to demonstrate an example of the larger terraces in the area
- Clear Creek – chosen as an example of a location which had been previously unrecorded

The recording of the data was undertaken using ESRI's field logging system/GIS, ArcPad 6. This received spatial information generated by a Garmin eTrex Vista handheld GPS. Data from the GPS was supplemented by WAAS corrections (when available), a barometric altimeter and fluxgate compass, all of which are built into the unit to create a useful low-grade survey tool. Data from the GPS was supplied via the NMEA 0183 protocol to an Ipaq Pocket PC. This handheld had been hardened using an Otter Armour pack, which proved its ability to resist shocks and moisture on many occasions during this project.

As data quality was to be important, a Maximum HPE (horizontal position error) was set at 6 metres. It was hoped that WAAS corrections could greatly improve the collected data. However, due to the incomplete nature of the coverage (due to the WAAS system being a Prototype), WAAS corrections were only obtained at locations with high elevation and extremely good sky view, and therefore was of little use when down on the river terraces. This did not greatly affect the data, however, as good satellite coverage and satellite constellations during the period of recording allowed for the HPE to drop to levels of 4 metres for a large proportion of the time. Similar height corrections from the barometric altimeter were observed to improve the vertical precision of the GPS system. This was calibrated to the local atmospheric pressure every day in an attempt to improve the accuracy of the results.

The data to be recorded in Arcpad was divided into three types to aid the recording process. The first type was the morphology of the river terraces to be recorded as polygons. This layer was to record all the terraces in the study blocks, irrespective of size. This layer was given the following attribute data:

- Terr_ID_ - a unique number generated for every terrace to aid data inquiry
- EST_AGE – the estimated age of that terrace, based on its position within the terrace complex of the area
- Height – to aid terrace identification, generated from the barometric altimeter
- NOTES – a field to record any distinguishing features of the terrace
- Z_992_Ter_ - the terrace type (i.e. T0, T1, T2) after Nordt's 1992 Survey

Small-scale structural features located on the terrace (i.e. Mound, Gully, Levee) were recorded as small polygons in the terrace features layer and were given the following attribute data:

- Feature_TY – the type of feature located on the terrace
- EST_AGE – the estimated age of the feature
- Notes – observations on the feature and its structure
- Z992_Ter – the terrace type that the feature is located on
- ET_ID – a unique number generated to aid data inquiry
- Elevation – generated from the barometric altimeter

The final data type recorded was the point features layer. This contained data types such as spot heights, locations of photographs or stratigraphic record sites. This was given a slightly different attribute dataset to reflect the different type of data being recorded:

- Attribute – the type of data being recorded
- Spot_ID - a unique number generated to aid data inquiry
- Hotlink – the name of any image file associated with the point (allows for hyper linking)
- Notes – any observations/ notes about the stratigraphy

As the point features are recorded as PointZ themes, the geography of these points contains their height information. All the points associated with stratigraphy were recorded in a systematic fashion, with field drawings and an associated photograph taken at each location where stratigraphy was found. The information from the points was then manually extracted from the GIS layer and entered into forms to act as a paper record of the exposed stratigraphy in the area that is associated with the GIS.

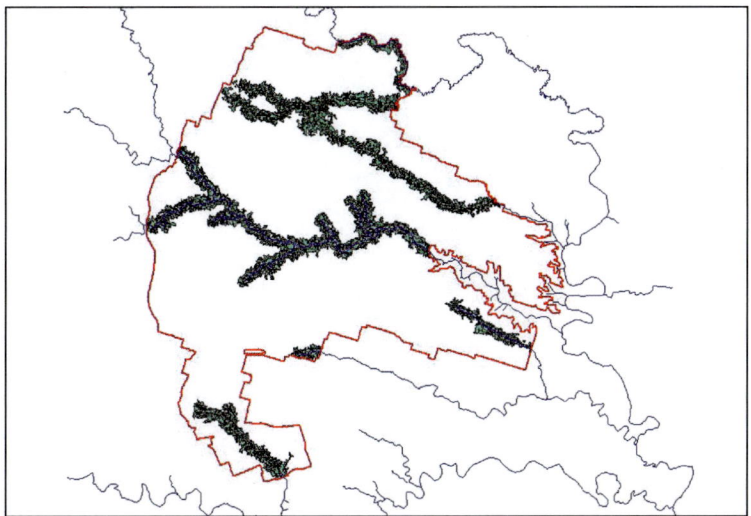

Figure 29: River proximity polygons

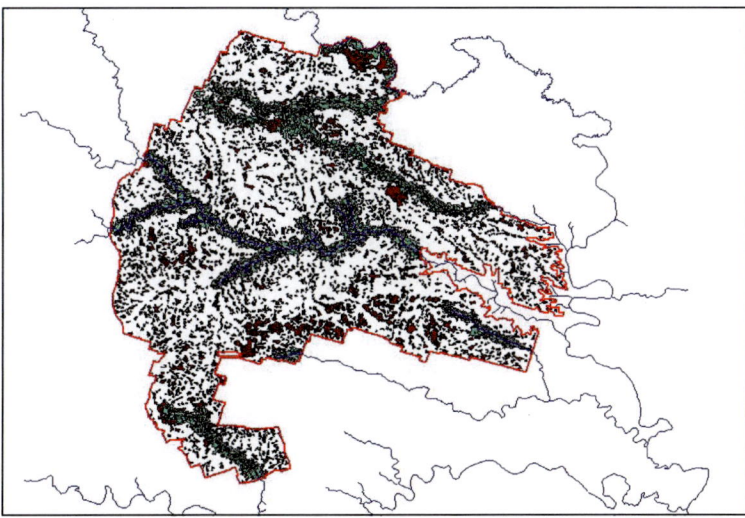

Figure 30: Flat area polygons and river proximity polygons

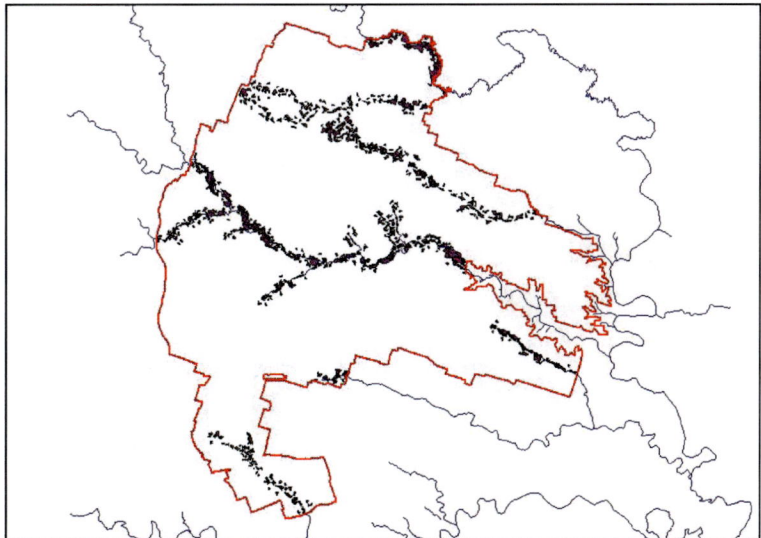

Figure 31: Potential river terraces

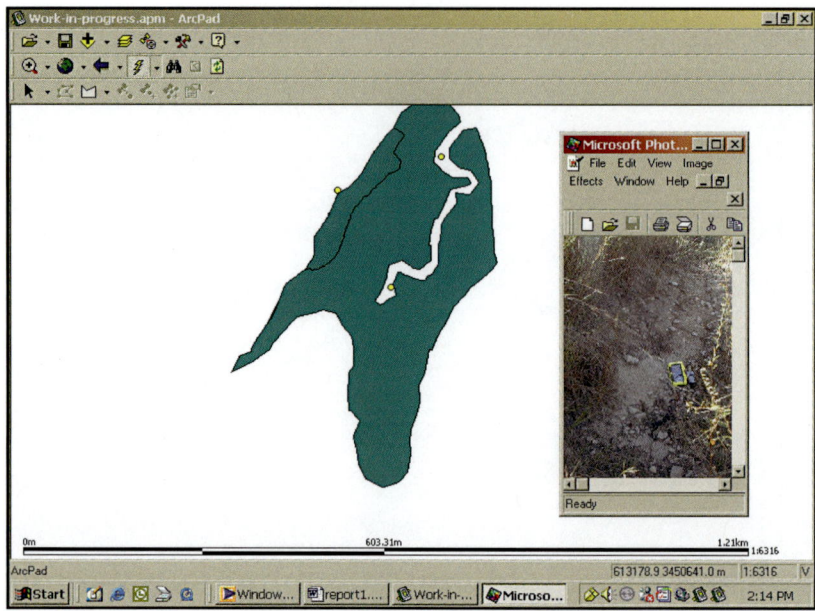

Figure 32: Hyperlinking in ArcPad

Figure 33: Clear Creek terraces

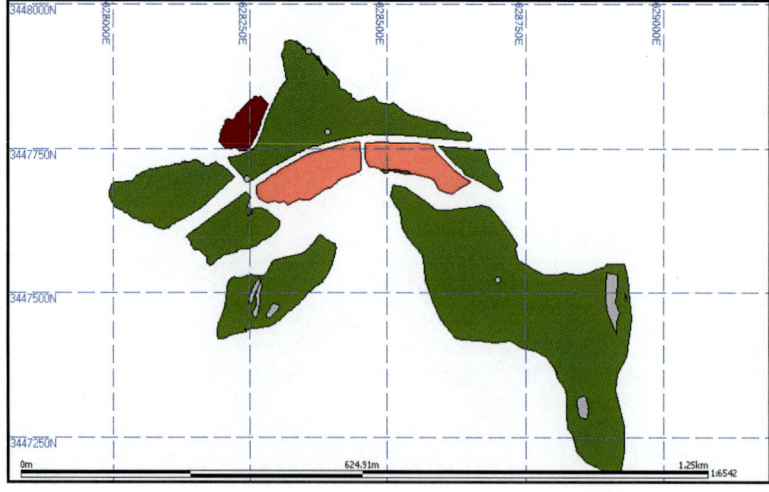

Figure 34: North Nolan terraces

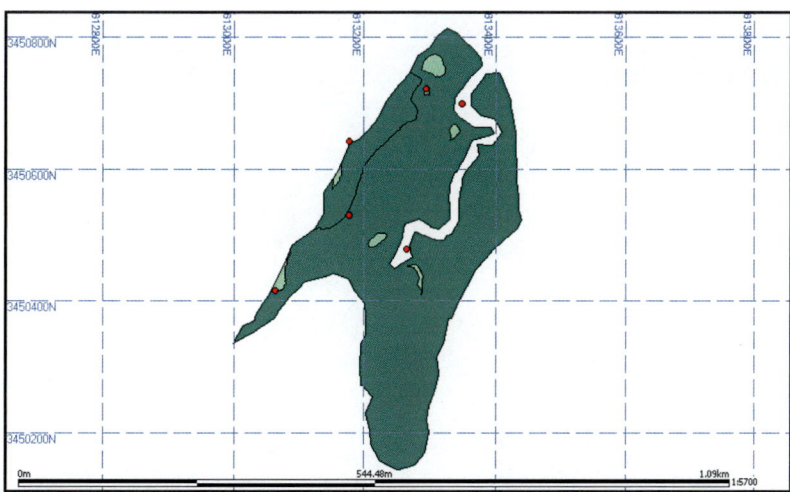

Figure 35: House Creek terrace

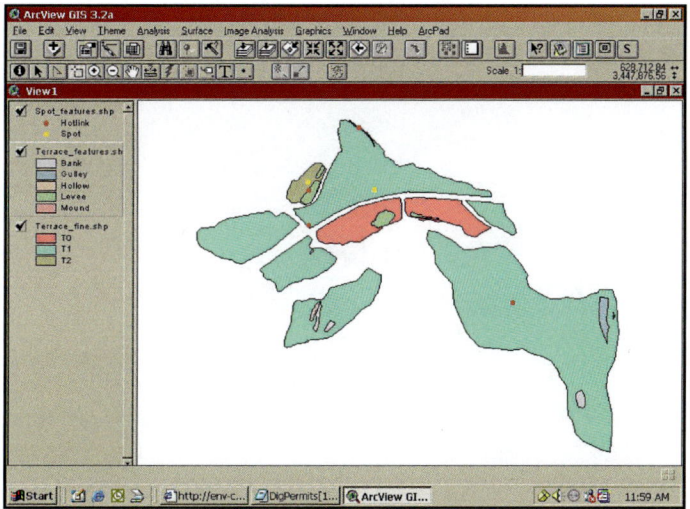

Figure 36: Diversity of the North Nolan Terrace

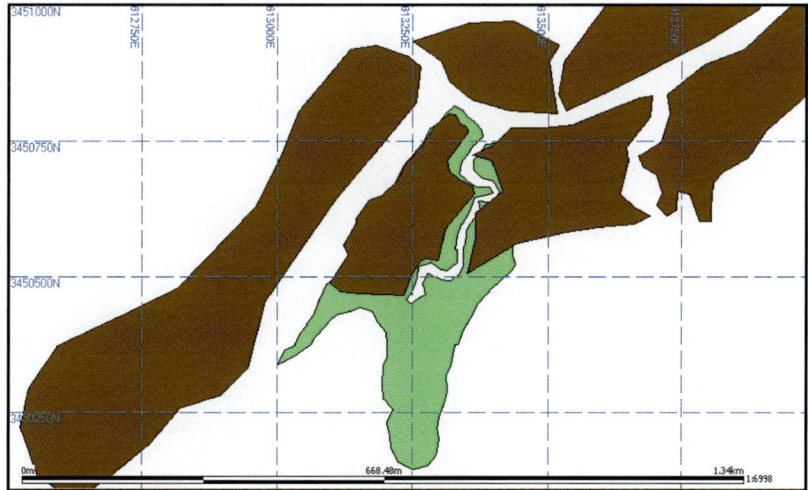

Figure 37: Desk-recorded terraces (brown) shown with field-recorded terraces (green)

Figure 38: Example of High Resolution Aerial Photography used in the study

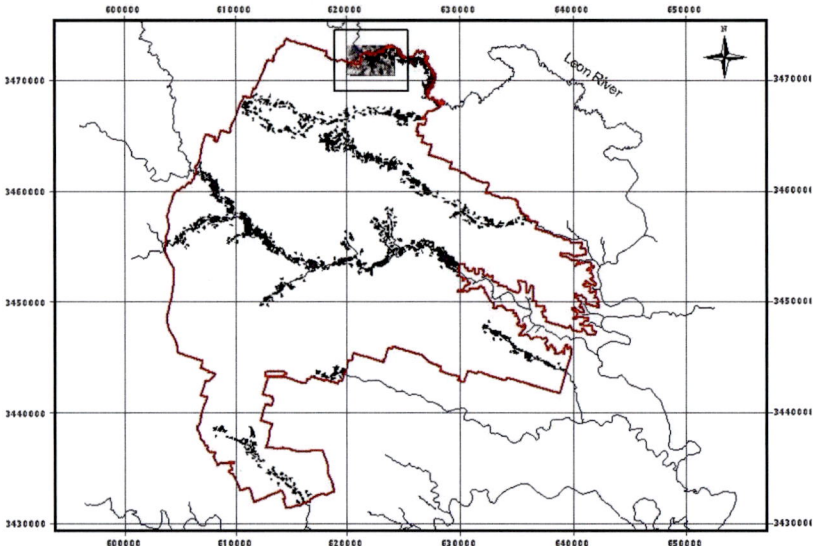

Figure 39: Location of Leon River study area

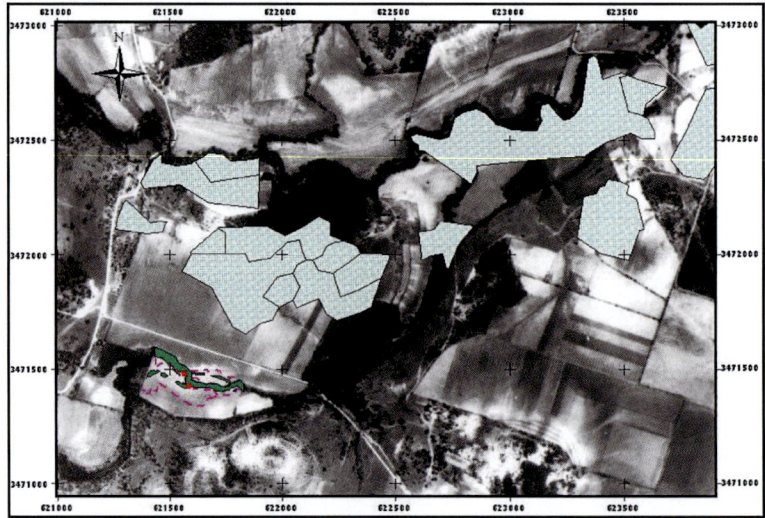

Figure 40: Extent of terraces extracted from the HLC data with AP-related field data

Once the polygon and point layers were created, the features were then recorded. Polygon features were generated by physically walking around them with the GPS, automatically adding vertices. In areas of poor sky view, manual vertices were observed with the GPS to improve their accuracy. Point features were recorded by stationary occupation to record their location. The spatial data of the point features was further improved by averaging a minimum of 10 points before the final reading was taken in an attempt to increase the reliability of the data recorded.

It was thought that there may have been a need for manual editing in ArcView of any attribute or topological errors with the data. ArcPad, however, proved able to cope with these corrections as the GIS coverage expanded. To enable the rapid visualisation of the exposures of stratigraphy in the test areas, ArcPad's hyper linking utility was used. First a point was recorded using the GPS in the standard manner, along with associated attribute data. The name of the photograph to be taken was entered into the database, in the 'hotlink' field. Once this had been achieved, scaled photographs of the exposures were taken using a digital camera. These files were then transferred to a PC and resized to fit on a handheld computer screen. These image files were then renamed to the 'hotlink' name, and transferred to the ArcPad project folder on the handheld computer. To enable hyper linking in ArcPad 6 the following functions are executed:
- the layer to be hyperlinked is selected in the layer info box,
- the properties box is then enabled
- the property tab 'hyperlink' is selected
- the hyperlink field is chosen from the attribute data

Once this has been done, the points are hyperlinked to the images. To observe a hyperlink, it is possible to choose the down arrow next to the identify button and select the hyperlink tool. Once this has been selected, tapping on a hyperlinked point will bring up the image recorded at that point (see figure 32). The results of this project are the three new layers of high-resolution data with associated attribute information for the selected terraces (see figures 33, 34 and 35).

The field-based recording, not surprisingly, displayed more complexity in the terraces than the HLC data. The North Nolan terraces were originally thought to be quite simple in structure. However the field survey revealed a small area of T1 terrace previously un-noticed, together with easily identifiable terrace features. Although the field-based recording is very time consuming, the benefits of such recording are clearly illustrated in Figure 37. The desk-acquired data is coloured brown, and the field-acquired data is coloured green. There are clearly areas of terrace that have been missed by the desk-based survey, and the resolution of features such as the channel that runs through the terrace is much lower. Although this shows additions to the desk-based characterisation data, the characterisation is broadly validated, and the figure is a good illustration of how broad-brush HLC data can be used as a basis for finer-grained studies.

In an attempt to examine the potential for the use of existing high-resolution vertical aerial photography to inform a finer-grained characterisation, a suitable target area was selected. The area selected was dictated by available photography and limited to one scene only as a test. The target site lay on a tributary of the Leon river in the extreme north of the Base. The aerial photograph was georectified to local detail within ArcView and then imported into ArcPad to enable it to be accessed in the field in a digital form. A hard copy of the image was also used while in the field as an aid to interpretation. The high-resolution aerial photography used in the testing picked up only modern features. However, the fact that these features were observed proves that it is possible to see features such as potentially man-made mounds in the aerial photography, indicating that the methodology for this style of work is sound and would be useful in future studies. The field-based study also located a previously unrecorded hearth structure (plate 21), which was recorded in a GIS layer, thus highlighting the potential of the HLC project for targeting areas for subsequent, more detailed ground investigation. However, few other visible archaeological remains were observed during the ground-truthing beyond those sites already recorded. This is probably due to the fact that most of the sites located on the terraces are buried. Heavy vegetation cover at some sites also prevented systematic examination of the terraces. However, from the sites visited in the course of the project, it should be noted that most of them are contained within/on a T1 (Holocene) Terrace.

The main height relationships between the terraces can be clearly observed and the height data was extremely useful in determining chronological sequence, especially in locations of heavy vegetation cover. Generally, trends observed by Nordt (1992) were in evidence, with T0 terraces being inset by 1 to 2 metres into T1 terraces. The height difference between the only T1 (high) and T1 terrace was 1 metre, similar to that illustrated by Nordt. One problem observed during this work with the GPS altimeter was that it often drifted off alignment. This may in part be due to the altimeter being set to the local air pressure, from the available weather forecast, which is probably not accurate, so may potentially cause errors. As a possible future improvement on this method, the GPS should be calibrated on a benchmark of known height in each study area. This would be far more effective at calibrating the GPS, and would possibly eliminate this potential source of error.

All of the findings from the ground-truthing program were incorporated into the existing HLC GIS data set, thus providing enhanced detail for the landscape areas examined. The program demonstrated the effectiveness of a combination of GPS and field-based GIS for rapidly updating and enhancing an HLC dataset. This technology can significantly expand the capabilities of a field worker, helping to cut down on the time between site discovery and investigation and recording, due to the ready availability of spatial data in a GIS format. In the main terrace data set, the spatial alignment of the selected terrace data was observed to be largely accurate, although it will not provide the level of accuracy that very high-resolution work would require (i.e. individual site maps). What the ground-truthing exercise does demonstrate is the validity and effectiveness of using the HLC data as a starting point for further, more fine-grained characterisation. Such further investigation would potentially be able to draw on data sources such as aerial photography and non-invasive survey as demonstrated, but also more dynamic techniques such as geophysical prospection and sample excavation. The ground-truthing exercise confirms that the HLC data functions as a useful potential cultural management tool. The benefits of real-time mapping in the field using a pocket GIS system are also obvious. Although the data collected by this project was not of survey-level precision, it does demonstrate the effectiveness of this type of GPS as a rapid mapping data collection tool. The availability of GIS layers in the field can greatly enhance accurate and appropriate decision-making, allowing little-visited or poorly-known sites to be revisited easily and accurately, whilst also enabling the direct access and updating of the GIS database at the site.

5.4 Results and discussion

5.4.1 The HLC data

Figures 43 and 44 show the mapped HLC data for Fort Hood. Figure 43 shows the division of the landscape into HLC broad types, and figure 44 shows the HLC sub types. Tables 24 and 25 show quantifications of the HLC broad and sub-types, as derived from the GIS.

HLC broad type	Count of polygons	Sum of area of polygons (square metres)	Area of polygons as % of entire base
Communications (CM)	1629	57277817	6.64
Defence (DF)	791	35668615	4.14
Field Patterns (FP)	1807	99774614	11.57
Natural Landscape (NL)	69	58202821	6.75
Open Land (OP)	5009	223852856	25.96
Ritual (RT)	28	1477247	0.17
Urban (UR)	646	31366442	3.64
Woodland-Related (WD)	6991	299092681	34.68
Water-Related (WR)	1324	55604436	6.45

Table 24: Quantification of HLC broad types

CLC SUB-TYPE	Count of Polygons	Sum of Area of Polygons (square metres)	Area of Polygons as % of entire base
CMAF	423	15063900	1.75
CMMR	1206	42213917	4.90
DFIM	791	35668615	4.14
FPEN	1807	99774614	11.57
NLKA	69	58202821	6.75
OPLF	716	19286583	2.24
OPLS	1987	95820655	11.11
OPUP	1707	82780418	9.60
OPVB	599	25965201	3.01
RTHC	26	1337355	0.16
RTNA	2	139892	0.02
URCA	420	21057141	2.44
URGC	77	2633643	0.31
URRS	149	7675658	0.89
WDLF	976	23303073	2.70
WDLS	2690	132979697	15.42
WDUP	2516	110742187	12.84
WDVB	809	32067724	3.72
WRLK	58	1823179	0.21
WRLS	110	2615733	0.30
WRRB	1156	51165524	5.93

Table 25: Quantification of HLC sub-types

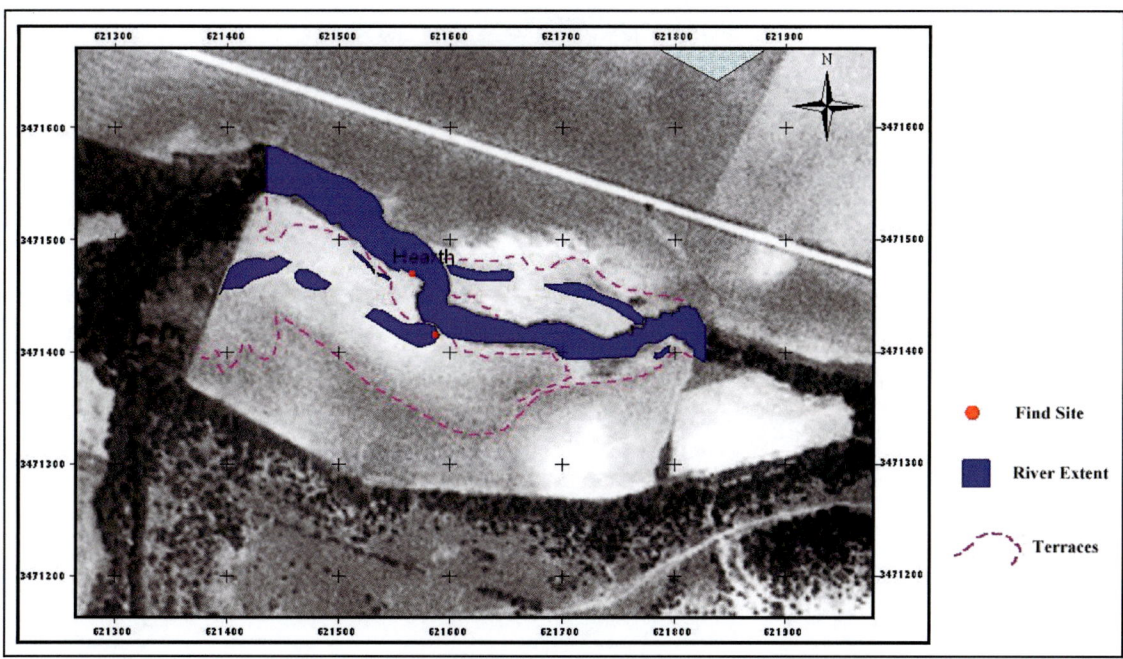

Figure 41: Detail of AP-related field data

Plate 21: Newly-discovered hearth site – photograph by Simon Fitch

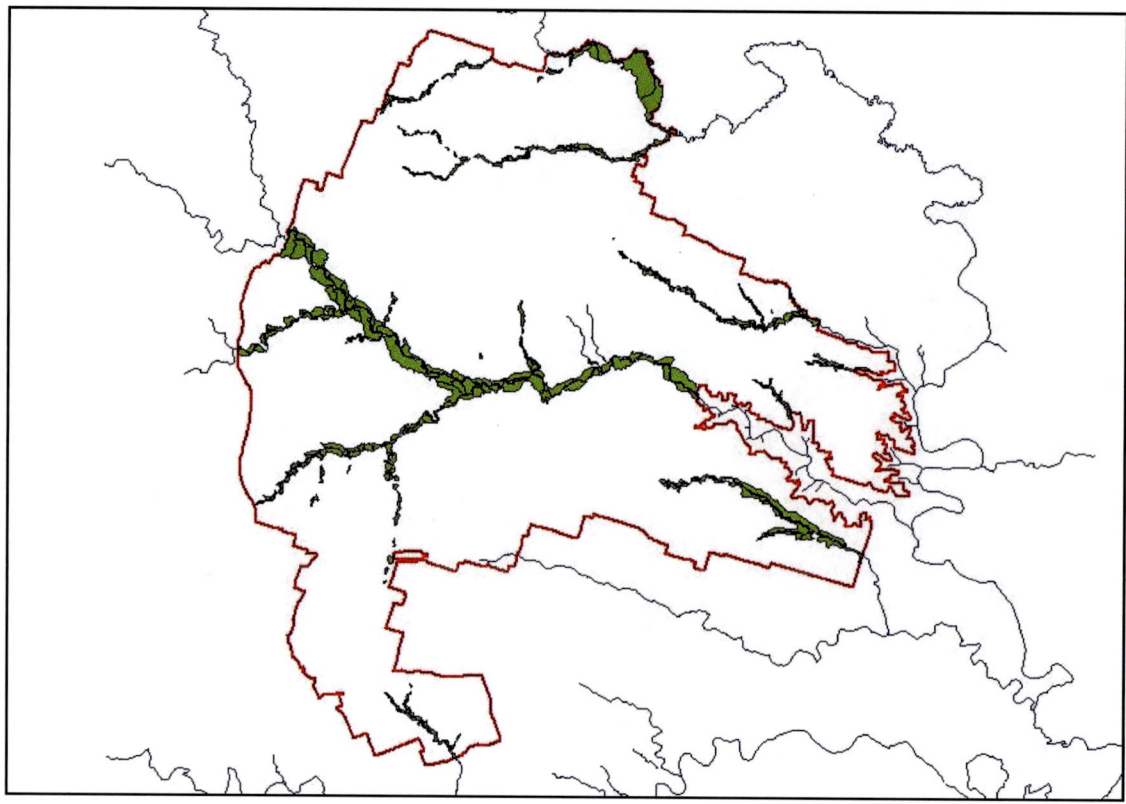

Figure 42: River terrace HLC data enhanced by ground-truthing

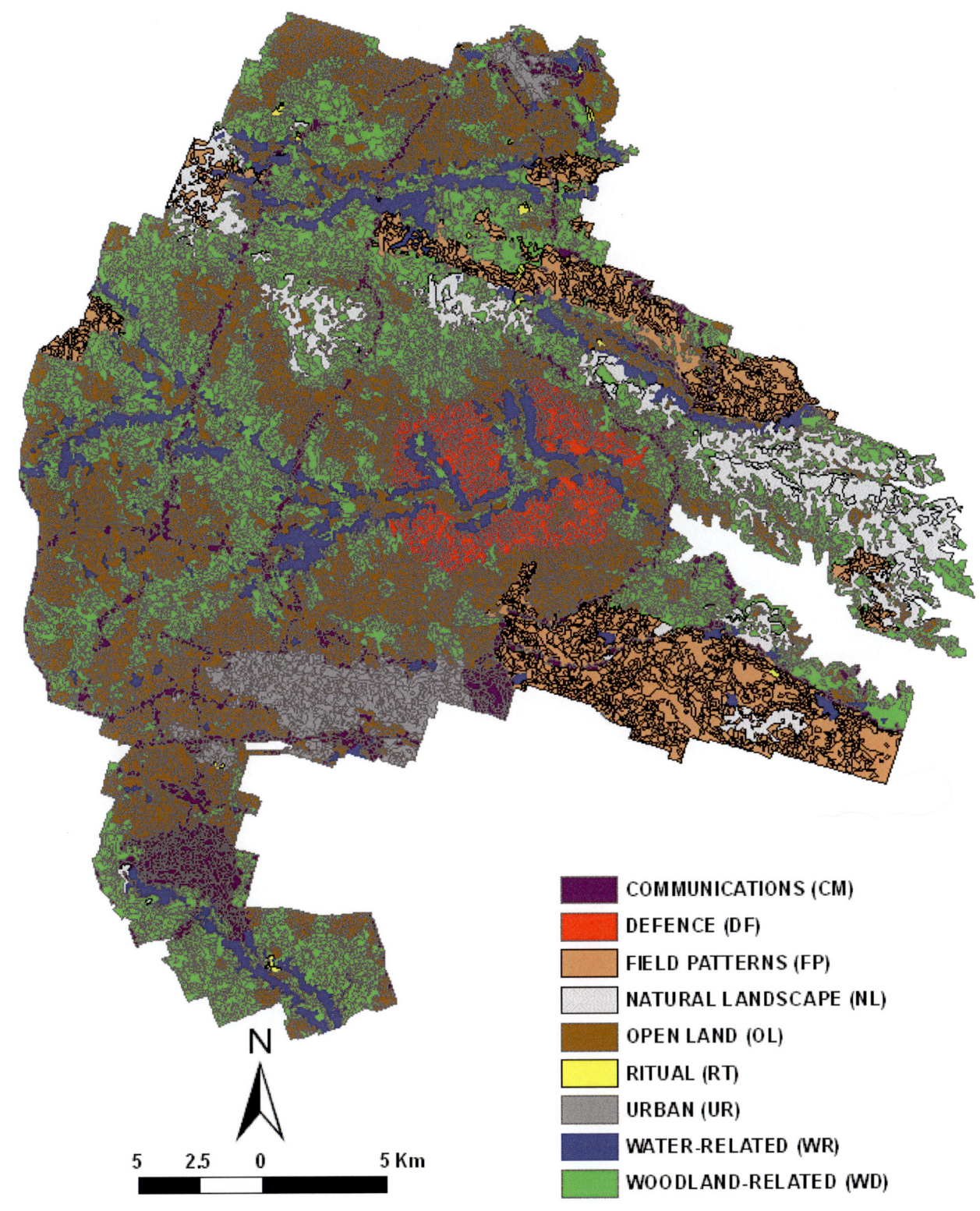

Figure 43: Study area mapped to HLC broad types

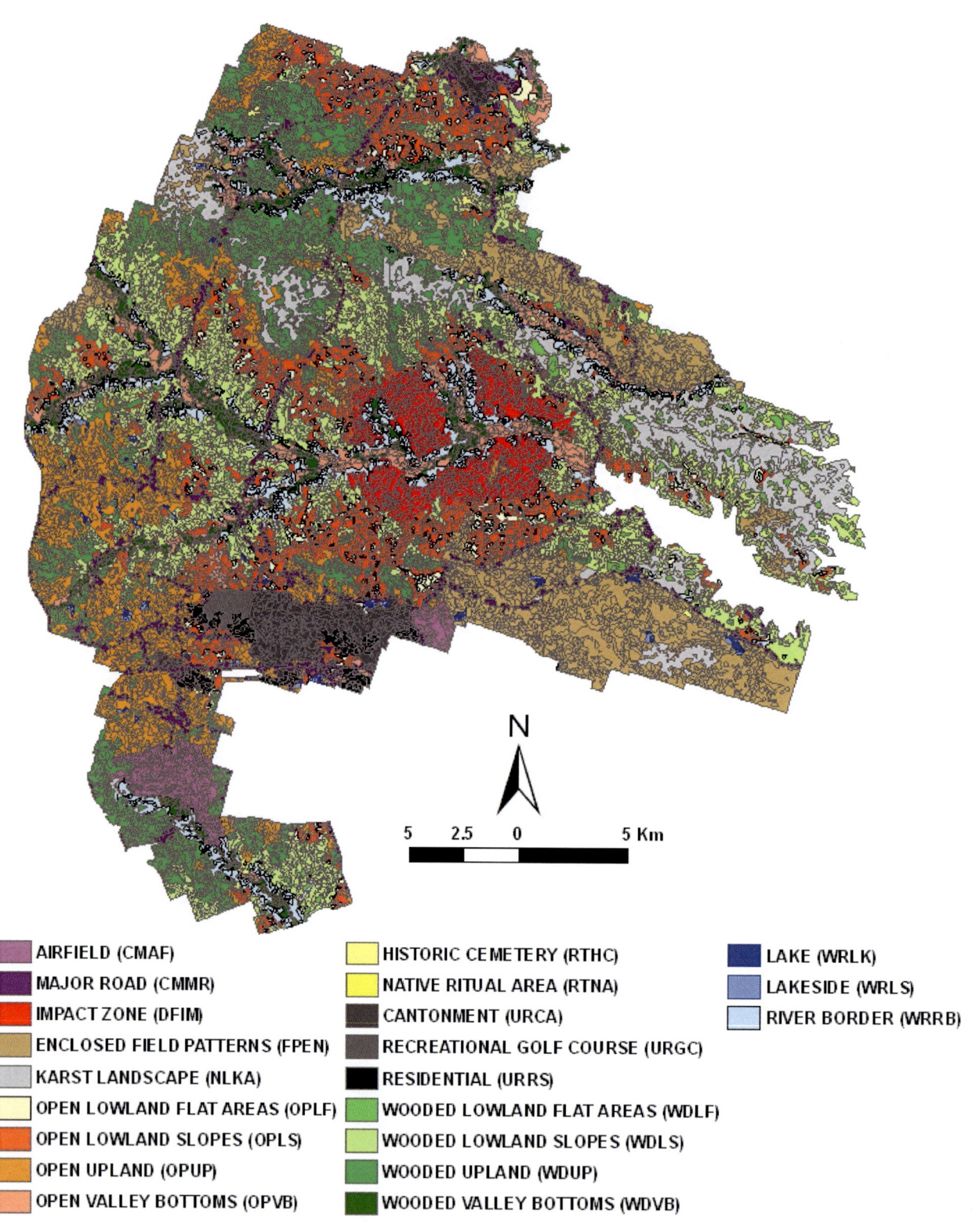

Figure 44: Study area mapped to HLC sub-types

The largest HLC broad type, by both polygon count and area, is Woodland, followed by Open Land. Together these two types comprise 60% of the total area of the base. It is interesting that Defence is one of the smallest categories, given that Fort Hood is a military installation, and it is, in fact, only the live-fire area where Defence occurs as the predominant landscape influence. This is partly due to the methodology used to determine HLC types, as it could be argued that every landscape polygon at Fort Hood should be assigned to a Defence HLC type.

However, for obvious reasons, this approach would not have provided meaningful data or fulfilled the aims of the project, so the methodology was deliberately devised so that significant non-military historic landscape influences would be proportionately reflected in the data. Despite this, it is clear that the military function has had a profound effect on almost every aspect of the present visible historic landscape. Although Fort Hood has a history of grazing and agriculture since the mid-19th century, with grazing concentrated along the eastern Cowhouse creek (Zeidler 2004, 124), the high proportion of un-settled and un-farmed land is directly related to military activity. Settlement is now exclusively in the cantonment and military residential areas, leaving the rest of the base uninhabited, and agricultural use is limited to cattle grazing. Although large areas of land on the base were leased back to ranchers after the establishment of the military base, the limited settlement and farming since the mid-20th century has led to a marked contrast in landscape character between the land within the base and that outside it. Within the base, the landscape character is more heavily influenced by natural vegetation, which has been able to re-establish itself due to the removal of farms and the elimination of crop-growing, and less influenced by agricultural land division than the land surrounding the base.

Landscape areas retaining elements relating to former land divisions appear largely in two blocks in the east, and it is surely significant that virtually all of the Field Pattern type polygons occur around the boundaries of the military base. An examination of the chronology of land acquisition for military use may shed some light on this, and an in-depth analysis of the spatial distribution of the Field Pattern HLC type would make a significant follow-on study to this project.

An interesting point to note is that although by the end of the 19th century there were around 32 small communities within the area now occupied by Fort Hood, the existence of these communities is not reflected in the HLC data other than in the ritual HLC type, which, other than the medicine wheel, comprises cemeteries from the historic period. This may be a result of the short-lived nature of these communities, which had largely disappeared in the early 20th century, some years before the establishment of the military base, due to the improvement in transport links to larger towns (Zeidler 2004, 124). Although it is clear that there are isolated remains of historic buildings still visible within the base, these are too ephemeral to be highlighted in a coarse-grained study such as the Fort Hood HLC project.

The Communication landscape areas are closely related to the Urban areas - the former are concentrated around the latter. The only dense block of Communication type polygons that is not immediately adjacent to an urban area occurs in the far south of the base and is due to the presence of the airfield in that area. The other Communication type polygons pick out roads running across the base.

The Natural Landscape type occurs mainly in a belt running Northwest-Southeast across the northern part of the base, in the Karst regions. The Natural Landscape type and the Field Pattern type both follow a broadly northwest-southeast orientation, reflecting the orientation of the major drainages across Fort Hood, such as Cowhouse Creek and Owl Creek.

Ritual landscape is centred on the Medicine Wheel, and a few other small areas, mostly in the north of the base, which coincide with historic cemeteries. There is only a very small proportion of HLC Type polygons (0.17%) where Ritual is the predominant influence on the landscape.

Other highly significant issues that emerge when studying the two HLC maps are the influence that choice of colour schemes can have on perceptions of the HLC data, and the way in which the HLC data can be used to create a range of different interpretations for different purposes. Both of these issues are particularly well-illustrated by the way in which drainages are discernible in the HLC maps. When the study area is mapped as HLC broad types, Cowhouse Creek, Henson Creek, Table Rock Creek and Reese Creek are clearly highlighted as the Water HLC type, whereas Owl Creek, Clear Creek and House Creek (at least at its western end), are not so easily distinguishable from the surrounding land. In fact, Clear Creek is not really differentiated from the surrounding landscape at all. However, once the area is mapped as HLC sub-types, House Creek in particular becomes much more obvious as a feature, and can be picked out by looking at a combination of Riverside, Open Valley Bottom and Wooded Valley Bottom sub-types. The difference is not so apparent for Clear Creek and Owl Creek, although the northern part of Clear Creek does emerge as a more distinct feature once sub-types are mapped. Clear Creek is obscured in the south largely by the predominance of the Urban HLC type in that area, and Owl Creek is less prominent than some of the other drainages because it is within one of the areas that is more heavily influenced by the Field Pattern HLC type. The latter point is significant in itself because the presence of Owl Creek may well have had a major influence on the historical trajectory of field patterns in that area. This possibility could be explored in more depth as part of a detailed analysis of field patterns, a potential future study that has already been mentioned above.

5.4.2 HLC data and archaeological site distribution

Together with the HLC data, the re-design of the Fort Hood database and the production of a suggested list of standard site type terms have provided a data structure that is more appropriate to the type of landscape-level analyses that are required for effective cultural resource management at Fort Hood than previously existed. A broad-brush quantification and visualisation study was undertaken using the HLC broad types and the standard archaeological site types assigned during the HLC project. As a basis for the study, quantifications of site types in relation to HLC broad types and sub-types were produced (tables 26 and 27). Also, distribution maps of archaeological sites in relation to HLC broad types were plotted (figures 45-52) using the same colour scheme for the HLC data as in figure 43, but without displaying the individual polygon boundaries.

Distribution maps of site types with HLC sub-types proved to be too visually complex to be of use, and it is more difficult to identify broad-brush trends from the sub-types quantification table, as the site numbers are smaller for each sub-type. However, the sub-type figures still provide very significant baseline data and could be used as the starting point for more in-depth, fine-grained landscape analyses at Fort Hood in the future.

Period information does not exist in the database in a format that can be used for distribution maps and quantifications, other than to differentiate between Prehistoric and Historic sites. This differentiation can be inferred from the site type distribution maps and quantification tables, as the site types themselves are specific to either the Prehistoric or Historic period.

The quantifications were achieved in the GIS using spatial intersection i.e. any archaeological sites that intersected a selected HLC type were included in the count for that HLC type. A site was counted once for each HLC type that it intersected, so some sites will have been counted several times. There are several other ways in which these figures could have been calculated, for example only counting a site if it lay completely within the selected HLC type, or only counting a site if more than 50% of its area lay within the selected HLC type. However, for the purposes of a broad-brush characterisation such as this, it was felt that a count on the basis of intersection would yield the most appropriate results. The site types used were those suggested and assigned in the new Fort Hood database (see Chapter 4), with the following exceptions:

- historic sites were amalgamated into military and non-military categories, as otherwise the numbers would have been too small to produce any meaningful figures
- the medicine wheel was not included in the quantification or visualisation as it is the only site in the category and would not produce sensible results
- sinkholes were not included in the quantification as there were only four recorded in the database, and again this number would have been too small to produce any meaningful figures. However, a distribution map was produced (Figure 47)

Table 26 shows a quantification of sites by type on each HLC broad type. There are two columns for each HLC broad type - the first shows a count of each site type on that particular broad type, and the second shows the site type as a percentage of all the occurrences of that site type over the base as a whole. Quantification of site types in relation to HLC sub-types was also carried out, as shown in Table 27. The figures for the site types were taken as representative of the archaeological record at a particular point in time, in this case June 2002.

Plate 22: Military presence in the landscape – photo by Gil Eckrich

Plate 23: Cattle grazing at Fort Hood – photo by Gil Eckrich

Plate 24: Site of the remains of a historic house at Fort Hood – photo from Fort hood CRM

Plate 25: Karst area at Fort Hood – photo from Fort Hood CRM

Plates 26 and 27: Cowhouse Creek (top) and Table Rock Creek (bottom) – photos from Fort hood CRM

	CM (6.64%)		DF (4.14%)		FP (11.57%)		NL (6.75%)		OP (25.96%)		*RT (0.17%)		UR (3.64%)		*WD (34.68%)		WT (6.45%)	
	Count	%	Count	%	Count	%	Count	%	Count	%	Count	%	Count	%	Count	%	Count	%
BR midden	4	3.60	0	0	20	18.02	6	5.41	25	22.52	0	0	0	0	34	30.63	22	19.82
BR mound	6	5.61	0	0	6	5.61	24	22.43	16	14.95	1	0.93	0	0	49	45.79	5	4.67
BR scatter	20	5.81	2	0.58	24	6.98	19	5.52	70	20.35	1	0.29	3	0.87	166	48.26	39	11.34
Historic Military	2	13.33	0	0	1	6.67	0	0	5	33.33	0	0	1	6.67	3	20.00	3	20.00
Historic Non-Military	122	7.74	41	2.60	206	13.07	110	6.98	394	25.00	27	1.71	6	0.38	550	34.90	120	7.61
LRPA	8	5.67	0	0	28	19.86	12	8.51	27	19.15	1	0.71	0	0	52	36.88	13	9.22
Lithic Scatter	35	6.64	8	1.52	70	13.28	64	12.14	94	17.84	3	0.57	4	0.76	197	37.38	52	9.87
Open Camp	14	4.09	2	0.58	33	9.65	30	8.77	76	22.22	2	0.58	3	0.88	142	41.52	40	11.70
Rock-shelter	5	2.70	0	0	10	5.41	61	32.97	9	4.86	0	0	0	0	97	52.43	3	1.62

Table 26: Quantification of sites by site type on each HLC broad type

*These two HLC types also contained the Medicine Wheel

	CMAF	CMMR	DFIM	FPEN	NLKA	OPLF	OPLS	OPUP	OPVB
BR midden		4		20	6	2	3	9	17
BR mound		6		6	24	2	4	11	3
BR scatter	2	18	2	24	19	6	34	27	23
Historic Military		2		1			2	2	2
Historic Non-Military	9	113	41	206	110	60	208	122	74
LRPA		8		28	12	5	15	8	5
Lithic Scatter	5	30	8	70	64	21	38	18	35
Open Camp		14	2	33	30	7	19	18	43
Rock Shelter		5		10	61	2	4	4	

	RTHC	RTNA	URCA	URGC	URRS	WDLF	WDLS	WDUP	WDVB	WTLK	WTLS	WTRV
BR midden	1					3	10	13	20	7	6	15
BR mound	1					10	25	20	8			5
BR scatter			1	2	1	30	86	54	46	4	5	33
Historic Military					1				3			3
Historic Non-Military	27		4	1	1	67	283	181	87	5	7	108
LRPA	2					16	25	27	5			13
Lithic Scatter	3		3		2	38	91	53	42	1		51
Open Camp	2					32	68	39	57	1	2	38
Rock Shelter				3		13	62	31				3

Table 27: Count of sites by site type on each HLC sub-type

Detailed statistical analysis of site types in relation to HLC types is beyond the remit of this project, but a discussion of the dominant trends is pertinent to the project, and demonstrates the potential of the HLC data and the new Fort Hood database for research and interpretation. Perhaps the most obvious trend is the disproportionately high percentage of Prehistoric archaeological sites occurring on the Woodland HLC type in relation to its area, especially Rock-shelters, Burned Rock Mounds, Burned Rock Scatters and Open Camps. The only site types that occur as disproportionately low percentages on this type are Burned Rock Middens (only slightly lower), and Historic Military Sites. The lower relative occurrence of Military sites on Woodland, and higher relative occurrence on Open Land, is possibly due to the greater difficulty of movement within Woodland as opposed to Open Land. There is also a lower percentage occurrence of Prehistoric sites on Open Land. This may be due to a number of factors, including greater vulnerability to destructive forces (particularly from military manoeuvres), or may actually be a true reflection of where Prehistoric activity occurred on the base.

Although it may not appear quite so obvious as the actual figures are lower, there are some significant trends in the Natural Landscape and Water HLC types. Despite comprising relatively small proportions of the area of the base as a whole, both of these HLC types have disproportionately high percentages of certain site types. The Natural Landscape HLC type, despite occupying only 6.75% of the base as a whole, has nearly 33% of the Rock-shelters, 22% of the Burned Rock Mounds (plate 29) and 12% of the Lithic Scatters. The high proportion of Rock-shelters must be a direct product of the Karst landscape (illustrated by the distribution map in figure 46), but the relatively high percentage occurrence of Burned Rock Mounds (three times higher than the percentage occurrence of the Natural Landscape HLC type) is more complex to explain, and would merit a separate, in-depth study in its own right.

Similarly, the Water HLC type, which occupies 6.45% of the base, contains nearly 20% of the Burned Rock Middens, 11% of the Burned Rock scatters, 20% of the Historic Military sites and 12% of the Open Camps. This may be due to a combination of factors including ease of detection, and concentration of archaeological work in particular areas, but may also be a reflection of high utilisation of these areas by both Prehistoric and Historic people, for example for their greater diversity of resources or for their military training potential.

The Communications HLC type contains a relatively high percentage of Military sites, largely because it includes airfields and roads, which are obviously critical to WW2 and post-WW2 military activity. The low percentage of sites occurring on the Defence HLC type is almost certainly not a true reflection of the level of archaeological activity in this area, and more a reflection of the limited fieldwork that has been carried out in the live-fire zone. The Field Patterns HLC type has a high percentage of Burned Rock Middens and LRPAs, and again, the reasons for this could form the basis of a separate, detailed study. The Ritual HLC type comprises such a small part of the base that it is difficult to define trends, as very small differences in site numbers will affect the relative percentages quite dramatically. However, a key feature of this HLC type is the relative percentage of Historic Non-military sites, of which a high proportion are historic cemeteries. It should also be noted that the Medicine Wheel occurs on this HLC type, but has not been included in the quantification for the reasons already mentioned. Likewise, the Urban HLC type comprises a very small part of the base as a whole, and no particularly significant trends are discernible.

Generally, Burned Rock sites seem to occur more densely in the west of the base, whilst Open Camps appear to be concentrated along river valleys and woodland (plates 30 and 31). Figures 45 and 46 show a correlation between Burned Rock sites and Rock-shelters, a relationship that has already been noted in the review section (see chapter 3). Figures 49 and 50 indicate a similarity between the distribution patterns of Lithic Scatters and LRPAs. They appear to be more concentrated in the north and east of the base, and are relatively sparse in the west and centre. This similarity may well be because the sites themselves are connected in terms of function and resource location. There are so few Military sites and Sinkholes that it is difficult to comment on their distribution. However, it is clear that this is not a true reflection of their numbers, but rather that they have not been systematically recorded in the archaeological database. The only site types that really show a fairly even distribution over the whole base are the Historic Non-military sites.

This analysis of HLC data and archaeological site distribution is by no means comprehensive, nor is it intended to be, as the project archaeologists would be the first to acknowledge that they are not the most appropriate people to undertake this work. Rather it is designed to provide a flavour of the type of landscape-level interpretive study that is possible with the data sets that are now in place at Fort Hood, and it is hoped that this type of study will be taken further by those who are best placed to do so, that is the archaeologists who live and work in the landscape around Fort Hood.

Plate 28: Woodland near Bear Creek – photo from Fort Hood CRM

Plate 29: Burned rock mound in the Karst landscape – photo from Fort Hood CRM

Plate 30: Prehistoric camp site by the Cowhouse Creek – photo from Fort hood CRM

Plate 31: Prehistoric camp site at Maple Canyon – photo by Gil Eckrich

Figures 45 - 52 illustrate distribution maps of archaeological site types with broad HLC types.

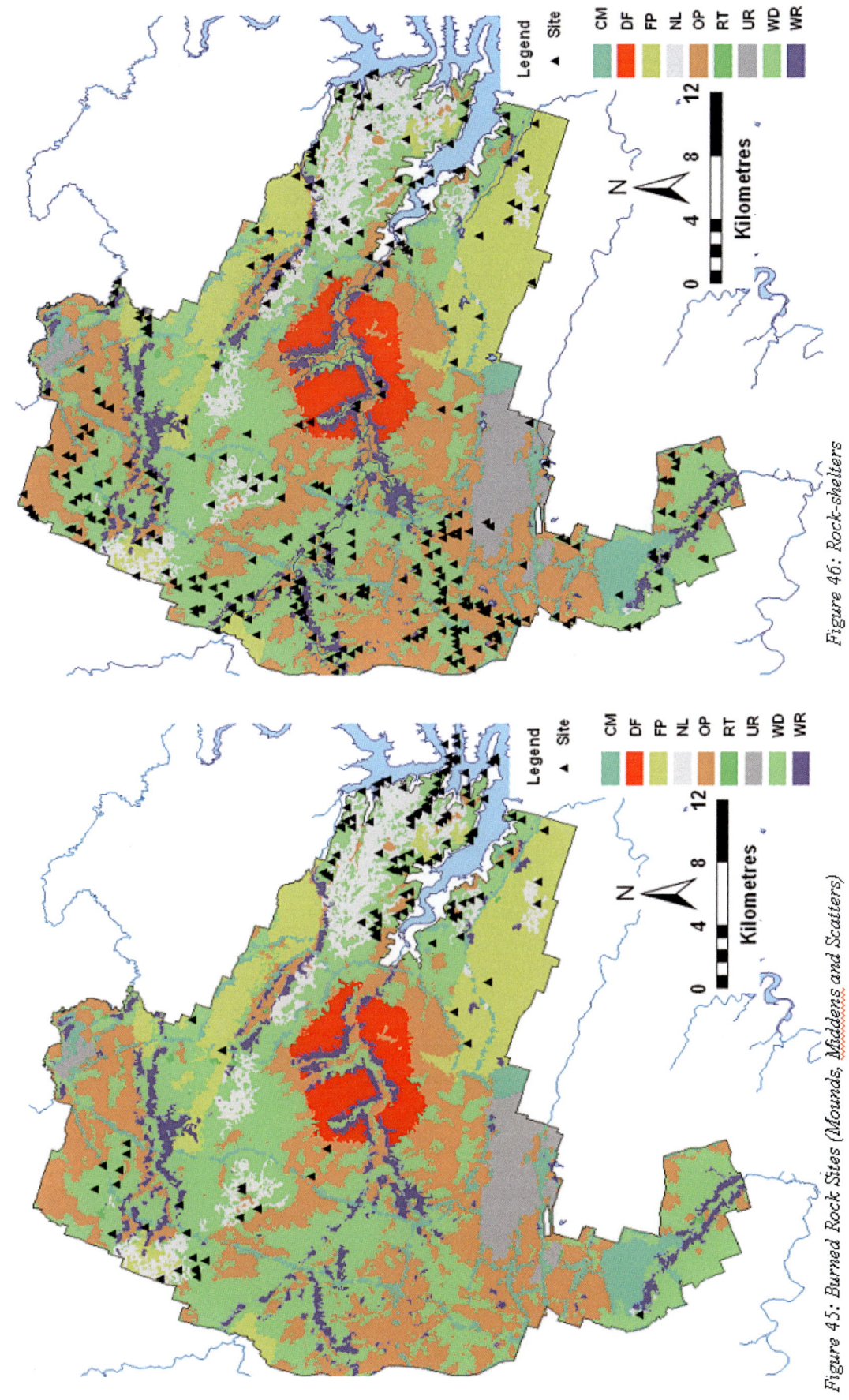

Figure 46: Rock-shelters

Figure 45: Burned Rock Sites (Mounds, Middens and Scatters)

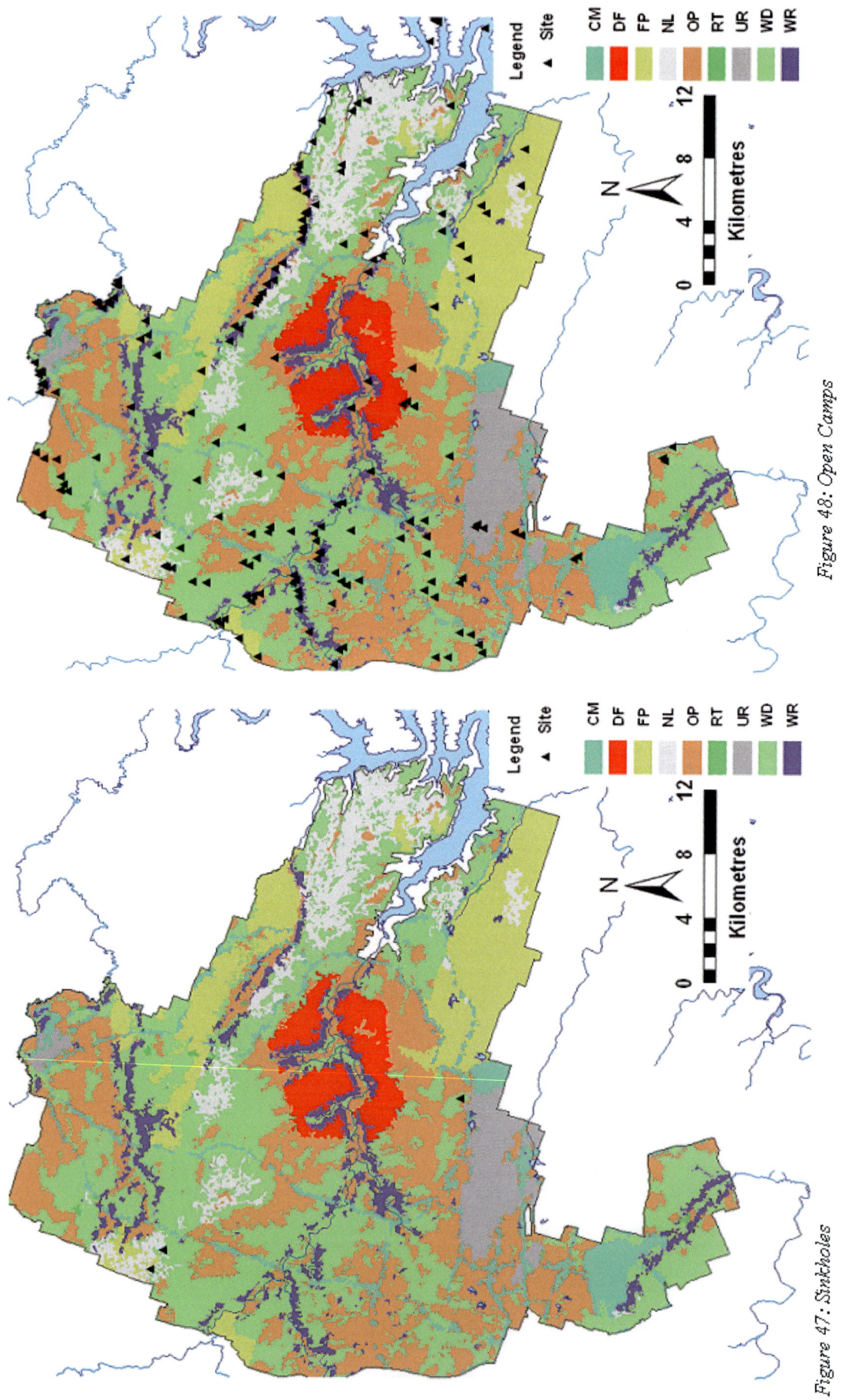

Figure 48: Open Camps

Figure 47: Sinkholes

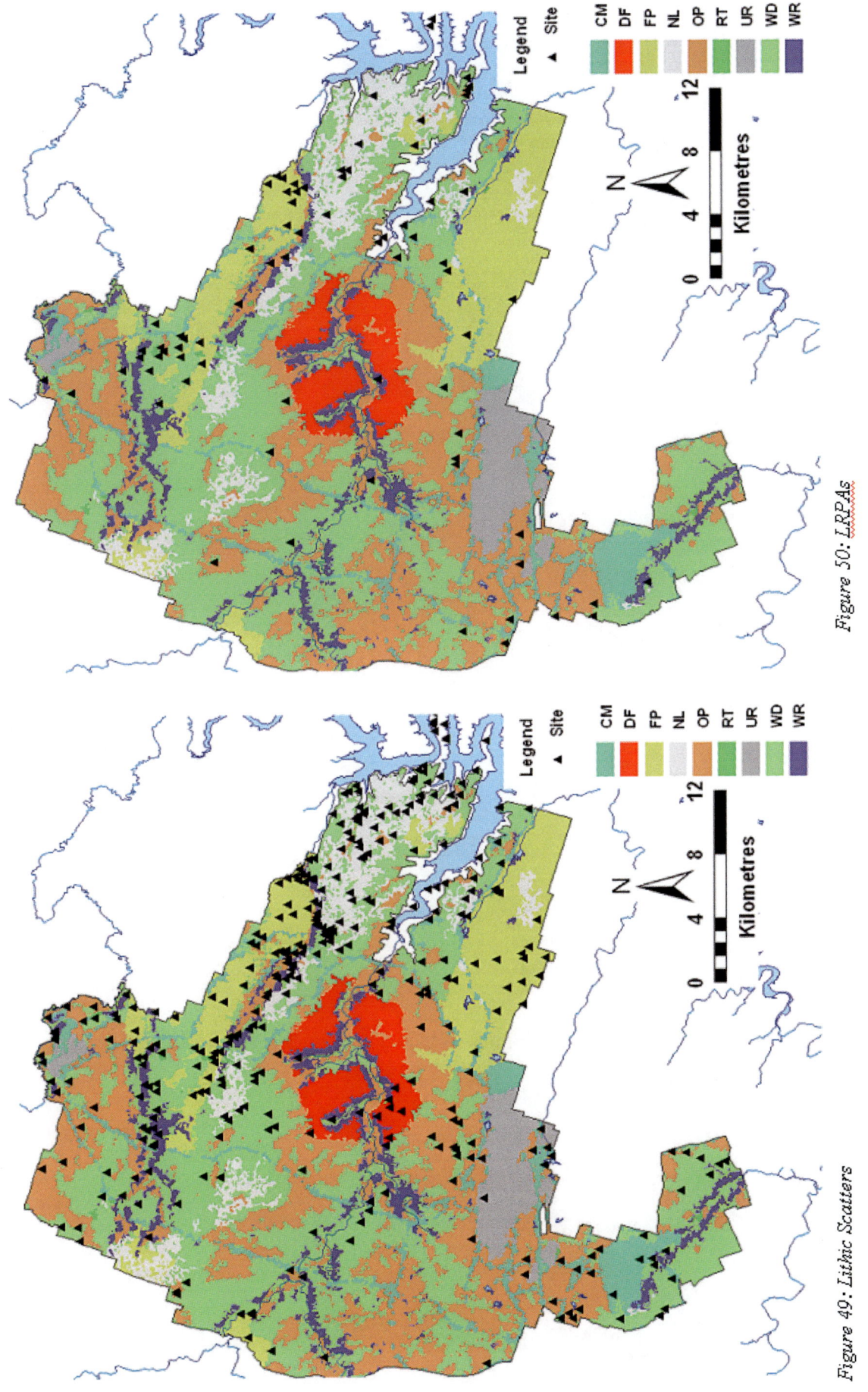

Figure 49: Lithic Scatters

Figure 50: LRPAs

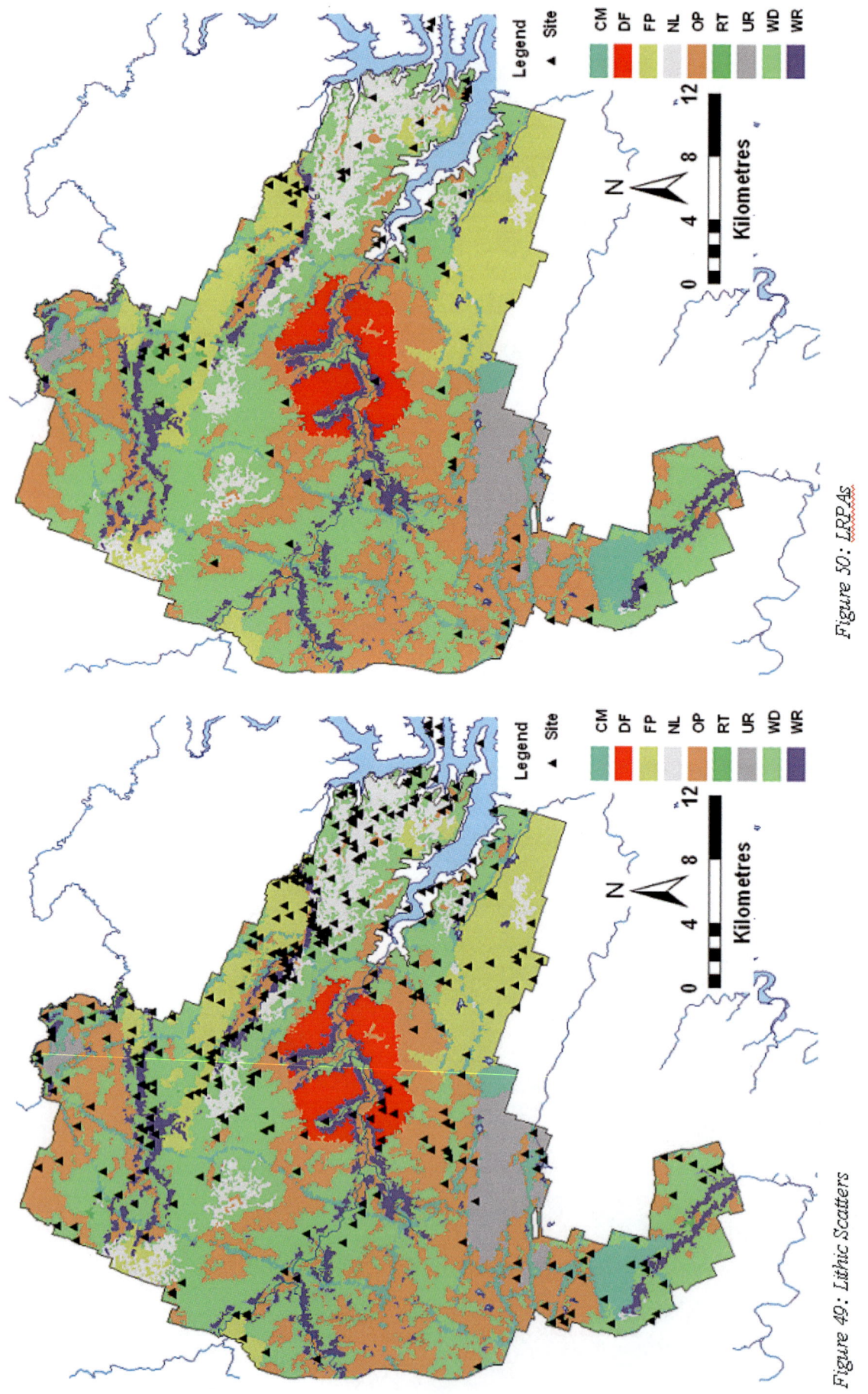

Figure 49: Lithic Scatters

Figure 50: LRPAs

6. Conclusions

"We keep digging up the same kinds of evidence using the same techniques. Targeting other aspects of the archaeological record and using a greater array of procedures are priorities"
Michael B. Collins (1995, 389) Forty Years of Archaeology in Central Texas

The principal aim of the Fort Hood Historic Landscape Characterisation (HLC) project was to apply historic landscape characterisation techniques to a landscape that is far removed geographically, environmentally and culturally from those landscapes for which the techniques were originally developed. The project was undertaken primarily to support the Fort Hood cultural resource management programme, which encompasses the management of a unique and complex historic landscape of international importance within the largest active armoured post in the USA. However, the aims and achievements of the project fit into a wider tradition of pioneering research carried out at Fort Hood, and should, therefore, also be examined within this context.

HLC as a methodology, was devised in England as a response to the need for monitoring and managing change in the historic landscape, and recognition of the major gap that existed in the management of the archaeological resource at a landscape level. This gap was impossible to address through the archaeological records maintained by the county Sites and Monuments Records, which were point based and site specific, and therefore unable to consider the spaces between, and by association, the relationships between sites. HLC techniques have also been utilised elsewhere in Europe, and although HLC methodology has changed and developed considerably over the years (Fairclough 1999, Aldred and Fairclough 2002, Darlington 2002, Dyson-Bruce 2002, Fairclough 2002, Clark et al. 2003), English HLC projects, virtually without exception, have used historic maps, usually Ordnance Survey maps, as the primary data source. Consequently, these projects have broken down the landscape into the necessary building blocks for characterisation by using polygons which are derived from existing land parcels on the maps, such as fields and woodlands.

Since HLC techniques were originally developed for English landscapes, it was a complex and thought-provoking task to transpose these ideas and techniques into a landscape with such a radically different historical trajectory. Whilst adhering to the fundamental principles of HLC methodology established for European use, the Fort Hood HLC methodology required extensive modification, and the experimental nature of much of the data processing and analysis has resulted in an HLC project that, in the spirit of previous research at Fort Hood, is unique in terms of methodology and application.

Probably the most obvious departure from English methodology involves the data sources used, as the project involved the characterisation of a landscape which was not already organised into easily accessible landscape units, and where no detailed mapping was available. A very large part of the project, therefore, consisted of the development of the methodology, and incorporated a considerable amount of experimentation with digital technologies and manipulation of very large data sets. It could be argued that the creation of base landscape polygons from classified Landsat satellite imagery and terrain data, and the fact that not all of those carrying out the characterisation were explicitly expert on the archaeology of the area, has led to a highly objective and transparent methodology and resulting HLC data set. This is not to deny that the project methodology involved interpretation, as HLC is interpretive by nature. However, the Fort Hood HLC methodology is systematic, justifiable and repeatable by anybody with access to the same data sources, and the data set can be easily re-analysed at any time. This is an important aspect of the characterisation programme, because the data set has to be, like the landscape that it characterises, dynamic and not static.

The Fort Hood HLC project is also unique in that, to the knowledge of the project team, HLC techniques have never been applied to a landscape that has seen land-use metamorphose from hunter-gathering to settled farming to wholesale military use within the space of 300 years. Reflecting aspects such as time-depth, non-site archaeology and local distinctiveness in a landscape of this type presented a huge challenge. However, it is entirely appropriate that HLC should be attempted within such a landscape, as issues of continuity and change are at the core of HLC theory.

The indigenous nature of prehistoric settlement at Fort Hood fuelled attempts to examine and incorporate intangible aspects of the landscape, primarily visibility and significant natural places in the landscape, into the project methodology. This was achieved through the incorporation of data relating to caves, sinkholes and viewsheds from mesas within the HLC attributes. This was never intended to be a comprehensive analysis of all intangible landscape aspects that may have been significant to the prehistoric population of Fort Hood, but rather a starting point. One hopes that our attempt to assess how such influences could be reflected in HLC data alongside the more 'traditional' aspects may assist in stimulating debate amongst the archaeological community as to how this aspect of our research could be taken forward.

A major outcome of the Fort Hood HLC project is the provision of a data structure that is more appropriate for the task of managing the Fort Hood archaeological resource and is in-line with current management trends. The re-design of the archaeological sites database and the production of a suggested list of standard site type terms has provided a framework for modelling the dynamic nature of the archaeological recording process, and has enabled utilisation of the concepts of group value and spatial relationships at a landscape level. The HLC data is the result of a systematic, evidence-based approach to data gathering, and covers the whole land surface of the base. It should be regarded as complementary to the archaeological site database, providing it with a context, filling a gap at the landscape level, and enabling new approaches to assessment that move beyond site-focused designations of significance. Although HLC is primarily a descriptive and interpretive approach and not simply a process of value judgements, the latter process can be facilitated by, for example, using the HLC data to create 'management zones', the significance of which can be evaluated using systematic assessment criteria, and appropriate management strategies. Such approaches will target resources for data recovery programmes, helping to ensure that the key sites in the most significant or representative landscape areas can be investigated should they come under threat.

The new data structure should also facilitate the integration of the cultural resource management programme with other environmental and conservation programmes at Fort Hood. In addition, Fort Hood maintains an active public outreach program, and the emphasis within HLC on the importance of the typical and commonplace in contributing to local distinctiveness of the landscape could encourage both local communities and interested groups from within the Native American population to take a more active role in conserving the landscape.

The new Fort Hood database and the HLC data produced as a result of this project form a baseline data set that can be built upon and improved by those who know more intimately the landscape characterised here. The broad-brush, rapid analysis of the occurrence of archaeological site types, in relation to the landscape analysis undertaken during the project term, provides a good illustration of how HLC data can be used to analyse the archaeological resource at a landscape level. The ground-truthing exercise undertaken along selected areas of river terraces as part of the project demonstrates how the established HLC framework can be used to identify and undertake a series of more detailed, in-depth landscape studies.

Of course, significant issues still remain to be considered. The current programme of work could not resolve important questions relating to the lack of appreciation of the role of group value or the larger significance of sites which are represented by palimpsests of archaeological activity over time. These are likely to remain issues for as long as sites are solely, or even primarily, assessed on the basis of their potential for inclusion in the National Register. Despite such concerns, the Fort Hood HLC project remains an achievement in the application of historic landscape characterisation methodologies at an international level. Regionally, it also acted as a forum for collaboration and exchange of ideas against the backdrop of a unique archaeological landscape with a strong tradition of innovative research. The authors' hope is that the project supports this tradition and, specifically, that the work will promote landscape research more generally. Together with the existing archaeological database, the product of numerous individuals over decades, this may provide a radically different perspective on the archaeology of Fort Hood and Central Texas: one that can play a significant role in defining the future direction of archaeological research and heritage management in the region.

7. Bibliography

Abbott, J T and Frederick, C D, 1990 Proton magnetometer investigations of burned rock middens in West-Central Texas: clues to formation processes, *Journal of Archaeological Science*, 17, 535-545

Abbott, J.T and Trierweiler, W N (eds.), 1995 *NRHP significance testing of 57 Prehistoric archeological sites on Fort Hood, Texas, volumes I and II*, United States Army Fort Hood, Archeological Resource Management Series, Research Report No. 34

Aldred, O and Fairclough, G, 2003 *Historic Landscape Characterisation: taking stock of the method*, English Heritage and Somerset County Council, London

Ashmore, W and Knapp, A B (eds.), 1999 *Archaeologies of landscape: contemporary perspectives*

Barratt, G and Litherland, S, 2003 *Cobham Park landscape evaluation*, Birmingham Archaeology Report for Kent County Council

Bellavia, G, 2006 Predicting Communication Routes, in Haldon, J (ed.) *General issues in the study of Medieval logistics*, Brill, Leiden, 185-198

Binford, L R, 1972. A consideration of archaeological research design, in Binford, L R (ed.), *An Archaeological Perspective*. Seminar Press New York. 135-164

Binford, L R, 1980 Willow smoke and dogs' tails: hunter-gatherer settlement systems and archaeological site formation, *American Antiquity*, 45, 4-20

Black, S L, 1989 Central Texas Plateau Prairie, in Hester, T R, Black, S L, Steele, D G, Olive, B W, Fox, A A, Reinhard, K J and Bement, L C, 1989 *From the Gulf to the Rio Grande: human adaptations in Central, South, and Lower Pecos, Texas*, 5-38, Research Series 33, Arkansas Archaeological Survey, Fayetteville

Black, S L, 1995 (Texas) Archaeology 1995, *Bulletin of the Texas Archeological Society*, 66, 17-45

Black, S L, Ellis, L W, Creel, D G and Goode, G T, 1997 Abstract, in *Hot rock cooking on the Greater Edwards Plateau: four burned rock midden sites in West Central Texas*, http://www.utexas.edu/research/tarl/publications/studies.html - 12

Blake, Marie E, 2001 *Archeological Investigations and Integrity Assessments of Historic Sites at Fort Hood, Texas*, United States Army Fort Hood, Archaeological Resource Management Series, Research Report No. 41

Bloemers, J H F, 2002 Past- and Future-oriented archaeology: protecting and developing the archaeological-historical landscape of the Netherlands, in Fairclough, G J and. Rippon, S (eds.), *Europe's Cultural Landscape: archaeologists and the management of change*, EAC Occasional Paper no 2, Brussels & London: Europae Archaeologiae Consilium & English Heritage, 89-96

Blum, M D, Abbott, J T and Valastro Jr, S, 1992 Preservation and visibility of the archaeological record, *Geoarchaeology*, 7, 339-370

Boyd, D K, Mehalchick, G and Scott, A M, 2000 *Planning document for the treatment of National Register-eligible Prehistoric sites under section 106 of the National Historic Preservation Act, Fort Hood, Texas*, United States Army Fort Hood, Cultural Resource Management Program, Environmental Division, Department of Public Works

Bradley, R, 1994 Symbols and signposts – understanding the prehistoric petroglyphs of the British Isles, in Renfrew, C and Zubrow, E B W (eds.), 1994 *The ancient mind: elements of cognitive archaeology*. Cambridge University Press.

Bradley, R, 1998 *The Significance of Monuments*, Routledge, London

Bradley, R, 2000 *An archaeology of natural places* Routledge

Bray, T, 2003 *Archaeology and Politics of Food and Feast*, Plenum. Springer.

Brown, J, Mitchell, N and Beresford, M (eds.), 2005 *The Protected Landscape Approach, Linking Nature, Culture and Community*, Cambridge (UK) and Gland (CH): IUCN

CAPT, nd *Historic Landscape in Wales*, http://www.cpat.org.uk/projects/longer/histland/histland.htm (6 July 2006)

Carlson, D L, 1993 *Archaeological site testing and evaluation on the Henson Mountain helicopter range AWSS project area, Fort Hood, Texas*, United States Army Fort Hood, Archaeological Resource Management Series, Research Report No. 26

Carlson, D L, Dockall, J E and Olive, B W, 1994 *Archeological survey at Fort Hood, Texas, fiscal year 1990: the northeastern perimeter area*, United States Army Fort Hood, Archaeological Resource Management Series, Research Report No. 24

Challis, K and Howard, A, In Press A review of trends within archaeological remote sensing in alluvial environments, *Archaeological Prospection*

Chapman, H, 2006 *Landscape Archaeology and GIS* Tempus

Clark, J, Darlington, J and Fairclough, G, 2003 *Pathways to Europe's Landscape (European Pathways to the Cultural Landscape 2002-2003)*, Heide.

Clark, J, Darlington, J and Fairclough, G, 2004 *Using Historic landscape characterisation: English Heritage's review of HLC Applications 2002 – 03*, English Heritage & Lancashire County Council

Collins, M B, 1995 Forty Years of Archeology in Central Texas, *Bulletin of the Texas Archeological Society*, 66, 361-400

Collins, M B, 1999 Quote, in Parvin, B 1999 *Peering into Texas' past*, http://www.tpwd.state.tx.us/expltx/eft/time/peering.htm

Collins, M B, 2000 Quote, in Wisner, G, 2000 Texas site suggests links with Europe's Upper Palaeolithic, *Mammoth Trumpet*, 15(1), http://www.peak.org/csfa/mt15-1.html - part5

Collins, M B and Hester, T R, 2001 *The Gault site*, http://www.utexas.edu/research/tarl/research/Gault/intro/intro.htm

Collins, M B and Weir, F A, 2001 *Wilson-Leonard site, the handbook of Texas online*, http://www.tsha.utexas.edu/handbook/online/articles/view/WW/bbw3.html

Connolly, J and Lake, M, 2006 *Geographical Information Systems in Archaeology – Cambridge Manuals in Archaeology*, Cambridge University Press, United Kingdom

Council of Europe, 2000 *European Landscape Convention, Florence,* European Treaty Series No. 176,. Available: http://conventions.coe.int/Treaty/en/Treaties/Html/176.htm

Countryside Commission, 1987 *Landscape assessment – a Countryside Commission approach,* CCD18, Cheltenham

Countryside Commission, 1993 *Landscape assessment guidance,* CCP423, Cheltenham

Countryside Commission, 1996 *Views from the past – historic landscape character in the English countryside,* CCW4, Cheltenham

Countryside Commission and Countryside Agency, 1998-99 *Countryside character volumes: vols 1-8*, Cheltenham, www.countryside.gov.uk/cci

Countryside Commission for Wales, 2004 *LANDMAP web site*, http://landmap.ccw.gov.uk/

DAKD, nd Digitalt Atlas over Kulturmiljøer i Danmark, available: http://www.humaniora.sdu.dk/kulturmiljoe/index.html (6 July 2006)

Darlington, J, 2002 Mapping Lancashire's historic landscape: the Lancashire HLC programme, in Fairclough, G J and Rippon, S J (eds.), 2002: *Europe's cultural landscape: archaeologists and the management of change*, 97-105, EAC Occasional Paper no 2, Europae Archaeologiae Consilium and English Heritage, Brussels and London

Dase, Amy E, Freeman, Martha Doty, Pugsley III, William S, Sitton, Thad and Blake, Marie, 2003 *Just Like Yesterday: Recollections of Life on Fort Hood Lands Volume 1 & Volume 2,* United States Army Fort Hood, Archaeological Resource Management Series, Research Report No. 49

Department of the Army, 2000 *Pamphlet 200-4, Director of environmental programs: cultural resources management*

Department for Culture, Media & Sport, 2001 *The Historic Environment: A Force for Our Future*, London, www.culture.gov.uk/heritage

Dixon, P, Dyson-Bruce, L, Hingley, R and Stevenson, J, 1999 *Historic Landuse Assessment (HLA): Development and Potential of a Technique for Assessing Historic Landscape patterns, report of the pilot project 1996-98*, Historic Scotland, RCHMS, Edinburgh.

Dockrill, S J, 1991 Geophysical Survey of Burnt Mounds in the Northern Isles: The Magnetic Response, in Hodder, M A and Barfield, L H, 1991 *Burnt mounds and hot stone technology: papers from the Second International Burnt Mound Conference*, West Bromwich, Sandwell Metropolitan Borough Council, 35-39

Dyson-Bruce, L, 2002 Historic Landscape Assessment – the East of England experience, in Burenhult, G (ed.), 2002 *Archaeological Informatics: Pushing the Envelope*, 35-42, Procs. 29th CAA Conference, Gotland, April 2001, BAR International Series 1016, Archaeopress

Ellis, G L, Lintz, C, Trierweiler, W N and Jackson, J M, 1994 *Significance standards for Prehistoric cultural resources: a case study from Fort Hood, Texas,* USACERL Technical Report CRC-94/04, United States Army Corps of Engineers, Construction Engineering Research Laboratories, Champaign, Illinois

English Heritage, 1994 *Archaeology review 1993-94*, English Heritage, London

English Heritage, 1996 *Sustaining the historic environment: new perspectives on the future*, English Heritage, London

English Heritage, 1998 *MIDAS: a Manual and Data Standard for Monument Inventories*, English Heritage, Data Standards Unit

English Heritage, 1999 *National Monuments Record Thesauri*, http://thesaurus.english-heritage.org.uk/

English Heritage, 2002 *Historic Landscape Characterisation: Template Project Design for EH-supported county-wide HLC projects*, English Heritage, London

English Heritage, 2003 *Twentieth-Century Military Sites: Current approaches to their recording and conservation*, English Heritage, London

English Heritage, 2005 Characterisation, *Conservation Bulletin* 46, Winter 2004/05, www/english-heritage.org.uk/characterisation

English Heritage, 2007 www.english-heritage.org.uk/characterisation

Exon, S, Gaffney, V, Yorston, R, and Woodward, A, 2001 *Stonehenge Landscapes: Journeys Through Real-And-Imagined Worlds*, Archaeopress, Oxford

Fairclough, G J, 1994 Landscapes from the past – only human nature, in Selman, P (ed.), 1994 *The ecology and management of cultural landscapes – proceedings of an IALE UK conference at Cheltenham, 1993*, Landscape Issues, vol. 11 no 1, 64-72, Cheltenham

Fairclough, G J, 2001 Boundless Horizons – Historic Landscape Characterisation, *English Heritage Conservation Bulletin*, 40, March 2001, 23-26

Fairclough, G J, 2002 Cultural landscape, computers and characterisation, in Burenhult, G (ed.), 2002 *Archaeological Informatics: Pushing the Envelope*, 123-149, Procs. 29th CAA Conference, Gotland, April 2001, BAR International Series 1016, Archaeopress

Fairclough, G J, 2003 Cultural Landscape, Sustainability and Living with Change?, in Teutonico, J M and Matero, F (eds.), 2003 *Managing Change: Sustainable approaches to the Conservation of the Built Environment*, 4th Annual US/ICOMOS International Symposium, Philadelphia, Los Angeles, Getty Conservation Institute, 23-46

Fairclough, G J, 2006, From assessment to characterisation, in Hunter, J and Ralston, I (eds.), *Archaeological Resource Management in the UK, Second Edition*, 250-270, Stroud: Sutton

Fairclough, G, Lambrick, G and McNab, A, 1999 *Yesterday's world, tomorrow's landscape: the English Heritage historic landscape project 1992-94*, English Heritage. London

Fairclough, G J and Rippon, S J (eds.), 2002: *Europe's cultural landscape: archaeologists and the management of change*, EAC Occasional Paper no 2, Europae Archaeologiae Consilium and English Heritage, Brussels and London

Fitch, S, 2002a *An examination of the Quaternary River Terraces at Fort Hood*, Unpublished masters dissertation, University of Birmingham

Fitch, S, 2002b *Fort Hood River Terrace Ground Truthing Project*, Unpublished internship project, University of Birmingham and Fort Hood

Francovich, R, and Patterson, H (eds.), 2000 *Extracting Meaning from Plough Soil Assemblages,* Oxbow, Oxford

Frederick, C D, Glascock, M D, Neff, H and Stevenson, C M, 1994 *Evaluation of Chert Patination as a Dating Technique: A Case Study from Fort Hood, Texas*, United States Army Fort Hood, Archeological Resource Management Series, Research Report No. 32

Frederick, C D and Abbott, J T, 1992 Magnetic prospection of Prehistoric sites in an alluvial environment: examples from NW and West-central Texas, *Journal of Field Archaeology* 19, 139-153

Freeman, M D, Dase, A E and Blake, M E, 2001 *Agriculture and rural development on Fort Hood lands, 1849-1942: National Register assessments of 710 historic archeological properties,* United States Army Fort Hood, Archeological Resource Management Series, Research Report No. 42

Gaffney, C and Gater, J, 2003 *Revealing the buried past : geophysics for archaeologists*, Stroud, Tempus

Gaffney, V and Tingle, M, 1984 The tyranny of the site: method and theory in field survey, *Scottish Archaeological Review* 3, 134-140

Gwyn, D, 2002 Associative landscape in a Welsh context, in Fairclough, G J and Rippon, S (eds.), *Europe's Cultural Landscape: archaeologists and the management of change*, EAC Occasional Paper no 2, Brussels & London, Europae Archaeologiae Consilium & English Heritage, 187-192

Historic Environment Review, 2000 *Power of Place, A future for the historic environment*, English Heritage, London

Herring, P, 1998 Cornwall's historic landscape (presenting a method of historic landscape character assessment), Cornwall Archaeological Unit

Hester, T R, 1986 Early Human Populations along the Balcones Escarpment, in Abbott, P C and Woodruff, C M (eds.), 1986 *The Balcones Escarpment: geology, hydrology, ecology and social development*, http://www.lib.utexas.edu/geo/BalconesEscarpment/pages 55-62.html

Hester, T R (ed), 1991 Abstract, in *The burned rock middens of Texas: an archeological symposium*, http://www.utexas.edu/research/tarl/publications/studies.html#13

Hey, G and Lacey, M, 2001 *Evaluation of archaeological decision-making processes and sampling strategies*, Oxford Archaeological Unit

Highways Agency guidance, 2007 *Assessing the Effect of Road schemes on Historic Landscapes Character*, Bristol (with EH, Halcrows and Landscape Institute)

Hill, R T 1901, Geography and geology of the Black and Grand Prairies, Texas, *United States Geological Survey, 21st annual report*, part V11, 666, Washington, D.C., GPO

Hodder, M A and Barfield, L H, 1991 *Burnt mounds and hot stone technology: papers from the Second International Burnt Mound Conference*, West Bromwich, Sandwell Metropolitan Borough Council

Hoskins, W G, 1955 *The Making of the English Landscape*, 14

Huckerby, C L, 2000 *Fort Hood cultural resource management program: status as of Sept 2000*

Huckerby, C L, 2001 Fort Hood, Texas – CRM in the Home of the Army's Largest Fighting Machines, in *CRM* 3 – 2001, 13-16

Hunter, J R, and Dockrill, S J, 1990 Recent Research into Burnt Mounds on Fair Isle, Shetland, and Sanday, Orkney, in Buckley, V (compiler), *Burnt Offerings: International Contributions to Burnt Mound Archaeology*, Wordwell Ltd., Academic Publishers, Dublin, Ireland., 62-68

Ingold, T, 1986 *The Appropriation of Nature*, Manchester University Press

Ingold, T, 1992 Culture and the perception of the environment, in Croll, E, and Parkin, D (eds.), *Bush Base: Forest Farm*, Routledge, London, 39-56

Ingold, T, 1993 The temporality of the landscape, *World Archaeology*, 25(2), 152-174

Jackson, J M, 1994 *United States Army cultural resources management plan for Fort Hood, Texas, fiscal years 1995 through 1999*, on file, Directorate of Engineering and Housing, Fort Hood, Texas

Johnson, L and Goode, G T, 1994 A new try at dating and characterizing Holocene climates, as well as archaeological periods, on the Eastern Edwards Plateau, *Bulletin of the Texas Archeological Society*, 65, 1-51

Kealhofer, L, 1999 Creating social identity in the landscape: Tidewater, Virginia, 1600-1750, in Ashmore, W and Knapp, A B (eds.), 1999 *Archaeologies of landscape: contemporary perspectives*

Kleinbach, K, Mehalchick, G, Boyd, D K and Kibler, K, 1999 *National Register testing of 42 Prehistoric archeological sites on Fort Hood, Texas: the 1996 season*, United States Army Fort Hood, Archeological Resource Management Series, Research Report No. 38

Lambrick, G, 1998 Hampshire historic landscape character and the community, in Fairclough, G, 1998 *Historic Landscape Characterisation, papers presented at an English Heritage seminar*

Landscape Atlas of Flanders, 2001 Ministry of the Flemish Community, Support Center GIS-Flanders, Bruxelles, available: http://geo-vlaanderen.gisvlaanderen.be/geo-vlaanderen/landschapsatlas/ (6 July 2006)

Macinnes, L., 2004 Historic Landscape Characterization, in Bishop and Phillips (eds.), *Countryside Planning: New approaches to Management and Conservation*, London, Earthscan, 155-169

McKinney, W, 1981 Early Holocene adaptations in Central and Southwestern Texas: the problem of the Paleoindian-Archaic transition, in *Bulletin of the Texas Archeological Society*, 52, 91-120

McMurry, R M, 1992 *John Bell Hood and the War for Southern Independence*, University of Nebraska Press

Mehalchick, G, Kleinbach, K, Boyd, D K and Kibler, K, 2000 *Geoarcheological investigations and National Register testing of 52 Prehistoric archeological sites on Fort Hood, Texas: the 1997 season*, United States Army Fort Hood, Archeological Resource Management Series, Research Report No. 39

Meltzer, D J, 1987 The Clovis Paleoindian occupation of Texas: results of the Texas Clovis fluted point survey, in *Bulletin of the Texas Archeological Society*, 57, 27-68

Meltzer, D J and Bever, M R, 1995 Paleoindians of Texas: an update on the Texas Clovis fluted point survey, in *Bulletin of the Texas Archeological Society*, 66, 47-82

Miller, P, 1995 How to look good and influence people: thoughts on the design and interpretation of an archaeological GIS, in Lock, G and Stančič, Z (eds.), *Archaeology and Geographic Information Systems,* London. Hodder and Stoughton. 319-334

Newcomb, W W 1993 Historic Indians of Central Texas, in *Bulletin of the Texas Archeological Society,* 64, 1-63

Nord, J M, 2006 Förhistoriska vägval och dagens väglandskap på Bjärehalvön i Nordvästra Skåne, in Qviström, M (ed), *Gångna landskap: möten mellan väghistoria och landskapshistoria,* 43-50, Alnarp: Institutionen för Landskapsplanering, Rapport 06:1, available: http://www2.lpal.slu.se/skyltfonstret/Mattias/Rapport%2006_1.pdf (17 July 2006)

Nord, J M, 2006 Landscape as heritage; the Bjäre Peninsula. I: Utskrift 8, Halmstad: Hallands Länsmuseer

Nordt, L C 1992 *Archaeological geology of the Fort Hood military reservation, Fort Hood, Texas,* United States Army Fort Hood, Archeological Resource Management Series, Research Report No. 25

Palang, H and Fry, G (eds.), 2003 *Landscape Interfaces: Cultural Heritage in Changing Landscapes,* Landscape Series 1, Kluwer Academic Publishers, Dordrecht

Parks Canada 2004 *An approach to aboriginal cultural landscapes: guidelines for the identification of aboriginal cultural landscapes,* http://www.pc.gc.ca/docs/r/pca-acl/index_e.asp

Pathways to Cultural Landscapes, 2004 *http://www.pcl-eu.de/indexen.php*

Prewitt, E R, 1981 Cultural Chronology in Central Texas, in *Bulletin of the Texas Archeological Society,* 52, 65-89

Prewitt, E R, 1985 From Circleville to Toyah: Comments on Central Texas Chronology, in *Bulletin of the Texas Archeological Society,* 54, 201-238

Pugsley, W S, 2001 *Imprint on the land, life before Camp Hood, 1820-1942,* Morgan Printing, Austin, Texas

Quigg, M J, Frederick, C D and Lippert, D, 1996 *Archeology and Native American religion at the Leon River medicine wheel,* United States Army Fort Hood, Archeological Resource Management Series, Research Report No. 33

RCAHMS, 2006 Historic Land-use Assessment web site, (http://jura.rcahms.gov.uk/HLA/start.jsp)

Ricklis, R A and Collins, M B, 1994 Abstract, in *Archaic and Late Prehistoric human ecology in the Middle Onion Creek Valley, Hays County, Texas,* Vol. 1: Archeological Components, and Vol. 2: Topical Studies, http://www.utexas.edu/research/tarl/publications/studies.html - 12

Selman, P, 2006 *Planning at Landscape Scale,* London: Routledge

Sitton, Thad, 2003 *Harder then Hardscrabble,* University of Texas Press, Austin, Texas

Stabler, Jennifer, 1999 *Evaluation of 710 Historic Sites on Fort Hood for Eligibility to the National Register of Historic Places: Bell and Coryell Counties, Texas,* United States Army Fort Hood, Archaeological Resource Management Series, Research Report No. 36

Stančič Z, Gaffney, V, Ostir-Sedej, K and Podobnikar, T, 1997 GIS analysis of land-use, settlement patterns and territories on the island of Brač, in Johnson, I and North, M (eds.), 1997 *Archaeological applications of GIS: Proceedings of Colloquium II, UISPP XIIIth Congress, Forli, Italy, September 1996,* Sydney University Archaeological Methods Series 5

Startin, B, 1994 Assessment of field remains, in Hunter, J R and Ralston, I (eds.), 1994 *Archaeological Resource Management in the UK,* 184-196

Tacon, P S.C, 1999 Identifying Ancient Sacred Landscapes in Australia: From Physical to Social, in Ashmore, W and Knapp, A B (eds.), 1999 *Archaeologies of landscape: contemporary perspectives*

Thoms, A V, 1993 *Archaeological survey at Fort Hood, Texas, fiscal years 1991 and 1992: the Cantonment and Belton Lake Periphery areas,* United States Army Fort Hood, Archeological Resource Management Series, Research Report No. 27

Tilley, C, 1994 *A Phenomenology of Landscape: places, paths and monuments,* Berg, Oxford

Trierweiler, W N (ed), 1996a *Archaeological Investigations on 571 Prehistoric Sites at Fort Hood, Bell and Coryell Counties, Texas,* United States Army Fort Hood, Archaeological Resource Management Series, Research Report No. 31

Trierweiler, N (ed), 1996b *Archeological testing at Fort Hood: 1994-1995, volumes I and II,* United States Army Fort Hood, Archaeological Resource Management Series, Research Report No. 35

Turner, S, 2001 *Devon HLC: draft (October 2001 draft),* Unpublished report by Devon County Council

Turner, S, 2006 Historic landscape characterisation: a landscape archaeology for research, management and planning, in *Landscape Research* 31, 385-398

United States Government, 1990 *Native American Graves Protection and Repatriation Act,* Public Law 101-601; 25 U.S.C. 3001 et seq.

Ward, R B, Blake, M E, Dase, A E and Freeman, M D, 2000 *Historical research of 401 sites at Fort Hood, Bell and Coryell Counties, Texas,* United States Army Fort Hood, Archeological Resource Management Series, Research Report No. 43

Waters, M R and Kuehn, D D, 1996 The geoarchaeology of place: the effect of geological processes on the preservation and interpretation of the archaeological record, in *American Antiquity,* 61, 483-497

Wesolowsky, Al B, Hester, T R and Brown, D R, 1976 Archeological investigations at the Jetta Court site (41 TV 151), Travis County, Texas, in *Bulletin of the Texas Archeological Society,* 47, 25-87

Williams, I, Briuer, F L and Limp, W F 1990a *The application of quantitative methodologies for the assessment of archeological site variability, Fort Hood military installation,* U. S. Army Corps of Engineers, Construction Engineering Research Labs

Williams, I, Briuer, F L and Limp, W F 1990b Using geographic information systems and exploratory data analysis for archaeological site classification and analysis, in Allen, K M S, Green, S W and Zubrow, E B W, 1990 *Interpreting Space: GIS and archaeology*

White, P and Ray, K, 2000 *A first interim progress report on the Herefordshire historic landscape characterisation project: end of January 2000,* unpublished report by Herefordshire County Council.

Wigley, A, 2001 *Interim report on the Shropshire historic landscape characterisation programme,* Shropshire County Council.

Williamson, T, 2006 'Mapping field patterns: a case study from eastern England', *Landscapes* 7(1), 55-67

Zeidler, J A, 2004 *Military impacts and archaeological site mitigation methods at the Firebreak site (41CV595), Fort Hood, Texas,* United States Army Fort Hood, Archeological Resource Management Series, Research Report No. 53

8. Appendix
The contents and use of the CD

Google Earth

One of the principal difficulties of publishing HLC data is the complexity of the GIS imagery that is generated by analysis. Although many of the results from the Fort Hood project have been reproduced in colour to assist the reader, it is accepted that this is still not entirely satisfactory. For this purpose selected data layers have been provided as Google Earth layers. Google Earth is a free spatial data viewer that can be downloaded in order to view the Fort Hood data from **http://earth.google.com/**.

Please note that the imagery provided for Google was **not** that used for classification in this publication. It does not represent the entire rule-based classification and cannot be directly compared in analytical terms.

IMPORTANT
The instructions provided here are for Google Earth 4. Full information on downloading, installing and using the viewer can be found at
http://earth.google.com/download-earth.html. If your computer specifications do not meet the specifications below or if the Fort Hood data does not display properly it may be that you require an earlier version of Google Earth. Google Earth 3 can be downloaded at **http://earth.google.com/download-earth3.html**
Google Earth 4 requires the following minimum specification for use;
- Operating System: Windows 2000 or Windows XP
- CPU: Pentium 3, 500Mhz
- System Memory (RAM): 128MB
- Hard Disk: 400MB free space
- Network Speed: 128 Kbits/sec
- Graphics Card: 3D-capable with 16MB of VRAM
- Screen: 1024x768, '16-bit High Colour'

However, the recommended specification is;
- Operating System: Windows XP
- CPU: Pentium 4 2.4GHz+ or AMD 2400xp+
- System Memory (RAM): 512MB RAM
- Hard Disk: 2GB free space
- Network Speed: 768 Kbits/sec
- Graphics Card: 3D-capable with 32MB of VRAM
- Screen: 1280x1024, '32-bit True Color' screen

Performance will vary according to the configuration of individual computers and graphic cards. Older machines or computers with a lower specification may be slow to draw images. Severe visual problems may be caused by issues with the installed graphic drivers or choice of graphic mode. See the Google support page at **http://earth.google.com/support/** for advice on graphic cards. If there are severe difficulties with viewing the Fort Hood data it may be that your machine requires an earlier version of Google Earth. Google Earth 3 can be downloaded at **http://earth.google.com/download-earth3.html**

Google Earth **must** be installed before opening the Fort Hood data files.

USING THE CD
On opening the CD the reader may either go straight to the **data** directory or open the default html page (**index.htm**). If the data directory is opened the following map and layer files can be extracted and used. These two file formats provide slightly different functionality. Only a select number of key layer files have been provided with complex data links via polygon nodes. Each map file is associate with a legend describing the contents. these files are generally smaller file and therefore can be loaded with relative ease. The primary Fort Hood Map file provides all the relevant data combined within a single file and a unified legend. Please be aware that data layers may take some time to load depending on the size of the file, the speed of the machine and network connections and whether data is accessed via the CD drive or copied onto the hard drive of the local machine. Please be patient when opening large files and consider copying the data onto your hard drive to speed up loading into Google earth.

Fort Hood Map File
The primary Fort Hood HLC data set with legend and incorporating;
- Archaeology polygons for the site
- Roads on the base
- Lakes on the base
- Rivers on the base
- The Impact zone
- The Live Fire zone
- HLC Broad classifications without labels.
- Boundary of Fort Hood

Map Files with Legends
- Archaeology - The surface area of all archaeological sites used in the study as polygons
- Roads - The Fort Hood road system as vectors
- Lakes - All substantial areas of water as polygons
- Rivers - All rivers and streams on the bas as vectors
- The Impact Zone - Artillery and live fire impact zone as a polygon
- The Live Fire Zone - Area of live fire as a polygon
- HLC Broad classifications - Broad historic landscape classifications as polygons
- HLC Sub-type classifications - All historic landscape sub-classes as polygons

Boundary of Fort Hood - The boundary of the Fort Hood as a polygon **Layer Files without Labels**
- Archaeology- The surface area of all archaeological sites used in the study as polygons
- Roads on the base - The Fort Hood road system as vectors
- Lakes on the base- All substantial areas of water as polygons
- Rivers - All rivers and streams on the bas as vectors
- The Impact Zone- Artillery and live fire impact zone as a polygon
- The Live Fire Zone - Area of live fire as a polygon
- HLC Broad classifications- Broad historic landscape classifications as polygons
- HLC Sub-type classifications- All historic landscape sub-classes as polygons
- HLC sample areas -Sample areas used to ground truth HLC classifications as polygons
- Boundary of Fort Hood- The boundary of the Fort Hood as a polygon

Layer Files with Labels.
- HLC sample areas-Sample areas used to ground truth HLC classifications as polygons and with attached data label.
- Full HLC classifications with labels- All historic landscape sub-classes as polygons and with attached data labels. **This file is large!**

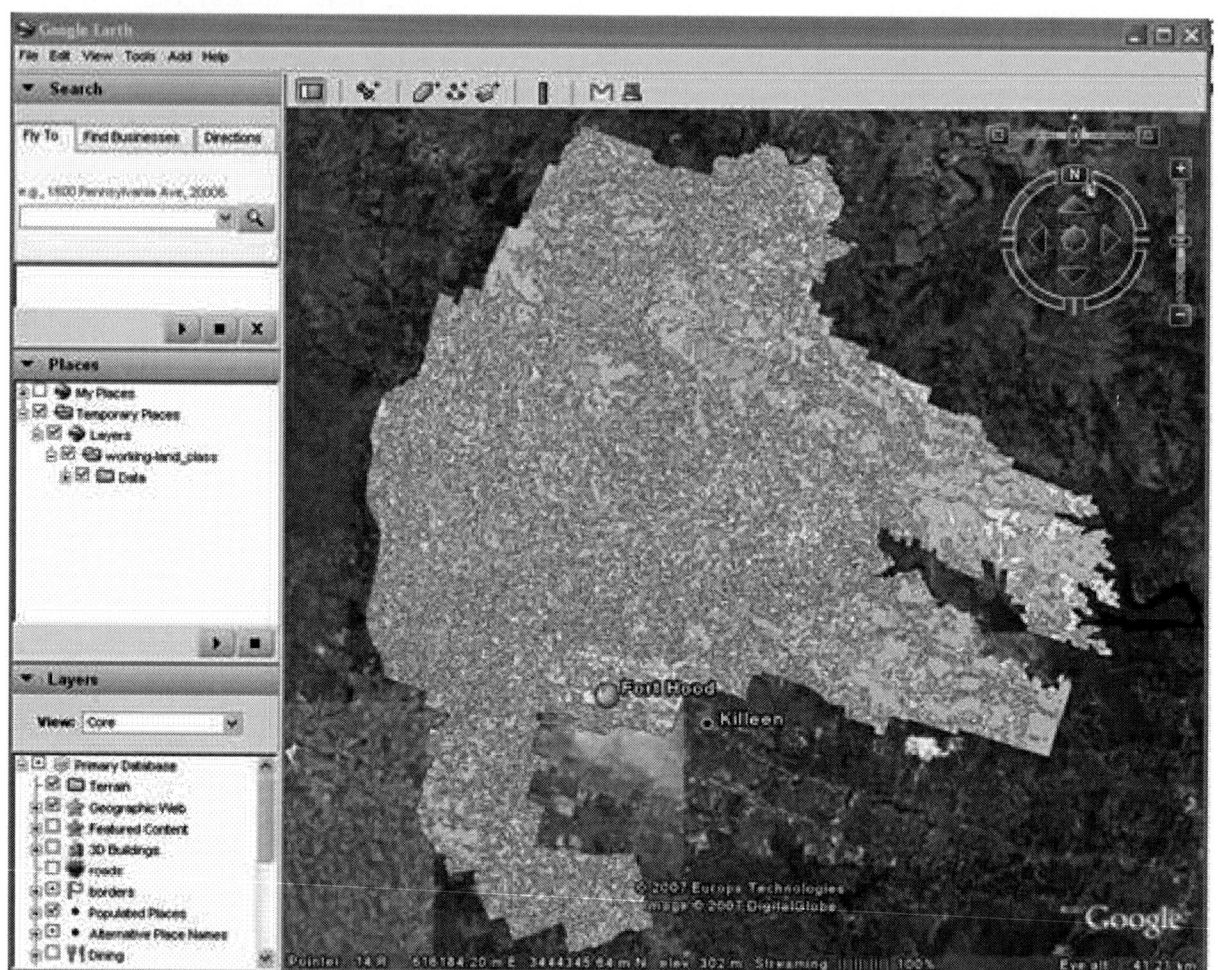

HLC data opened in Google Earth 4

Heritage Management at Fort Hood, Texas: Experiments in Historic Landscape Characterisation

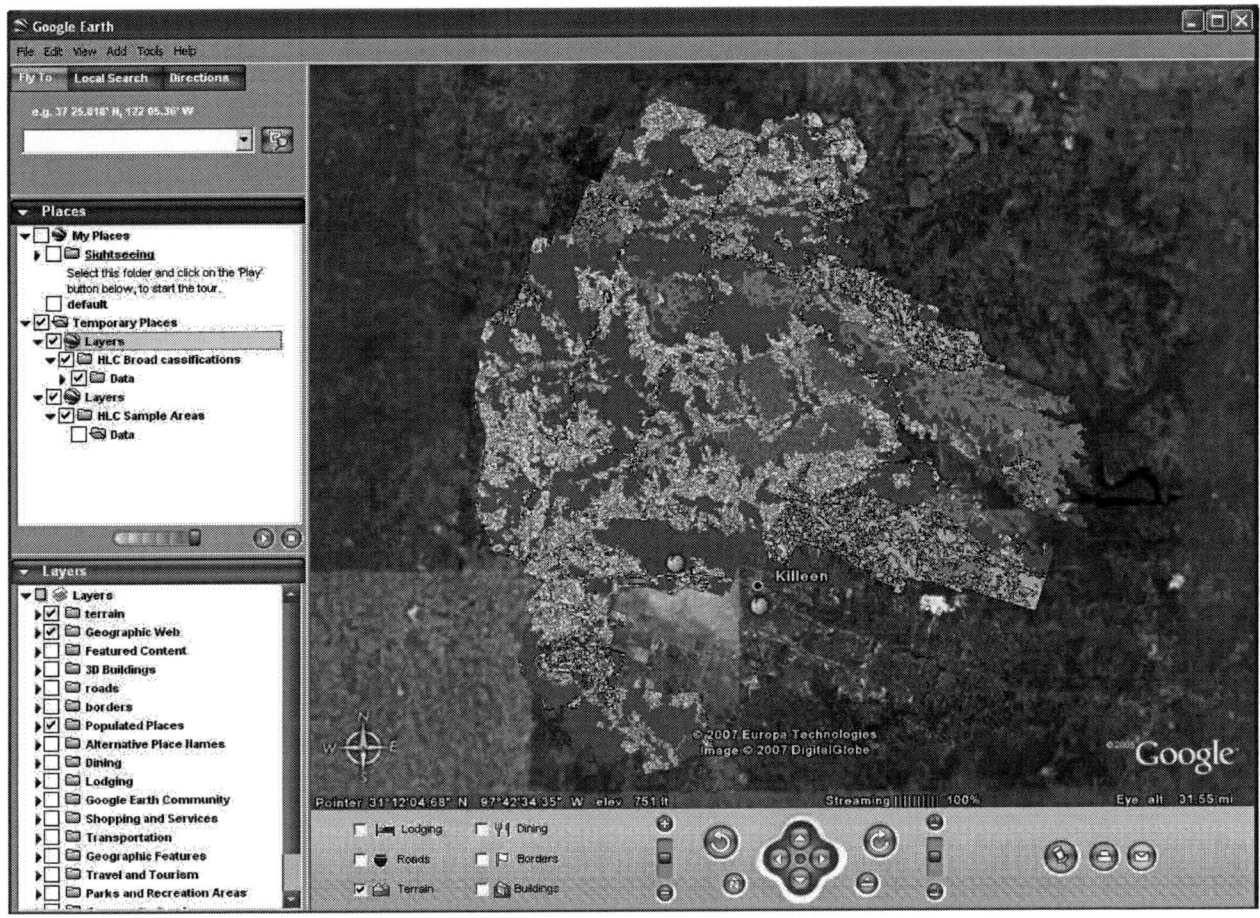

HLC data opened in Google Earth 3

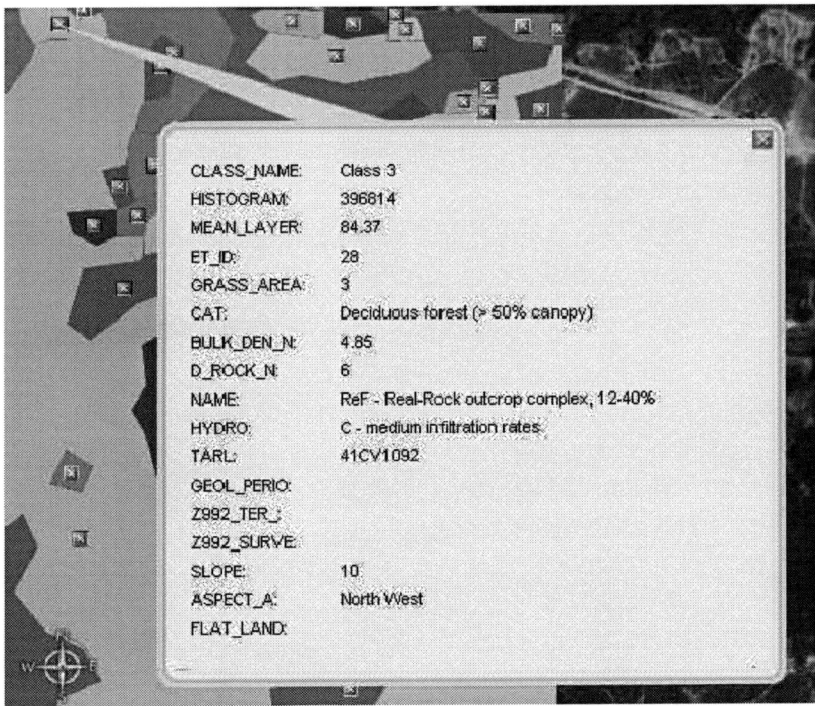

Label attached to node in Google Earth 3

Any of the files, or links to files, provided may be double clicked to start Google Earth (when installed). Alternately, the data can be copied to a directory on the PC and used from there. This will speed up the reading of the data. If the default HTML page is opened first, a separate data page can be accessed via the appropriate hyperlink and each file copied to your PC or opened by double clicking the file.

The ordering of the files used will dictate the way in which data is displayed in Google Earth and some data may not be visible or be partially visible when using the default settings. This is particularly true when using the 3D options of Google earth. Visibility issues can be overcome by turning individual layers on and off as required but also by altering the transparency settings of individual layers or their altitude setting. The altitude setting in particular is important and some layers may have to be placed above the the ground to ensure full visibility. In **Google Earth 4** layers and their property settings are accessed in the 'places' pane. Check individual layers to view, and right-click individual data to choose the layer property option. In **Google Earth 3** layers should be selected from the 'places' pane for editing and the advanced options selected to provide similar options.

If layer files with labels have been opened, clicking on the the label polygon node will provide details of the underlying database. Please note that these files in particular may be large and very slow to load. The density of label nodes clutter the image when viewed across the entire base. The viewer must zooms into the image to identify specific nodes for interrogation!

Whilst it is accepted that this does not provide a perfect solution to the viewing of complex digital imagery, the authors do hope that this does assist the reader in viewing and interpreting the data and the value of HLC procedures and output for the purposes of heritage management.